Dryden's Final Poetic Mode

Dryden's Final Poetic Mode

The *Fables*

CEDRIC D. REVERAND II

UNIVERSITY OF PENNSYLVANIA PRESS *upp* Philadelphia

Library of Congress Cataloging-in-Publication Data

Reverand, Cedric D.
  Dryden's final poetic mode.

  Bibliography: p.
  Includes index.
    1. Dryden, John, 1631–1700. Fables.   I. Title.
PR3418.F5R48   1988   821'.4   88-10768
ISBN 0-8122-8121-7

69901

For My Parents

CONTENTS

TABLE OF CONTENTS FOR *FABLES*

The full title of Dryden's collection, as it appears in the folio first-edition, is *Fables Ancient and Modern; Translated into Verse, from Homer, Ovid, Boccace, & Chaucer: With Original Poems* (London: Jacob Tonson, 1700). What follows is a table of contents for *Fables* (Tonson, or Dryden, included such a table as the last page in the 1700 volume), indicating the original sources of the translated poems:

Contents for Fables

After the tales themselves, Dryden includes Middle English texts of the following (from Thomas Speght's 1687 edition of Chaucer):

FREQUENTLY USED

ABBREVIATIONS

Chapman: *Chapman's Homer: The Iliad, the Odyssey, and the Lesser Homerica*. Trans. George Chapman, ed. Allardyce Nicoll. Bollingen Series, 41. 2 vols. New York: Pantheon Books, 1956 [*Iliad* appears in vol. 1].

Kinsley: *The Poems of John Dryden*. Ed. James Kinsley. 4 vols. Oxford: Clarendon Press, 1958 [*Fables* appears in vol. 4 of Kinsley, excepting "Alexander's Feast" which, since it was first published in 1697, appears in vol. 3].

Lattimore: *The Iliad of Homer*. Trans. Richard Lattimore. 1951; rpt. Chicago: University of Chicago Press, 1963.

Letters: *The Letters of John Dryden: With Letters Addressed to Him*. Ed. Charles E. Ward. Durham, NC: Duke University Press, 1942.

Life: Ward, Charles E. *The Life of John Dryden*. Chapel Hill: University of North Carolina Press, 1961.

Loeb: *Cicero: Letters to Atticus* [Loeb Classical Library]. Trans. E. O. Winstedt. 3 vols. New York: Macmillan, 1912–18.

        Ovid: Metamorphoses [Loeb Classical Library]. Trans. Frank Justus Miller. 3rd ed., rev. G. P. Goold. 2 vols. 1st ed., 1916; 3rd ed., 1977; rpt. Cambridge, MA: Harvard University Press, 1984.

Winn: Winn, James Anderson. *John Dryden and His World*. New Haven: Yale University Press, 1987.

Works: *The Works of John Dryden* [the California Dryden]. Ed. Edward Niles Hooker, H. T. Swedenberg, et al. 20 vols. Berkeley: University of California Press, 1955– .

Since the California Dryden (*Works*) has only reached 1696, citations to *Fables* (1700) follow the text of Kinsley. All other citations to Dryden's poetry and prose use the text of *Works*.

ACKNOWLEDGMENTS

$\mathcal{T}$HE NOTES will bear witness to the many scholars and critics to whom I am indebted, both those upon whose insights and findings I build and those with whom I on occasion disagree (I hope without ill will). In addition, I would like to offer thanks to Morris R. Brownell and Sanford Budick, who first inspired me to explore this whole period of literature; to the William Andrews Clark Library and the Andrew Mellon Foundation, which, by kindly offering me a Mellon Fellowship, provided me with the opportunity and scholarly resources to begin this study of Dryden; to Thomas R. Preston, George R. Guffey, and David M. Vieth, who, at the early stages of this project, offered both encouragement and wise scholarly advice; to my colleagues, John D. Dorst, Walter F. Eggers, Duncan S. Harris, Janice H. Harris, Richard Howey, Keith N. Hull, Eric W. Nye, Bruce Richardson, Fred Slater, Robert Torry, and John Warnock, who had the patience to listen attentively to my ramblings in progress, and who repeatedly offered constructive suggestions and useful information; to both the College of Arts and Sciences, and the English Department of the University of Wyoming, which provided a subsidy that partially supported publication of this book. I am also indebted to Philip Holt and Gerard Reedy, for assistance particularly in the tricky business of dealing with Dryden's source texts for his classical material, and to James A. Winn, who generously provided me with the manuscript of his forthcoming biography of Dryden and later compounded my debt to him by reading my manuscript. Professor Winn's perceptive criticism helped me significantly in sharpening my own argument, and also on more than one occasion rescued me from error. What errors and oversights remain are, of course, my own responsibility, but there would have been more had it not been for the generosity and knowledge of this far-flung community of scholar-teachers.

Acknowledgments

One portion of this book has already appeared, in a considerably different form, in "Dryden's Final Poetic Mode: 'To the Dutchess of Ormond' and *Fables*," *The Eighteenth Century: Theory and Interpretation* 26 (1985):3–21. My thanks to the editors of that journal, Robert M. Markley and Jeffrey R. Smitten, for their kind and knowledgeable assistance. Finally, I would like to thank my wife for her continual help, support, patience, and also for her expertise: as a professional editor of great talent and skill, she constantly puts me in mind of the virtues of clear prose.

Chapter One

DRYDEN'S MOST MEMORABLE
AND LEAST REMEMBERED WORK

It is to his fables, though wrote in his old age, that Dryden will owe
his immortality . . . The warmth and melody of these pieces, has never
been excelled in our language.—Joseph Warton [1]

*W*H E N we think about what our favorite passages from Dryden
might be, how often do these lines come to mind:

> While list'ning to the murm'ring Leaves he stood,
> More than a Mile immers'd within the Wood,
> At once the Wind was laid; the whisp'ring sound
> Was dumb; a rising Earthquake rock'd the Ground:
> With deeper Brown the Grove was overspred:
> A suddain Horror seiz'd his giddy Head,
> And his Ears tinckled, and his Colour fled.
> Nature was in alarm; some Danger nigh
> Seem'd threaten'd, though unseen to mortal Eye.
> (88–96)

I would guess that these lines come to mind not at all. Had I begun by
quoting "In pious times, e'r Priest-craft did begin, / Before *Polygamy*
was made a sin," or "Trust Nature, do not labour to be dull," or even "I
am as free as Nature first made man, / 'Ere the base Laws of Servitude
began," I would have hit upon passages well known by most informed
readers. But I suspect that the above quotation, far from being memorable, is something that even Dryden aficionados would at this point be
struggling to identify. The lines come from "Theodore and Honoria,"
translated from the *Decameron*, one of the twenty-one tales in Dryden's
last collection of poems, *Fables Ancient and Modern* (1700).

I did not choose the passage at random. Joseph Warton, in his praise

I

of *Fables* (part of which is quoted above), included a number of illustrative quotations, capped off by these very lines, which "I place . . . last, as I think them the most lofty of any part of Dryden's works" (Warton, 2 : 19). Sir Walter Scott, whose knowledge of Dryden is still impressive after a century and a half, singled out these lines as memorable in his *Life of Dryden* (1808). Henry Hallam, reviewing Scott's edition of Dryden in the same year for the *Edinburgh Review*, cited the same passage as being especially popular.[2] And Byron, in his letters and his journal kept at Ravenna, repeatedly seemed inspired by these "murm'ring Leaves"; he mentions several times the pleasant prospect of strolling through "the famous forest of Boccaccio's story—and Dryden's fable."[3] What these authors consider as memorable Dryden will perhaps come as something of a surprise to those of us who do not remember it. Equally surprising is the enthusiasm accorded such Dryden selections. Scott also cited another passage from *Fables*, in these glowing terms:

> There is not in our language a strain of more beautiful and melodious poetry, than that so often quoted, in which Dryden describes the sleeping nymph, and the effect of her beauty upon the clownish Cymon. But it is only sufficient to mention that passage, to recal it to the recollection of every general reader, and of most who have read any poetry at all.[4]

Needless to say, this oft quoted passage that every general reader knows is just as solidly forgotten as the other memorable passage. I will not quote it here; it's somewhat racy.[5]

The fact is that *Fables*, which few of us have read all the way through, and few of us teach as a major Dryden work, was the work by which Dryden was once best known, the work for which he was once most admired.[6] Certainly tastes change. In Poet's Corner, the name Cowley appears in large letters, while in the upper right-hand corner of the same stone, the names of Spenser, Sidney, and Dryden appear in small letters, now nearly indistinct. *Pericles* was once exceedingly popular, and few of us now think of that as quintessential Shakespeare; it is more like optional Shakespeare, which one might assign once the major tragedies and comedies have been adequately covered. Perhaps *Fables* is a parallel case. It appealed to the Romantics—Wordsworth, by the way, called it the "most poetical" of Dryden's works—and now we know better.[7] We have learned to appreciate occasional poetry and satire; they, naturally, preferred narrative and fable. However, I do not think the matter is all that simple. For one thing, the generation immediately following Dryden, whose tastes were not like those of Wordsworth or Scott, also admired *Fables*; the eighteenth century saw at least a dozen editions of the work, implying a general popularity. As to its popularity among individual readers, we have Congreve's remark that Dryden's "Parts did not decline with his Years: . . . he was an improving Writer to his last, even to near seventy Years of Age; improving in Fire and Imagination, as well as in Judgement: Witness his Ode on St. *Cecilia*'s Day, and his Fables, his latest Performances."[8] Pope, whom we usually connect to Dryden through their verse satires (the *Dunciad* is indebted to "MacFlecknoe," and so on), also had a high regard for Dryden's final work: "those Scribblers who attack'd him in his latter times, were only like Gnats in a Summer's evening, which are never very troublesome but in the finest and the most glorious Season; (for his fire, like the Sun's, shin'd clearest towards its setting)."[9] Later on in the century, Sheridan liked *Fables* so much that he had long passages by heart and was fond of reciting them (*his* favorite passage, however, was from "Palamon and Arcite").[10]

Furthermore, modern critics have been no less appreciative. Mark Van Doren, whose 1920 book, *The Poetry of John Dryden*, helped rescue Dryden from the outer darkness into which Arnold had attempted to cast such poets of statement, begins his discussion of *Fables* by quoting Dryden's remark from the Preface, "I have built a House, where I intended but a Lodge" (Kinsley, 4:1444), and then commenting: "If he had thought of the lodge as a green retreat for a fading muse, he found the house a bustling hall built for the entertainment of his ripest powers; there had been no fading."[11] In the appreciation that follows (215–32), by the way, Van Doren quotes about twenty passages, including both the memorable passages that Scott and Hallam found so appealing. Fifty years later, one discovers Earl Miner continuing the praise, calling *Fables* "the *second* greatest narrative of the seventeenth century," second only to *Paradise Lost*.[12] A work second only to *Paradise Lost* that few of us read or teach? When Miner speaks, most Dryden scholars listen carefully, and yet few have pursued this inviting lead.

I am naturally curious as to what it is in a work that can appeal to diverse tastes across the ages, from satirists like Congreve and Pope, to a spectrum of Romantics, Wordsworth, Scott, Byron, and Hunt, to notable twentieth-century scholar-critics from Van Doren to Miner. Indeed, what kind of work is it that could strike a responsive chord in both Wordsworth and Byron, who were seldom in accord on critical issues (with Byron preferring to think of Wordsworth and his ilk as the "pond" poets). One suspects that different readers are attracted to different aspects of *Fables* (and that Byron probably never read the anthology all the way through), yet the collection is apparently rich enough to accommodate a diversity of interests. I am equally curious as to why a work that is still warmly admired is, for the most part, warmly ignored. There is more written on Dryden's heroic drama, dead as it is to our generation, than on *Fables*. We have complete books on "Religio Laici," on the esoteric "Hind and the Panther," and even, of late, a book on "Annus Mirabilis," but *Fables*, a major work comprising nearly twelve thousand lines of poetry, seems to keep slipping out of the critical nets. There exists only a handful of articles, usually on individual poems, most of which consider the poems as separate entities rather than as parts of a longer work, and there is no book-length study (excepting Judith Sloman's unpublished dissertation).[13]

James D. Garrison, another admirer of *Fables*, suggests that the reasons for this lie in the nature of the work itself: *Fables* "has evoked remarkably little sustained commentary, primarily because the collection is so difficult to grasp as an imaginative whole" (Garrison, 411). True. Those few modern critics who have dealt with *Fables* accord it the same high praise as previous generations, yet they tend to combine their appreciation with a surrender to the elusive quality of the work. Earl Miner, for instance, gives a table of the individual poems and their connections, discusses larger thematic relations, insists on Dryden's "unifying conception" (*Dryden's Poetry*, 290), his "principles of integration" (300), but then goes on to admit that he has not fully explained how *Fables* is integrated.[14] Instead, he falls back on praising Dryden's variety, "comprehensiveness," and "spacious imagination" (300, 317–19). William Myers, similarly, considers *Fables* "Dryden's richest work," claims it embodies "a unification of classical, mediaeval and modern experience," and ends his summary of the tales and their connections by confessing that "the deliberately rambling associative nature of their construction makes explication a singularly self-defeating activity."[15] Such critics typically find *Fables* capacious, integrated, unified, comprehensive; however, nobody seems able to say, precisely, what is being integrated and what comprehended.

In part, this enthusiasm for a rich, capacious text is a standard scholarly justification; we especially admire inexhaustible literary works, and we

4

can add *Fables* to that list. We can also humbly admit that we are unable to account for a work so rich. I admire and share that enthusiasm, but I sense more than the genial, pro forma submission to an inexhaustible or richly ambiguous text. *Fables* is more than comprehensive and capacious; it is tantalizingly subversive. What it gives, it also takes away. As some of the modern critical responses quoted above suggest, *Fables* engages the reader, invites him to synthesize and connect, only to discover ultimately the limits of that whole enterprise.[16] I would argue that it is this process itself, which has made *Fables* so elusive, that is at the very heart of the work. Attempting to make connections, discover inherent systems of value, and build theories are all part of a normal, critical approach that seeks coherence and integration. It is that entire approach that *Fables* calls into question by demolishing the connections, contradicting the systems of values, undercutting the very theories it invites us to build. Ultimately, as I will argue, I think this is part of a strategy of personal expression Dryden developed, amounting to a new poetic mode that emerged when he changed from laureate, public spokesman for king and country, to outcast, minority voice. The subversive process that characterizes *Fables* is an expression of Dryden's experience in dealing with a changed and changing world, where the various systems of values he had long cherished are now crumbling, and he himself is caught in the trap of trying to reconcile the irreconcilable.[17]

To examine this subversive process, I will look at possible connections, themes, and systems of value that I think Dryden deliberately weaves together only to unravel. However, I will not follow the obvious strategy of considering the tales one after the other, in the order of their appearance in *Fables*, a method I find unsatisfactory for a number of reasons. It makes more sense to me to read *Fables* as most readers would, playing with different groupings, reflecting on a previously read tale in light of a later tale, not merely heading forward toward a conclusion, but moving back and forth, reexamining, readjusting.[18] The disadvantage of this procedure is that it entails unavoidable repetition, since a tale studied in one context may be reconsidered later in connection with other tales, yet if the reexamination reveals something different (which it usually does), this can be a fruitful approach. *Fables* is not in the same mold as a *Paradise Lost* leading upward toward redemption or as a *Dunciad* leading downward to the inexorable return of Chaos and Night; it is more like

The Canterbury Tales, one of Dryden's models for a miscellany of tales and translations that resonate in complex ways against one another. It is likely that we look back at "The Knight's Tale" after finishing "The Miller's Tale," and that we look back again to both after reading "The Wife of Bath's Tale," and so forth, readjusting and perhaps reevaluating our earlier conclusions. That seems to be the way Dryden read Chaucer, not looking at a sequence of tales, but rather seeing the whole set and not knowing where to start or which way to move, which Dryden implies when he assumes the pose of an eager hunter seeing in Chaucer "such a Variety of Game springing up before me, that I am distracted in my Choice, and know not which to follow" (Kinsley, 4:1455).[19]

Another reason for adopting a non-sequential approach to examining *Fables* is that this seems to be true to Dryden's own method. He confesses in his Preface that "the Nature of a Preface is rambling; never wholly out of the Way, nor in it" (Kinsley, 4:1450), and that applies as well to the way in which Dryden selects his tales, beginning with the first book of the *Iliad*, then moving on to the twelfth book of the *Metamorphoses*, "because it contains, among other Things, the Causes, the Beginning, and Ending, of the *Trojan* War," from that to the "Speeches of *Ajax* and *Ulysses* lying next in my way," from that to the fifteenth book of the *Metamorphoses*, then "looking backward" to "Meleager and Atalanta," then to "Cinyras and Myrrha," next to "Baucis and Philemon," then to Boccaccio, and so forth (Kinsley, 4:1444–45). As these remarks suggest, Dryden continually stresses the process of connection by association. He justifies his being "led" from Chaucer to "think on *Boccace*" by remarking that "Thoughts, according to Mr. *Hobbs*, have always some Connexion" (Kinsley, 4:1446); one tale reminds him of another, which reminds him of yet another, and gradually a collection grows, not linearly, but by accretion, until his translations "began to swell into a little Volume" (Kinsley, 4:1445).

As is often the case with Dryden's disarming explanations, his description of himself as rambling should be taken with a grain of salt.[20] It turns out that the process of association happens to lead him through authors in chronological order, which makes this a subtly organized kind of rambling — first Homer, then Ovid, then Chaucer, then Boccaccio, "who was not only his Contemporary, but also pursu'd the same Studies" (Kinsley, 4:1446). And while he is rambling, Dryden manages to assemble a lineage of authors, making a case as he often did for the English tradition; he describes Milton as "the Poetical Son of *Spencer*, and Mr. *Waller* of *Fairfax*," remarks that "the Soul of *Chaucer* was transfus'd" into Spenser (Kinsley, 4:1445). Dryden not only raises Chaucer to the status of "the Father of *English* Poetry" (Kinsley, 4:1452), but more, Dryden locates Chaucer among his classical literary forbears, and at the same time inscribes the name of Dryden in the family tree by alluding to Chaucer as "my Country-man, and Predecessor in the Laurel" (Kinsley, 4:1445). This may be rambling, yet there is method in it.

In the ensuing discussion, I have provided summaries of the tales, ample quotations, and clear explanations of Dryden's alterations, even though some scholarly readers will doubtlessly find this unnecessary and perhaps even annoying. However, it is my contention that few readers, and even only a handful of Dryden scholars, are familiar with *Fables*; the only complete version currently in print is in volume four of the 1958 Kinsley edition (the California Dryden has not yet reached 1697–1700), which is not on everyone's bookshelf. There are many readers who do not recall what happens in "Meleager and Atalanta," or "Sigismonda and Guiscardo," or the twelfth book of the *Metamorphoses*, and who will not remember either the originals or the earlier translations sufficiently to recognize Dryden's alterations (who, I wonder, remembers the pseudo-Chaucerian "The Flower and the Leaf"?). I offer apologies to the Dryden scholars who do not require such complete information, but I hope they will indulge me if they consider that they are a small company, and that one of my hopes is to invite the literary general reader who does *not* know *Fables* to join that company.

To discover the special qualities of *Fables* and why it has remained elusive, the best place to enter, perhaps, would be where the water seems most transparent, where there seems to be, by common consent, a clear, coherent thematic concern—just how clear will become clearer as we proceed.

NOTES

1. Joseph Warton, *Essay on the Genius and Writings of Pope*, 4th ed., 2 vols. (London: J. Dodsley, 1782), 2:12. The actual individual tales Warton cites are "particularly Palamon and Arcite, Sigismonda and Guiscardo, Theodore and Honoria; and above all, . . . his exquisite music ode ["Alexander's Feast"]."

Most Memorable and Least Remembered Work

2. Upali Amarasinghe, in *Dryden and Pope in the Early Nineteenth Century: A Study of Changing Literary Taste, 1800–1830* (Cambridge: Cambridge University Press, 1962), discusses and quotes the responses of Scott, Hallam, and Warton (23–35).

3. From a 20 July 1819 letter to Lady Byron, *Byron's Letters and Journals*, ed. Leslie A. Marchand, 10 vols. (Cambridge, MA: Harvard University Press, 1973–80), 6:181. See also 6:166 (26 June 1819) and 7:253 (22 October 1820). At one point (20 February 1821), Byron, invited to a dinner in this forest near Ravenna, playfully hopes to see the spectre of Guido Cavalcanti, galloping right out of Dryden's tale (from Byron's Ravenna journal, Marchand, 8:48).

4. Walter Scott, ed., *The Works of John Dryden*, 18 vols. (London: William Miller, 1808), 11:452. Leigh Hunt used the exact same two passages, one from "Theodore and Honoria," the other from "Cymon and Iphigenia," to illustrate Dryden's admirable variety. See Amarasinghe, 25n.

5. For those who may be interested, see lines 79–106 from "Cymon and Iphigenia"; Dryden's version is racier than Boccaccio's.

6. This is essentially Amarasinghe's conclusion (see especially 23, 185, 193).

7. Wordsworth specifically praises the Boccaccio translations, although he does so begrudgingly, partially because he regards Dryden as "not . . . any great favourite of mine," and partially because he is offended at Dryden's explicit treatment of sexual encounters. Letter to Sir Walter Scott, 7 November 1805, quoted in *Dryden: The Critical Heritage*, ed. James Kinsley and Helen Kinsley (London: Routledge & Kegan Paul, 1971), 323–25.

8. Congreve, "Preface to Dryden's Dramatick Works" (1717), from *The Works of William Congreve*, ed. Montague Summers, 4 vols. (1924; rpt. New York: Russell & Russell, 1964), 4:181. The ode on St. Cecilia's Day to which Congreve alludes is "Alexander's Feast" (1697), which remained one of Dryden's most popular poems throughout the next century, and which Dryden reprinted in *Fables*.

9. Letter to Wycherley, 26 December 1704, in *The Correspondence of Alexander Pope*, ed. George Sherburn, 5 vols. (Oxford: Clarendon Press, 1956), 1:2.

10. The appreciative comment by Sheridan as well as the begrudgingly kind comment by Wordsworth referred to earlier are both cited by Amarasinghe (193, 23).

11. Mark Van Doren, *The Poetry of John Dryden* (New York: Harcourt, Brace & Howe, 1920); rev. and retitled *John Dryden: A Study of His Poetry* (New York: Holt Rinehart, 1946; rpt. Bloomington: Indiana University Press, 1963), 215.

12. Earl Miner devotes a chapter to *Fables* in *Dryden's Poetry* (Bloomington: Indiana University Press, 1967), 287–323, and returns to *Fables* repeatedly: see his "Forms and Motives of Narrative Poetry," in *Writers and Their Background: John Dryden*, ed. Miner (Athens: Ohio University Press, 1972), 234–66; *The Restoration Mode from Milton to Dryden* (Princeton: Princeton University Press, 1974), 541–57; and "Time, Sequence, and Plot in Restoration Literature," in *Studies in Eighteenth-Century Culture*, vol. 5, ed. Ronald C. Rosbottom (Madison: University of Wisconsin Press, 1976), 67–85. The judgment that *Fables* is the second greatest seventeenth-century narrative appears both in the

concluding paragraphs of *Restoration Mode* (556–57), and in another Earl Miner article, "Dryden's Admired Acquaintance, Mr. Milton," *Milton Studies* 11 (1978):25.

13. The most significant critical studies of *Fables*, besides those by Earl Miner cited in the previous note, are: James D. Garrison's "The Universe of Dryden's *Fables*," *Studies in English Literature* 21 (1981):409–23; Judith Sloman's "The Structure of Dryden's *Fables*," Ph.D. diss., University of Minnesota, 1968; and Steven N. Zwicker's *Politics and Language in Dryden's Poetry: The Arts of Disguise* (Princeton: Princeton University Press, 1984), 158–76. Sloman has developed her ideas in two subsequent articles: "An Interpretation of Dryden's *Fables*," *Eighteenth-Century Studies* 4 (1970/71):199–211, and "Dryden's Originality in *Sigismonda and Guiscardo*," *Studies in English Literature* 12 (1972): 445–457. Sloman's posthumously published book, *Dryden: The Poetics of Translation* (Toronto: University of Toronto Press, 1985), further extends her ideas on *Fables* in the two concluding chapters (125–219).

14. While he consistently speaks in terms of integration, Dryden's unifying conception, and the like, Miner also consistently hedges his bets, admitting that "in any event the *Fables* is not a completely integrated whole" (*Dryden's Poetry*, 291). At one point, after speaking of "a unity achieved from highly diverse elements" (289) and asserting that *Fables* embodies "a special, original harmony," Miner begins the next paragraph: "To urge so much is not to deny that our impression of the *Fables* is apt to be one of variety to the point of disorder" (289). Similarly, Judith Sloman, in *Dryden: The Poetics*, does the same kind of hedging, in the opposite direction, calling *Fables* "obviously not a single unified narrative," but later in the same sentence claiming that "it works by creating an illusion of narrative with a collection so well integrated that we experience it as a tightly constructed sequence" (207). No sooner does Sloman comment that *Fables* "displays a range of fragmentary perceptions" than she welds the fragmentary into a "complex wholeness" (23). I regard these reactions not as inconsistency, but as a testament to the power of *Fables* to push astute critics toward integrating, while at the same time subverting their attempts to discover an ultimate unity.

15. William Myers, *Dryden* (London: Hutchinson, 1973), 171, 190. Similarly Zwicker, in *Politics and Language*, finds that "*Fables*, whatever its genesis, is not a haphazard collection" (165). Like Miner and Sloman, Zwicker responds to contradictions, and like them he relies upon terms like "balance," "reconcile," and "transcend" (see especially 173–75), which demonstrate the instinct to pull together something that one feels to be "haphazard." In moving toward his concluding remarks, Zwicker summarizes: "By meditating on those truths and wrongs, the poet finally transcended them through fable, through fiction, through a world in which the powers of the imagination reconciled change with constancy" (175). I would ask, transcended into what? And how can change be reconciled with constancy?

16. Norman Rabkin, in *Shakespeare and the Problem of Meaning* (Chicago: University of Chicago Press, 1981), observes that "the essence of our experience" in dealing with Shakespeare's tragedies "is our haunting sense of what doesn't fit the thesis we are tempted at every moment to derive" (23). I think this is also true of *Fables*; consequently, I disagree with Rabkin's subsequent argument that

this "irreducible multivalence" (63) is what distinguishes Shakespeare from the closed, consistent, rationally ordered Dryden (63–112). *Fables* particularly has resisted critical attempts to close it.

17. Although I will have occasion to refer to the effect of text upon reader, I remain wary about the pure subjectivity and the solipsism implicit in much reader-response criticism, and for that reason I remain attentive both to the events surrounding the poem and to Dryden's personal circumstances, which I think account for his subversive strategies of expression. Such an approach accords with David M. Vieth's work on reader-entrapment, which consistently stresses the need to view works not in a vacuum (or merely within the confines of one reader's mind), but in historical and biographical contexts. See Vieth's "Introduction" to *Papers on Language and Literature* 18 (1982):227–33 (volume 18 is a special issue devoted to entrapment in Restoration and early eighteenth-century literature).

18. I disagree with Judith Sloman, who "think[s] of Dryden's collections as 'sequences' because they have a cumulative effect if read from beginning to end and because the sense of development contributes to their meaning. Each poem functions almost as a stage in an argument or a thought process" (*Dryden: The Poetics*, 53–54). However, Sloman also acknowledges another possible kind of ordering, which seems to me more useful in dealing with a miscellany: "A specific kind of meaning emerges in a 'structure of structures' [a term borrowed from N. E. Collinge who uses it to describe a book of Horace's odes], since the individual poem may read one way when considered alone but have entirely different implications when it is compared to others in the collection" (53).

19. One might note that Dryden includes "The Wife of Bath's Tale" in his *Fables*, as well as an original poem about a dutiful wife, another about a worthy bachelor, another about a pure virgin, and several other tales from other sources about married couples. Thus, in addition to playing with intriguing echoes, and rearranging Chaucerian groups into Drydenian groups, Dryden seems to have anticipated by two hundred years George L. Kittredge's idea of the "Marriage Group."

20. Robert D. Hume, in *Dryden's Criticism* (Ithaca: Cornell University Press, 1970), describes this approach as "the deliberate digressiveness" of Dryden's essays (35). Speaking specifically of the Preface to *Fables*, Hume remarks that "the organization gives the impression of casual discourse" (54–55), which neatly characterizes both the casual apparent rambling I have been describing, and the organization inherent within it.

Chapter Two

THE ANTI-HEROIC FABLES

O N E O F Dryden's principal concerns in *Fables* is the heroic code, a good starting point for exploring what I have referred to as the elusiveness of *Fables*. It is also Dryden's starting point, as the opening verse paragraph of the first poem, "To the Dutchess of Ormond," reveals:

> The Bard who first adorn'd our Native Tongue
> Tun'd to his *British* Lyre this ancient Song:
> Which *Homer* might without a Blush reherse,
> And leaves a doubtful Palm in *Virgil*'s Verse:
> He match'd their Beauties, where they most excell;
> Of Love sung better, and of Arms as well.
> (1–6)

With such an opening, we can reasonably expect that we are going to hear a great deal more about love and arms. Another reason for starting with heroism in *Fables*, aside from its conspicuousness and its centrality to Dryden's career, is that it is one issue on which modern scholars of Dryden seem to agree: *Fables* is, by common consent, anti-heroic. Some contend that Dryden believed deeply in the validity of heroic values early in his career, when he was writing heroic plays, but became disenchanted as he matured; since *Fables* is his last major work, such critics regard it (often without examining it) as the final stage in the process of disillusionment.[1] What makes that interpretation especially attractive is that it offers an explanation as to why it is Dryden always wanted to write an original epic and yet never did write one: when he was mature enough to do so, he no longer believed in the whole enterprise. *Fables*, then, becomes the epic he never wrote, that is, the anti-heroic substitute for the heroic poem he could no longer believe in. Of course, there are other plausible explanations for Dryden's missing epic. Perhaps he never got around to it: in the Preface to *Fables*, he still talks about his "Intentions ... to translate the whole *Ilias*," if God grants him "longer Life, and moderate Health" (Kinsley, 4:1448). A grand translation of Homer might have been the equivalent to Dryden's epic. Or, he may have already achieved that equivalent in his translation of the *Aeneid*.[2]

The evidence for Dryden's implicit anti-heroism in *Fables* is abundant, and it is worth examining both to validate this accepted view (which is usually assumed rather than demonstrated) and to show its possible limitations. Dryden not only selected tales that would allow him to attack the old heroic code, but also altered heroic material so as to make Homer unwittingly denigrate Homer. Equally important, but not sought out by those intent upon finding Dryden's anti-heroic strain, is Dryden's honoring of heroic values, which gives us back something that he has just taken away.

THE FIRST BOOK OF HOMER'S ILIAS

Perhaps the most salient example of the anti-heroic in *Fables* is the first book of the *Iliad*, which Dryden translated with the aid of two trots, the expansive Chapman translation (1598–1610) and the plodding John Ogilby translation (1660–69) done in dreadfully contorted heroic couplets, a literal-minded, illustrated, large-print version suitable for children (Pope read it when he was a child).[3] Dryden relied a little on both authors, yet his own version, rather than steering a middle course between realms of gold and realms of nonsense absolute, ventures off in a different direction, toward the lowlands of burlesque.[4] The first book, just to review the familiar plot, centers on two debates, one between Agamemnon and Achilles, the other between Juno and Jupiter.[5] Agamemnon has been urged to surrender his captive, Chryseis, in order to remove a curse on the Greeks; he insists that he be compensated, which he achieves by seizing Achilles' captive, Briseis. This causes an angered Achilles to refuse to fight, and to implore his mother, Thetis, to ask Jove to punish the Greeks for depriving him of Briseis. Thetis, accordingly, offers her petition, and Jove grants it, which causes Juno to protest vigorously, until Vulcan intervenes and reconciles the gods. The two central arguments give both Homer and Dryden an opportunity to interrelate the world of men with the divine order, although the net effect for each author is quite different.

First, Dryden adds details that reduce both Achilles and Agamemnon.

Instead of Homeric wrath and grief, we see uncontrollable rage and passion, with both heroes appearing as helpless victims of their emotions. At one point in the Homeric original, when Athena appears to Achilles, "amaze strooke everie facultie" (Chapman, line 202), which sounds like an appropriate response to direct divine intervention.[6] In Dryden this becomes: "Tam'd by superiour Force he turn'd his Eyes / Aghast at first, and stupid with Surprize" (304–5). Emphasizing Athena's superior force rather than her divinity is a nice touch, one that changes the character of Achilles. Instead of being a warrior properly awed by a god, he appears more the bully, somebody who thinks in terms of power and will alter his course only when a superior power tames him; when this one arrives, Achilles is rendered "stupid," which means awed or stunned, of course, but is scarcely the most flattering adjective for a hero, since stupid also means stupid.[7] When Athena leaves, Achilles obeys her injunction to put away his sword, and he resumes his verbal denunciation of Agamemnon, which Athena had specifically approved: "Draw no sword; Use words, and such as may / Be bitter to his pride, but just" (Chapman, lines 211–12). Dryden's description of Achilles' behavior after Athena's departure twists things slightly:

> At her departure his Disdain return'd:
> The Fire she fan'd, with greater Fury burn'd;
> Rumbling within till thus it found a vent:
> Dastard, and Drunkard, Mean and Insolent:
> Tongue-valiant Hero, Vaunter of thy Might . . .
> (332–36)

The last two lines are the beginning of Achilles' tirade against Agamemnon, "Vaunter of thy Might" being a Dryden addition that again implies that Achilles is more concerned with power than with honor. Where in the original and Chapman versions Achilles is following divine instructions, "Burne[ing] in just anger" (Chapman, line 216), and continuing to express himself in such words as may be bitter "but just," Dryden's Achilles seems out of control. "Just anger" has been replaced by "turbulence of Mind" (311), and what could be a heroic virtue is replaced by what seems to be a mental disorder. Best of all, Dryden adds the image of Achilles as erupting volcano. Altogether, Achilles appears as a victim of his own uncontrollable rage, temporarily rendered stupid, and now about to explode once Athena's superior restraining force is removed.

Agamemnon, if anything, fares worse. Achilles ends the above speech by throwing his staff onto the ground and sitting down, and we turn to watch Agamemnon's reaction: "Atrides' [i.e., Agamemnon's] breast was drownd / In rising choler" (Chapman, lines 244–45). Both are mightily angry. Dryden renders this as:

Against the Ground his golden Scepter threw;
Then sate: with boiling Rage *Atrides* burn'd:
And Foam betwixt his gnashing Grinders churn'd.
(359–61)

The one hero is volcanic, the other like a mad dog; noble wrath starts looking ridiculous. Not only are both figures apparently possessed by forces they cannot control, but those forces render them distinctly less than human, a point Dryden pursues elsewhere. Earlier in the quarrel, Agamemnon upbraided Achilles with these words:

Debates, Dissentions, Uproars are thy Joy;
Provok'd without Offence, and practis'd to destroy.
Strength is of Brutes; and not thy Boast alone;
At least 'tis lent from Heav'n; and not thy own.
(265–68)

Agamemnon's purpose is, in part, to puncture Achilles' pride in his strength by telling him that his power is not his own; Dryden's Agamemnon, however, points out something else, that Achilles' strength is bestial. When several lines later we discover the hero who denounces Achilles as a brute himself foaming at the mouth and gnashing his teeth, we are likely to laugh; on Dryden's scale, both heroes are not just sub-human, but ludicrously so, rather like cartoon villains in their comically exaggerated displays of anger. The point is all the more significant, I think, when we consider this in the context of *Fables* as a whole, for it has not been long since Theseus in "Palamon and Arcite" delivered his speech on the Chain of Being, on the natural hierarchy that testifies to God's presence:

He perfect, stable; but imperfect We,
Subject to Change, and diff'rent in Degree.
Plants, Beasts, and Man; and as our Organs are,
We more or less of his Perfection share.
(3:1046–49)

Bestial Agamemnon and Achilles share less of "his Perfection," apparently; the heroic code they comprise looks crude and primitive in the light of the Boethian universe Theseus defines.

14

One could cite any number of small touches whereby Dryden diminishes his heroes, but one more, I think, will suffice. In the following extended passage, we can actually see Dryden reworking Chapman, for Chapman makes a subtle addition that imparts an added dignity to Agamemnon, which Dryden manages to rip away completely. We are at the point in the first book where, having returned Chryseis to palliate Apollo, Agamemnon orders the proper sacrifices to "reconcile the shooter God" (Dryden, 431). In Chapman, the passage runs as follows:

> And now the king of men
> Bad all the hoast to sacrifice. They sacrific'd and cast
> The offal of all to the deepes; the angrie God they grac't
> With perfect Hecatombs—some buls, some goates along the shore
> Of the unfruitfull sea inflam'd. To heaven the thicke fumes bore
> Enwrapped savours. Thus though all the politique king made shew
> Respects to heaven, yet he himselfe all that time did pursue
> His owne affections. The late jarre, in which he thunderd threats
> Against Achilles, still he fed, and his affections' heats
> Thus vented.
>
> (Chapman, lines 308–17)

I take "politique king," a Chapman addition, as a mildly favorable piece of description; Agamemnon is behaving as a responsible king ought, offering his respects to heaven, which might be called the indirect approach, while at the same time continuing in his wrath (the direct approach). Not so in Dryden's version:

> *Atrides* then his outward Zeal to boast,
> Bade purify the Sin-polluted Host.
> With perfect Hecatombs the God they grac'd;
> Whose offer'd Entrails in the Main were cast.
> Black Bulls, and bearded Goats on Altars lie;
> And clouds of sav'ry stench, involve the Sky.
> These Pomps the Royal Hypocrite design'd,
> For Shew; But harbour'd Vengeance in his Mind:
> Till holy Malice, longing for a vent,
> At length, discover'd his conceal'd Intent.
>
> (436–45)[8]

Dryden's Agamemnon is a hypocrite, his sacrifice a total sham "design'd, / For Shew"; all the while his foremost motive has been to get back at Achilles. Dryden not only adds hypocrisy as a motive, but makes the passage pivot around it. He starts by stressing the "outward" behavior, building up to a grand show of clouds that fill the sky. Then, after using the word "Hypocrite," Dryden reveals what has been going on inwardly—the "harbour'd Vengeance," the malice somewhere underneath "longing for a vent," the "conceal'd Intent"—all of which the outward pomp had been meant to hide, but which now comes rushing out in the last four lines.

Worse, Agamemnon is not just a hypocrite, but also a king, a "Royal Hypocrite," and, as Achilles remarks when accusing him of selfishness, Agamemnon was "Advanc'd to Sovereign Sway, for better Ends / Than thus like abject Slaves to treat thy Friends" (227–28, a couplet added by Dryden). As these additions imply, in Dryden's translation the issue of kingship assumes a central position, with "sovereign sway" becoming a veritable leitmotif. As Achilles' comment above attests, Dryden's characters are in the habit of trying to teach political lessons to this "haughty" (38) king, this "King of Men . . . swoln with Pride" (13, both Dryden additions), not that it ever does much good. Thus, Chapman's Nestor advises Agamemnon to "give not streame / To all thy powre, nor force his prise" (Chapman, lines 272–73), but Dryden's Nestor turns this into: "Thou, King of Men, stretch not thy sovereign Sway / Beyond, the Bounds free Subjects can obey" (389–90). And a few lines later, after advising Achilles to calm down, Chapman's Nestor turns back to Agamemnon for a final reminder:

> King of men,
> Command thou then thy selfe, and I with my prayres will obtaine
> Grace of Achilles to subdue his furie; whose parts are
> Worth our intreatie.
> (Chapman, lines 279–82)

Dryden transforms this plea for self-restraint into a mini-lecture on the responsibilities of kingship, the wisdom of political restraint, the relationship of king to people, and the moral authority behind laws:

> Thou first, O King, release the rights of Sway,
> Pow'r, self-restrain'd, the People best obey.
> Sanctions of Law from Thee derive their Source;
> Command thy Self, whom no Commands can force.
> The Son of *Thetis* Rampire of our Host,
> Is worth our Care to keep; nor shall my Pray'rs be lost.
> (397–402)

That Dryden should repeat the "Sway/obey" rhyme within ten lines (389–90; 397–98) suggests his concern with kingly power as an issue in itself, a familiar Dryden preoccupation. We hear something similar at the end of "Britannia Rediviva" (1688), where Dryden turns from celebrating the birth of an heir to the throne, to advising the current monarch on how thrones should be held in the first place: James II, like Agamemnon, should restrain himself and avoid the dangerous consequences of "boundless pow'r" (341) and "Resistless Force" (349).

Agamemnon, like James, does not listen. While Dryden's Nestor and Achilles incline toward pithy morals on how a king should behave, Agamemnon stubbornly ignores their comments; he has his own view of sovereign right, upon which he continually relies in justifying his actions. When Agamemnon finds he must surrender his captive, he demands a recompense; in Homer, Chapman, and Ogilby, the idea is that Agamemnon should not be the only one not to have a prize:

> Wouldst thou maintaine in sure abode
> Thine owne prise and sleight me of mine? Resolve this: if our friends
> (As fits in equitie my worth) will right me with amends,
> So rest it; otherwise, my selfe will enter personally
> On thy prise.
> (Chapman, lines 134–38)

Dryden's royal hypocrite, however, is much more concerned with what is due him *as king*, as Dryden's translation of this passage reveals:

> Shall I release the Prize I gain'd by Right,
> In taken Towns, and many a bloody Fight,
> While thou detain'st *Briseis* in thy Bands,
> By priestly glossing on the God's Commands?
> Resolve on this, (a short Alternative)
> Quit mine, or, in exchange, another give;
> Else I, assure thy Soul, by Sov'reign Right
> Will seize thy Captive in thy own Despight.
> (200–207)

No longer is this a matter of equity—we all deserve prizes, including me. Rather, Dryden's Agamemnon is eager to insist that seizing the captive is his "Sov'reign Right"; earlier, he had referred to his "Slave" as "my Sov'reign Prize" (165). When Dryden's prophet Calchas cynically classifies Agamemnon among those "Sov'reigns ever jealous of their State" (116, a Dryden insertion), and when Achilles refers to Agamemnon as "still tenacious of thy Hold" (184), they have grasped this Agamemnon's motivation. His hold over Chryseis is his petty way of asserting his hold over the throne.

17

Agamemnon *is* ever jealous of his State, ever aware of possible threats to his power. When Calchas tells him he must relinquish his captive, Agamemnon's response in Chapman, Ogilby, and Homer is an irritated denunciation of nuisance prophecies, but in Dryden this turns into sheer paranoia: "And now thou dost with Lies the Throne invade" (159). Petty, cunning, selfish, arbitrary, foaming at the mouth, seeing threats to his throne behind every bush, ever eager to assert and consolidate his authority, this Agamemnon is a chilling picture of kingship.[9] This is not to say that Homer's royal figures are entirely bathed in glory; Homer has a Thersites to comment cynically on kingship, although the querulous prophet does not appear in the first book. Dryden, however, manages to achieve the same effect without a Thersites, but more, he amplifies it: his Nestor, Achilles, and Calchas all tend to sound like Thersites, and his paranoid Agamemnon fulfills their mean-spirited descriptions of kingly behavior.

Dryden's world of selfish, brutal rulers, immature warriors subject to uncontrollable passions, cynical commentators on the arbitrary exercise of kingly power, stands the classical heroic mode on its head.[10] But by far the greatest changes in Dryden's translation occur at the end when Dryden deals with the pagan gods; here he reduces the epic to the level of burlesque. The scene shifts from the Grecian camp to Mount Olympus, and we watch Thetis begging Jove to avenge the dishonor done to her son Achilles. Jove is reluctant to grant her request, knowing that to do so will anger Juno; nonetheless, he promises to punish the Greeks, reminding everybody that his vow once given is irrevocable and is inevitably fulfilled. As Jove has predicted, Juno becomes incensed, upbraids Jove with "sharpe invective" (Chapman, line 522), accuses him of "being seduc't" (Chapman, line 538) by Thetis into honoring Achilles, and attacks Jove for making judgments in secret, apart from his wife. Jove asserts his authority; without actually acknowledging what he has vowed, he tells Juno that she cannot "prevent" his "designes" and warns her that "Thy curiositie / Makes thee lesse car'd for at my hands, and horrible the end / Shall make thy humor" (Chapman, lines 544–46). This frightens Juno and troubles all the gods, but Vulcan intervenes, as Nestor had in the power struggle between Agamemnon and Achilles, in an attempt to reconcile both parties.

Just as Nestor had argued that the personal strife threatened to damage the common cause, so does Vulcan argue that "these words will breed wounds beyond our powres to beare / If thus for mortals ye fall out" (Chapman, lines 555–56). And just as Nestor had advised Achilles not to resist Agamemnon, "since no king that ever Jove allowd / Grace of a scepter equals him" (Chapman, lines 275–76), so Vulcan warns Juno not to resist Jove, "his power Olympian / Is so surpassing" (Chapman, lines 562–63), which Vulcan demonstrates by telling of his own injury, suffered when Jove hurled him from heaven. Unlike Nestor, Vulcan succeeds as mediator. He pours wine, passes the cup around, induces Juno to smile and the gods to laugh; what might have been a day of wrath turns instead into a day of celebration, feasting, and singing, ending with Jove returning to his couch at sunset and falling asleep with Juno at his side. Her position as consort is intact, as is Jove's power and authority, and sweet sleep and celebration becalm all.

Dryden's version, which includes all of the above, has a totally different effect, with timely shifts of emphasis changing everything. For instance, when Jove insists on his right to make decisions without consulting Juno, he tells her:

> Have never hope to know
> My whole intentions, though my wife. It fits not, nor would show
> Well to thine owne thoughts; but what fits thy woman's eare to heare,
> Woman nor God shall know before it grace thine eare.
> (Chapman, lines 528–31)

In Dryden, this becomes:

> Ev'n Goddesses are Women: And no Wife
> Has Pow'r to regulate her Husband's Life:
> Counsel she may; and I will give thy Ear
> The Knowledge first, of what is fit to hear.
> (735–38)

Dryden has not really added anything, but he has taken the throwaway qualification "though my wife," and the statement (not in Homer) about what fits a woman's ear, and made from them a new, central issue. Jove's pronouncement of what it is fit that Juno know becomes instead an anti-feminist remark about uppity wives knowing their places. Just as Dryden had expanded on the theme of sovereign power earlier, so does he here develop the theme of marriage, which also resonates throughout *Fables.* When Vulcan urges Juno not to resist so powerful a god as Jove, he asks her to "Suffer, beare, though your great bosome grieve, / And lest blowes force you" (Chapman, lines 567–68). In Dryden this becomes advice that Juno should know and keep her subservient, wifely place:

Be, as becomes a Wife, obedient still;
Though griev'd, yet subject to her Husband's Will.
I wou'd not see you beaten . . .
(788–90)

The dangerous possibility that Jove will smite a fellow god becomes the more mundane, and despicable, possibility that a husband will beat his disobedient wife.[11]

Homer's Jove (Zeus), prior to making his vow for Thetis, expects strife from Juno: "Juno will storme and all my powers inflame with contumelies. /Ever she wrangles, charging me in eare of all the Gods / That I am partiall still" (Chapman, lines 501–3). A little later, when he gets from Juno the tirade he anticipated, he begins one of his heated speeches with "Wretch! . . . Thy subtle jealousies / Are still exploring; my designes can never scape thine eye" (Chapman, lines 542–43). Dryden renders the first speech, addressed to Thetis, as:

Know'st thou what Clamors will disturb my Reign,
What my stun'd Ears from *Juno* must sustain?
In Council she gives Licence to her Tongue,
Loquacious, Brawling, ever in the wrong.
(697–700)

And the second speech, to ever-in-the-wrong Juno, becomes:

My Household Curse, my lawful Plague, the Spy
Of *Jove's* Designs, his other squinting Eye;
Why this vain prying, and for what avail?
(752–54)

Jovian wrath has been transformed into Juvenalian tirade. One might be led to pity the target of these anti-feminist shafts, except that Dryden has so altered Juno's character that she fulfills Jove's Juvenalian expectations. In one of her speeches, for example, the original Juno complains that Thetis, "daughter of the sea's ancient," has "won over" Jove (Lattimore, lines 555–56), which, in Chapman's less sedate translation, becomes more insulting: she accuses Jove of "being seduc't by this old sea-God's seed / That could so early use her knees, embracing thine" (Chapman, lines 538–39). Since Thetis did fall to her knees and clasp Jove's legs, Juno's guess as to what happened is accurate, and also may be a nice piece of innuendo, since there are other ways Thetis could have used her knees to embrace Jove's legs. What may hover above Chapman's lines as innuendo becomes frontal assault in Dryden's expanded version of the speech:

> Which of thy Dames, what Prostitute of Love,
> Has held thy Ear so long and begg'd so hard
> For some old Service done, some new Reward?
> Apart you talk'd, for that's your special care
> The Consort never must the Council share.
> One gracious Word is for a Wife too much:
> Such is a Marriage-vow, and *Jove*'s own Faith is such.
> (726–32)

There is nothing here that is invented out of thin air, for in the classics Jove has a history of infidelity and Juno a reputation for nagging and at times avenging herself on her husband. But it is Dryden who brings this into the foreground, who narrows Juno's motives, which in the original include a concern for the Trojans, to a jealous accusation that Jove has once again been messing around. What could have been a power struggle with disastrous consequences is nothing more than a marital spat between stereotypical shrewish wife and wife-hating husband.[12]

Since this dangerous power struggle between Jove and Juno has degenerated into an exchange of domestic insults, it follows that Dryden's Vulcan performs a slightly different function; no longer do two implacable and mighty forces require a tactful mediator, but rather a comic exchange of insults requires a comic interlocutor, and Dryden changes Vulcan into something of a buffoon. "Heaven's famous Artizan" (Chapman, line 553) enters instead as "The Limping smith . . . / hopping here and there (himself a Jest)" (768–69). Dryden uses Vulcan to degrade everybody; as we have seen, Dryden adds lines that make Vulcan tell Juno to know her place as a wife, thereby confirming rather than mitigating Jove's demeaning anti-feminism. Vulcan manages to insult Jove too, indirectly, by suggesting that Juno humor him: "But one submissive Word, which you let fall, / Will make him in good Humour with us All" (782–83: Chapman says "Soften then with gentle speech his splene," line 563). Dryden's Vulcan seems not to be advising tactful submission but rather an insincere gesture, making it appear that Jove is the kind of person who can best be handled with what might be called child psychology.

Nor does Dryden's Vulcan ennoble the rest of the gods. In passing around "The sweete-peace-making draught . . . [of] Nectar" (Chapman, lines 578–79), the original Vulcan brings about general good cheer and celebration: "A laughter never left / Shooke all the blessed deities," and "They banqueted and had such cheere as did their wishes crowne" (Chapman, lines 579–80, 582). Dryden transforms this mellow ceremony of harmony among the gods into a drunken orgy. The "Clown" (801) fills the bowl, and "Loud Fits of Laughter seiz'd the Guests" (804), which makes the gods seem out of control, seized by fits, rather than crowning their wishes with cheer. Banqueting becomes drinking, with results suitable to rakes: "They drank, they laugh'd, they lov'd, and then 'twas Night / . . . Drunken at last, and drowsy they depart" (807, 810). The sweet nectar seems to have gotten stronger in the translation.

The first book of the *Iliad* moves toward a final scene of reconciliation between Jove and Juno. After a day of celebration, or heavy drinking, depending on which version we are reading, Jove goes to his couch, which Chapman, oozing Keatsian sibilants, renders as:

> Even he to sleepe went by whose hand heaven is with lightning guilt,
> High Jove, where he had usd to rest when sweet sleepe seisd his eyes.
> By him the golden-thron'd Queene slept, the Queene of deities.
> (Chapman, lines 588–90)[13]

Dryden ends with:

> The thund'ring God
> Ev'n he withdrew to rest, and had his Load.
> His swimming Head to needful Sleep apply'd;
> And *Juno* lay unheeded by his Side.
> (812–15)

Conjugal reconciliation is replaced by conjugal indifference, a becalmed Jupiter turns into a drunken thunderer collapsing at the end of a day of heavy drinking, and the famed craftsman, parallel to wise Nestor, becomes a jest, an "obsequious" (771) clown, a "Rude Skinker" (803). Of course, the classical gods are notoriously imperfect, which is part of their charm; but Dryden has expanded on their foibles, has rendered them comic. If the heroic warriors are turned into selfish bullies, the pagan gods seem even lower on the scale of intrinsic nobility.

THE TWELFTH BOOK OF OVID'S METAMORPHOSES

A few years earlier, in the Dedication to *Examen Poeticum* (1693), Dryden remarked on what he felt to be the failings in Homer: he "provokes to Murther, and the destruction of God's Images; he forms and equips those ungodly Man-killers, whom we Poets, when we flatter them, call Heroes; a race of Men who can never enjoy quiet in themselves, 'till they have taken it from all the World" (*Works*, 4:374). Those seeking Dryden's anti-heroism are fond of citing this brief statement.[14] All in all, Dryden's translation of the opening of the *Iliad* allows him to flesh out the remark and, in the process, disembowel Homer. When we end Dryden's version of the first book with the sight of squabbling gods now drunk, orgied into oblivion, we realize why it is that Dryden might have been unable to continue the epic he has begun, and undone.[15] True, but in a way, Dryden *did* finish. The variety in *Fables* is so great that we are perhaps likely to overlook one of Dryden's many "links"; his headnote to "The Twelfth Book of Ovid His Metamorphoses" reminds us that Ovid "naturally falls into the Story of the *Trojan* War, which is summ'd up, in the present Book" (Kinsley, 4:1666). The twelfth book is like a Chinese box of stories within stories within stories, with the longest section devoted to Nestor's tale of a bloody fight between the Lapithae and the centaurs. This and other digressions take such precedence that we scarcely notice Ovid's recounting the Trojan War, in passing, from the landing of the Greeks and the death of the first Greek (Dryden, 94), to the death of Achilles ten years later (Dryden, 805). By turning to book twelve, Dryden does, in a way, complete the story of the Trojan War he had begun with "The First Book of Homer's Ilias"; he just shifts from Homer to Ovid.

Of the twenty-one tales in *Fables*, eight are from *Metamorphoses*, which is cause enough to reflect on the possible reasons Dryden gravitated toward Ovid. For one thing, both writers became political outcasts late in their careers. Augustus banished Ovid to Thomis on the Black Sea and arranged for all copies of *Ars Amatoria* to be expelled from public libraries;[16] Dryden too was a kind of exile, in spirit, for with his loss of the laureateship in 1688, he shifted from official spokesman called upon to proclaim his views to the public, to deposed laureate, "strugling with Wants, oppress'd with Sickness, curb'd in my Genius, lyable to be misconstrued in all I write" (Postscript to the *Aeneis*, Kinsley, 3:1424). We have an Augustan poet and a Stuart poet, both of whom intended to write epics of their own, both of whom were deposed; such a parallel could scarcely escape Dryden, who was especially alert to possible connections between himself and the great authors of the past. In his Preface to "Eleonora," published in 1692, Dryden explicitly likened himself to Ovid, who, "going to his Banishment, and Writing from on Shipbord to his Friends, excus'd the Faults of his Poetry by his Misfortunes" (Kinsley, 2:582). By turning to Ovid, Dryden turns to a congenial alter ego, another dispossessed poet who had grown estranged from the whole world of heroic virtue.[17] That *Fables* includes but one book of Homer, severely altered, and eight tales from Ovid, several of which are already anti-heroic in import, indicates the nature of Dryden's shift. And if it is significant to observe the changes Dryden made to square Homer with his own perceptions of the epic world, it is equally significant to observe that Dryden's translation of Ovid is "straight"—the details, the tone, even the hero-puncturing metaphors that Dryden found himself adding to Homer, were already there in Ovid, ready to be honed into couplets. Dryden did not have to change much (except to sharpen a point here and there); Ovid already expressed a distrust of the heroic code.[18]

The twelfth book of the *Metamorphoses* is a Sternian ramble, with digressions on top of digressions, episodes dangled loosely from other episodes, flashes backwards and forwards, not to mention an occasional sex change by a character who starts out female, changes to a male, and ends up as a bird. The narrative is free from the constraints of necessary, or even plausible, connections, as a plot summary will perhaps illustrate. Book twelve starts with the Greeks awaiting a wind, moves toward another of those sacrifices advised by the seer Calchas to propitiate the gods, and then the battle itself begins, with most of our attention focused on one fight, that between Achilles and the invulnerable Cygnus. Spears bounce off Cygnus, much to Achilles' discontent; he cannot believe his eyes and even pauses to test his spear on some other hapless warrior, who crumbles instantly to the ground. Having convinced himself that his aim and spear are still sound, Achilles tries again, and when the spear again fails, resorts to a backup plan: he uses his buckler to pin Cygnus to the ground, and while kneeling on his opponent, Achilles uses his own chinstrap to strangle the impenetrable warrior.

When the day's battle is over, the victors celebrate with a sacrifice and a feast. The discourse turns to "Deeds of Arms" (222), and Nestor is asked to recount the story of Caeneus, another presumably invulnerable warrior who was nonetheless killed. Nestor's story starts with Neptune ravishing the lovely woman Caenis; in compensation for this injury, Neptune grants her a wish, and she wishes she were a man. Neptune turns her into one and makes her invulnerable into the bargain. Next, Nestor abruptly begins the apparently unrelated story of the wedding between Perithous and Hippodame, attended by the Lapithae and the centaurs. At the nuptial feast one of the centaurs, Eurytus, impelled by wine, lust, and his own bestial nature, tactlessly attempts to rape the bride-to-be, for which he is swiftly killed. His death is avenged, and the killing spreads, with warriors using eating utensils, altars, furniture, and nearby trees as weapons. Nestor eventually returns to Caeneus (in line 609—he/she was last mentioned in line 291), who was involved in this fight and who, like Cygnus, was killed though invulnerable. And like Cygnus, who was turned into a swan, Caeneus turns into a yellow bird. At the end of Nestor's tale, Tlepolemus complains that Nestor had not included Hercules, who was there at that very fight, which allows Nestor to explain that he had omitted Hercules intentionally, because Hercules killed Nestor's kinsmen.

Once Nestor has finished speaking, book twelve shifts to Neptune, the sire of Cygnus, who appeals to Apollo for vengeance on his son's murderer, Achilles. Apollo helps Paris slay the supposedly invulnerable Achilles, and we end with the death of Achilles and a mention of the new "Strife, betwixt contending Kings" (821), Ulysses and Ajax, as to who should be awarded Achilles' armor and shield. The debate between these two rivals is the subject of Dryden's next fable, "The Speeches of Ajax and Ulysses," from the beginning of book thirteen of the *Metamorphoses*. By his own account, Dryden had turned to book twelve in order to complete the story of the Trojan War, but his enthusiasm for Ovid, or his momentum, carried him beyond the compass of that book. Having reached the "Ending, of the *Trojan* War," Dryden admits in his Preface, "Here I ought in reason to have stopp'd; but the Speeches of *Ajax* and *Ulysses* lying next in my way, I could not balk 'em" (Kinsley, 4: 1444).

This is scarcely a plot that would have pleased Aristotle, but it is not plot that sustains book twelve. Rather the episodes are all like the analogous events typologists find in comparing stories from the Old and New Testaments: Ovid's rambling, like Dryden's, has a method to it, and we discover that all the episodes comprise variations on the theme "Deeds of Arms" (222). Nestor's story of Caeneus is but another version of the Cygnus story; both demonstrate that the invulnerable are not exactly invulnerable. That Nestor should tell the Caeneus story in celebration of Achilles' victory is ironic, for this is Achilles' story too. "The Terror of the *Trojan* Field" (812) is reduced to "small Remains / A little Urn, . . . scarcely fill'd, contains" (816–17; Dryden takes the rhyme and most of the words straight from Sandys, lines 615–16). Ultimately, there are no victors; invulnerable Achilles ends up as dead as the invulnerable warrior he slew. And Achilles' fame only causes more bloodshed, for it leads to the death of Ajax, who, in book thirteen, kills himself once Achilles' armor is awarded to Ulysses.

The consequences are bad, but at least Achilles' fame, if not Achilles, lives on; Hercules is not so lucky. When reminded by Tlepolemus that he had omitted Hercules' exploits from his narration, Nestor explains that it is "Better to pass him o'er, than to relate / The Cause I have your mighty Sire to hate" (717–18). Nestor then tells how Hercules killed Nestor's brothers, eleven of them, "All Youths of early Promise" (729), and Nestor gives a detailed account of just one death, the slaying of Periclymenos. When he was "Vanquish'd on Earth" (737, a Dryden addition), Periclymenos, like Cygnus and Caeneus, turned into a bird, an eagle, but the new form provided no sanctuary. Hercules, "bending his inevitable Bow" (744), killed Periclymenos, and Nestor, the same Nestor who had described death after death, concludes this final account of his brother's death at the hands of Hercules with these lines:

> Now, brave Commander of the *Rhodian* Seas [Tlepolemus],
> What Praise is Due from me, to *Hercules*?
> Silence is all the Vengeance I decree
> For my slain Brothers; but 'tis Peace with thee.
> (757–60)

Tlepolemus gets his wish: Nestor finally does include Hercules, mentioning his exploits only to explain why he is not mentioning them. Nestor says his vengeance is "Silence" rather than more killing, but that is not quite true; in his own way, he destroys Hercules by taking away his glory, debunks the hero in an afterthought rather than deify him. Hercules is just another indiscriminate destroyer, one who "levell'd to the Ground / *Messenia*'s Tow'rs" (723–24), and did the same to Elis and Pylos, "Both guiltless of their Fate" (726). What makes this all the more appropriate is that the eloquent, elderly Nestor often serves as Dryden's alter ego, as we perhaps notice when in the first book of the *Iliad* we hear this same character delivering distinctly Drydenian advice to Agamemnon about how kings should exercise their power (397–402). In defaming Hercules, Nestor does to him what Dryden had already done in his translation of Homer to heroic-volcanic Achilles, and, for that matter, to power-hungry Agamemnon as well. One might add that in avenging himself on a heroic figure while maintaining that he is taking no vengeance, Nestor also manages to accomplish what Dryden seems to accomplish in his incessant attacks upon William III throughout *Fables*.

This story of Periclymenos' death, then, adds to the impact of the whole in a number of ways. In addition to debunking yet another hero, and piling up more examples of murder upon murder, the episode demonstrates that vengeance once begun breeds more vengeance. Furthermore, the character speaking these words becomes subject to his own theme; Nestor, "first for Prudence in repute" (245), is not immune from the consequences of bloodshed, nor free from the desire for revenge.[19] But of course the idea that bloodshed once begun knows no limits is what the Lapithae and the centaurs demonstrate, with bloody death after bloody death, in the central piece of action in book twelve. In the background, the real Trojan War takes place; in the foreground, we witness a parody. Instead of Paris impelled by love to steal another man's wife, we get the beast Eurytus, drunken and filled with lust, raping a bride-to-be; instead of the noble warriors glorified by Homer, we get beasts fighting with furniture, a ludicrous, reductive commentary on heroism. Since the battle of the Lapithae and centaurs takes place in a cave, this is not merely parody, but "is quite literally a grotesque of heroic literature."[20]

Both Dryden and Ovid seem to revel in describing gore; the deaths are not merely bloody, although they are that, but also ingenious, acro-

27

batic, and bizarre, which makes book twelve not so much chilling as humorous, in an appropriately grotesque way. Eurytus, the "foul Ravisher" (333), is the first to fall, struck by "An ample Goblet, . . . of antick Mold" (330):

> He falls; and falling vomits forth a Flood
> Of Wine, and Foam and Brains, and mingled Blood.
> Half roaring, and half neighing through the Hall,
> Arms, Arms, the double form'd with Fury call;
> To wreak their Brother's death: A Medley-Flight
> Of Bowls and Jars, at first supply the Fight.
>
> (334–39)

We no sooner accept the characters as warriors than Dryden reminds us they are "neighing," or are "double-form'd" centaurs; the latter is straight from Ovid's "bimembres,"[21] but Dryden heightens the implicit bestiality by adding roaring and neighing. The non-centaurs are no less bestial;[22] Celadon, the next to fall, is likened to an ox led to the sacrificial altar:

> On *Celadon* the Ruin fell; and left
> His Face of Feature and of Form bereft:
> So, when some brawny Sacrificer knocks
> Before an Altar led, an offer'd Oxe,
> His Eye-balls rooted out, are thrown to Ground;
> His Nose dismantled, in his Mouth is found,
> His Jaws, Cheeks, Front, one undistinguish'd Wound.
>
> (348–54)

Not only is Celadon indistinguishable from a brute, but he also dies in a singularly stupid way, never aware that he is being "dismantled." Dryden's verb, "knocks," makes the gore seem off-handed (more so than Ovid's "rumpere . . . molitur,"[23] which means "he strives to break"), and we are surprised at the detailed consequences, with dangling eyeballs and whatnot spilling over the ground after a seemingly effortless gesture. The implements of death are comically inappropriate: a goblet, bowls, jars, and in Celadon's case, a heavenly chalice, a sconce, and tapers, a miscellany of "holy Things" (343) stolen from the vestry and hurled amidst the Lapithae. All the trappings of civilization, from its "Instruments of Feasts" (340) to its religious artifacts, have been converted to ammunition for the purposes of slaughter. The actual functions of eating utensils and sacred vessels in this brutal world are as far from their ostensible civilized uses as is the aimless death of Celadon from the religious sacrifice to which it is compared.

I do not think Dryden evokes pity for the victims, in part because there are so many and they keep piling up too swiftly for us to distinguish individuals, and in part because rather than emphasize their suffering, Dryden emphasizes their surprise, the surprise of Eurytus who dies in his wine cup, or of Aphidas:

> Snoring, and drunk with Wine, *Aphidas* lay.
> Ev'n then the Bowl within his Hand he kept:
> And on a Bear's rough Hide securely slept.
> Him *Phorbas* with his flying Dart, transfix'd;
> Take the next Draught, with *Stygian* Waters mix'd,
> And sleep thy fill, th' insulting Victor cry'd;
> Surpris'd with Death unfelt, the Centaur dy'd;
> The ruddy Vomit, as he breath'd his Soul,
> Repass'd his Throat; and fill'd his empty Bowl.
> (436–44)

Death is both abundant and unexpected. Just as Petraeus has his weapon, an uprooted oak tree, at the ready, he finds himself "nail'd . . . to the Wood" by "*Perithous'* Dart" (450). In some cases, the surprise comes because the death is semi-accidental. Not only do chalices and altar stones hit random targets (like Celadon), but at times a warrior will aim at A and hit B by mistake. At one point, Charaxus, whose hair has been set on fire, lifts a "Threshold-Stone" (393) in hopes of throwing it. Alas, it is too heavy to throw:

> The Weight it self, forbad the threaten'd Blow,
> Which dropping from his lifted Arms, came down,
> Full on *Cometes* Head; and crush'd his Crown.
> (394–96)

At least it kills somebody. Similarly, Demoleon uproots a pine tree, and swings it toward Theseus, who steps aside in such a fashion that the tree accidentally sunders Crantor's body at the waist (487–88). Nobody is safe; Dictys, luckily, escapes from the fray, but in the act of leaping to safety, he accidentally impales himself on an ash tree (455–59).

There is gore aplenty here, with ingenious variations. Exadius wrenches stag horns from a wall and uses them to pierce both eyes of Grineus simultaneously (372–79); Helops has a spear go through one ear and come out the other (453–54); Dorylas dies on an empty stomach, literally:

> Him *Peleus* finish'd, with a second Wound,
> Which through the Navel pierc'd; He reel'd around;
> And drag'd his dangling Bowels on the Ground.
> Trod what he drag'd; and what he trod he crush'd:
> And to his Mother-Earth, with empty Belly rush'd.
> (519–23)

Throughout, death is remarkably casual; it happens at random, by mistake, in passing. Even when the death is the result of a direct, purposeful aim, it still seems offhanded:

> He [Phaeocomes] threw at *Pholon*; the descending Blow
> Divides the Skull, and cleaves his Head in two.
> The Brains, from Nose and Mouth, and either Ear
> Came issuing out, as through a Colendar
> The curdled Milk: or from the Press the Whey
> Driv'n down by Weights above, is drain'd away.
> (585–90)

Likening squashed brains to milk pressed through a colander makes the gore seem as ordinary as a domestic chore (this is also the case in Ovid's version).[24]

Since death occurs abundantly, suddenly, accidentally, we discover that those who dare to think they are secure, whether feasting, or sleeping, or powerfully wielding a weapon, or even escaping, are in for the ultimate surprise. This was the case for Cygnus, who had boasted:

> For Ornament, not Use, these Arms are worn;
> This Helm, and heavy Buckler I can spare;
> As only Decorations of the War:
> So *Mars* is arm'd for Glory, not for Need.
> 'Tis somewhat more from *Neptune* to proceed,
> Than from a Daughter of the Sea to spring:
> Thy Sire is Mortal; mine is Ocean's King.
> Secure of Death, I shou'd contemn thy Dart.
> Tho' naked; and impassable depart.
> (118–26)

Secure and proud, Cygnus is strangled by Achilles, whose power he has just dismissed. The above boast rings hollow.[25] It also rings true. As it turns out, it *is* somewhat better to have Neptune as one's sire, as Achilles finally discovers when Neptune enacts his revenge for Cygnus's death.

Achilles, like Cygnus, like Eurytus, Celadon, Aphasius, Crantor, Dictys, Caeneus, and others I have not even mentioned, are all surprised by death, although it is difficult to tell without a scorecard who is getting vengeance upon whom.

THE SPEECHES OF AJAX AND ULYSSES

Book twelve ends with the announcement of the strife between Ajax and Ulysses over the armor of Achilles. Rather than ending here, which would leave the story somewhat up in the air, in the middle of Ovid's transition to the next book, Dryden goes on to translate the warriors' debate. As Brooks Otis points out, this *"controversia"* was "a stock subject of the rhetorical schools and gave Ovid a fine opportunity to show his *ingenium*" (Otis, 282). It affords Dryden the same opportunity, and allows him to end his treatment of the Trojan War as he began it, with an argument between warriors. Unlike the initial debate between Achilles and Agamemnon, this one needs no twisting to make the heroes seem more selfish; the basic issue, who better deserves the armor he is arguing for, is inescapably selfish, the participants unavoidably self-serving. The antithesis between "Eloquence" and "Brute Force" is in itself appealing; what better way of demonstrating ingenium than by cleverly presenting an argument where the ingenious orator wins over the brawny man of deeds.

Ajax admits at the outset: "By different Methods we maintain our Right, / Nor am I made to Talk, nor he to Fight" (15–16). His argument proves him correct. Considered as a piece of rhetoric, it is deficient; he leaves wide openings for his opponent; he introduces issues that he fails to pursue to best advantage; he makes tactless suggestions.[26] At one point, while trying to insult Ulysses, Ajax inadvertently insults the armor for which he is arguing: "Great is the Prize demanded, I confess, / But such an abject Rival makes it less" (23–24). In Ajax we see another raging figure scarcely under control, reminiscent of Achilles the volcano:

> To these the Master of the sevenfold Shield,
> Upstarted fierce: And kindled with Disdain
> Eager to speak, unable to contain
> His boiling Rage, he rowl'd his Eyes around
> The Shore, and *Grecian* Gallies hall'd a-ground.
> (2–6)

The kindling and boiling are Dryden additions (to Ovid's more general "inpatiens irae").[27] Ajax's argument—"In bloody Fields I labour to be great" (17)—amounts to a verbal justification of all the slaughter we have witnessed in the preceding narrative. As Dryden puts it in the dedication, this "Man-killing Ideot" is "one of those Athletick Brutes whom undeservedly we call Heroes" (Kinsley, 4:1442). Ulysses, as the voice of reason, is by contrast cool, and for once we have a warrior emerging as controlled instead of volcanic, reasonable rather than animalistic. "Brawn without Brain is thine" (553), he remarks of Ajax, and that remark certainly has a bearing on all the brainless brawn we have witnessed, most of it piled up in bloody heaps in book twelve.

Yet, though eloquence triumphs, it does not behave quite the way we might expect. Ulysses wins the argument, as any reputed orator would in a debate against an enraged brute, but there remains a doubt as to whether Ulysses is the worthier candidate for the honor. When Ajax finishes his address with a challenge—

> So cast the glorious Prize amid the Foes:
> Then send us to redeem both Arms and Shield,
> And let him wear who wins 'em in the Field.
> (194–96)

—relying ultimately on his only strength, physical action, Ulysses stands up to begin his response:

> Till from his Seat arose *Laertes* Son,
> Look'd down awhile, and paus'd e'er he begun;
> Then to th' expecting Audience rais'd his Look,
> And not without prepar'd Attention spoke.
> (199–202)

The dramatic pause (also in Ovid) is telling; like an actor who has the gift of good timing, Ulysses waits for the applauding "Multitude" (197) to quiet down. And he begins not by pressing his own claims, but rather by lamenting the loss of "great *Achilles*" (208):

> But since hard Fate, and Heav'ns severe Decree
> Have ravish'd him away from you and me,
> (At this he sigh'd, and wip'd his Eyes, and drew
> Or seem'd to draw some Drops of kindly Dew)
> Who better can succeed *Achilles* lost,
> Than He who gave *Achilles* to your Hoast?
> (209–14)

As a rule of oratory, both Cicero and Quintilian recommend beginning "with an air of modesty or even diffidence" (Brewer, 1418), which is precisely what Ulysses is doing. However, it is very much "an air," and we discover not merely a master of eloquence, but a hypocrite, an actor replete with dramatic tricks, waiting for the audience to settle down, feigning grief.[28] Later, in a marvelous theatrical gesture, he actually bares his chest and shows his scars (408–11). The voice of eloquence, the one example of a warrior in control, is also manipulative, deceptive, and cold-blooded. Ajax is right about Ulysses: "His Arms are a smooth Tongue; and soft Deceit" (18).

Even though he wins the argument and the armor, Ulysses never completely exculpates himself from all of Ajax's specific charges. Ajax accuses Ulysses of deserting Nestor in the field and intentionally ignoring Nestor's cries for aid. In what appears to be a point-for-point rebuttal, Ulysses skips this point altogether; the charge of cowardice lingers. Ajax also accuses Ulysses of deserting Philoctetes and betraying Palamede: "Thus of two Champions he depriv'd our Hoast, / By Exile one, and one by Treason lost" (85–86). It was Ulysses who counselled the Greeks to leave Philoctetes behind

> In a bare Isle to Wants and Pains expos'd,
> Where to the Rocks, with solitary Groans
> His Suff'rings and our Baseness he bemoans.
> (64–66)

Palamede's fate was worse. He had outsmarted Ulysses, had "sham'd him out of Madness into Fight" (80); Ulysses out of "immortal Spight" (79)

> Accus'd him first of Treason to the State;
> And then for proof produc'd the golden Store,
> Himself had hidden in his Tent before.
> (82–84)

Ulysses responds to the charges concerning his treatment of Philoctetes and Palamede, but does so in a cunning and not completely satisfactory way. Yes, he counselled that Philoctetes be left behind, but

> That *Philoctetes* is on *Lemnos* left
> Wounded, forlorn, of human Aid bereft,
> Is not my Crime, or not my Crime alone,
> Defend your Justice, for the Fact's your own.
> (484–87)

33

Where Ajax responded sympathetically to Philoctetes' plight, mentioning his pains, groans, sufferings, Ulysses describes that plight almost clinically: no tears for dead Achilles (that is, no real tears), and no fellow-feeling here either, just a detached description of the man's unfortunate predicament. Most chilling of all, however, is the way that Ulysses shifts the blame, making the desertion of Philoctetes a Greek responsibility. In defending himself from the charge that he framed Palamede, Ulysses uses the same strategy:

> If *Palamede* unjustly fell by me,
> Your Honour suffer'd in th' unjust Decree:
> I but accus'd, you doom'd: And yet he dy'd,
> Convinc'd of Treason, and was fairly try'd:
> You heard not he was false; your Eyes beheld
> The Traytor manifest; the Bribe reveal'd.
> (478–83)

These are not denials. Leaving Philoctetes may have been a crime, convicting Palamede may have been unjust (and Ulysses may have framed him), but whatever the truth of the matter, Ulysses has made these Greek sins rather than exclusively his own.[29]

In answering Ajax's denunciation of Ulysses for feigning madness in order to avoid having to fight at Troy, Ulysses makes the obvious response (and upbraids Ajax in passing for being too stupid to anticipate the obvious):

> Does not the Fool perceive his Argument
> Is with more force against *Achilles* bent?
> For if Dissembling be so great a Crime,
> The Fault is common, and the same in him.
> . . . .
> But grant me guilty, 'tis not much my care,
> When with so great a Man my Guilt I share.
> (462–65, 472–73)

One has to admit that Ulysses has a good point, but he has also just defended dissembling, not by asserting his honesty, but by again implicating somebody else.

Ulysses walks away with the armor, but Ajax's accusations are still resonating in the air; Ulysses has defended himself persuasively, but has also defended lying, cheating, stealing, and betrayal, usually by pointing his finger at others who, if he is guilty, are equally guilty. It is your fault, not just mine; your crime, not mine; I only accused, you doomed. In addition, one of the many positive pieces of evidence Ulysses gives to justify his cause is that he persuaded Agamemnon to sacrifice his daughter, Iphigenia, when it was necessary to appease the gods. Ulysses stresses that he did this, properly, for "the common Good" (304), that he dared face the king and make him act as king rather than father. As reasonable as this is—and all the arguments he advances are reasonable—it is a dehumanizing virtue: persuading a father to kill his own daughter. Agamemnon struggled, but Ulysses "durst th'Imperial Pow'r controul, / And undermin'd the Parent in his Soul" (302–3). Luckily for the Greeks, Ulysses was heartless, and when he discusses his action for the common good, he expresses no sympathy, no feeling, but instead pride in his eloquence. Persuading a man to murder his daughter becomes the ultimate challenge to the clever lawyer, an impossible case that only consummate eloquence could win:

> Never was Cause more difficult to plead,
> Than where the Judge against himself decreed:
> Yet this I won by dint of Argument.
> (306–8)

If this debate ends as a victory for eloquence, that victory has a price: the loss of human feeling. Brains and brawn have clashed, but in a way, ingenium or no ingenium, both figures lose.[30] They demean each other, they demean themselves, and, in a nonchalant way, Ulysses manages to demean all the Greeks by making them share his guilt.

I have discussed these particular tales at length because between them they cover the Trojan War, or perhaps bury it.[31] The pattern does not stop here, however; elsewhere in *Fables* we discover purposeless slaughter, redundant vengeance, dehumanized heroes, unworthy Helens, and other ruined Troys. For instance, "Alexander's Feast," a poem dealing primarily with the power of music and the power of poetry, includes a vain, easily manipulated monarch who marches off to destroy Persepolis for the sake of his courtesan, Thais, "another *Hellen*" who "fir'd another *Troy*" (150). Alexander the Great becomes another debunked warrior-hero, not unlike the none-too-great "Cymon," whom Dryden explicitly likens to Paris (318–19) in "Cymon and Iphigenia" (from Boccaccio). This tale is another anti-heroic gem. Cymon the love-struck brute joins forces with the equally love-struck Lysymachus so they can efficiently coordinate their rapes of the ladies, both of whom are seized just as they are about to be married to other men. Again, a "Nuptial Feast" (541) turns into a scene of carnage, plunging two nations into a war that drags on until exhaustion leads to peace. And the original cause of all the bloodshed, rather than being the love of Paris and Helen, is the uncontrollable passion of Cymon the "slavering Cudden" (179) for a dissembling woman who is also something of a nag.

As these two tales suggest, even when the setting is not the Trojan War, Dryden manages to work in further attacks upon the heroic code, further instances where would-be heroes are diminished, often by passion, and where deeds of love look less than glorious. If Cymon demonstrates this, with a passion, another Dryden character, Theodore, demonstrates the same thing, in a more subtle, less extreme way. His passion does not exactly render him bestial. Not exactly. But almost. The tale of "Theodore and Honoria" (also from Boccaccio) is another love story, this one tracing the quest of an honorable man for a "lofty Maid" (20) who scorns him but finally marries him. That much is the bare plot, but the twists and turns along the way make this a rather complicated love story; although Theodore wins the woman he loves, by the time this occurs, Theodore is less than an honorable man, is more hating than loving, and his victory is more a conquest over a relentless rock than it is an idyllic joining of paramours.

First, Theodore's love is "Madness" (9, a word Dryden adds to his version), and when he is rejected, "his next Endeavour was to Hate" (30). He does not actually turn hatred into vengeance, but he witnesses a dream vision that handily does this for him: he sees a knight, accompanied by mastiffs, chase and disembowel the woman whose haughty rejection of the knight drove him to suicide. He explains to Theodore that this is a daily event, a punishment the knight considers "eternal Justice" (138). Theodore, ever the opportunist, uses this dream vision for his own benefit by arranging a feast for Honoria and her family where he slyly pretends he has given up his pursuit of her. Actually, the feast is merely an occasion to allow Honoria to witness the slaughtering knight, who appears on schedule—Theodore so disposes the guests that Honoria has a good seat—and rips out his victim's heart and entrails "just when the Dessert, and Fruits were plac'd" (263). This, like the fight between the centaurs and Lapithae at the nuptial feast, pretty much ruins the celebration. The scheme works, and Honoria, who sees in Theodore "the grisly Ghost that spurr'd th' infernal Steed" (345), who recognizes that this dream may come true, is literally driven to distraction, which Dryden emphasizes by adding a passage (345–79) that charts her progress from anxiety to bad dreams to fevered blood. Entirely out of fear, she begs Theodore to take her (it seems to be a toss-up between that and suicide), and he quickly accepts her before she can change her mind.

This tale becomes another story about the consequences of uncontrollable passion, and if the main characters do not behave like beasts, there are mastiffs disemboweling a young lady in the background, a kind of external dramatization of what the embittered Theodore feels within himself. It is another celebratory feast gone completely awry.[32] In this case, the consequences are not literally destructive, since the evisceration of the reluctant lady is part of a dream vision, but vengeance is destructive nonetheless, for it destroys love and diminishes both central figures. Theodore, who could not love Honoria, ends up threatening her, frightening her, manipulating her, and finally controlling her, and Honoria, rather than softening to a willing wife, finally rushes to Theodore "Resistless in her Love, as in her Hate" (424), desperately acquiescing to marriage because she fears being devoured, repeatedly, by dogs. She is reduced to a victim, and her conqueror shrinks from excellence to selfish schemings. At the beginning of the tale, he was a noble knight,

> . . . *Theodore* the Brave, above the rest,
> With Gifts of Fortune, and of Nature bless'd,
> The foremost Place, for Wealth and Honour held,
> And all in Feats of Chivalry excell'd.
> (5–8)

But he becomes as vindictive as the squabbling gods (who were also last seen at a feast), as cunningly self-serving in his stratagems as Ulysses, as unheroic as the debased Achilles and Agamemnon, who also incline toward madness in part because of love for a woman.

"Meleager and Atalanta" (from Ovid) provides an especially interesting case, because it serves so many functions. First, it provides Dryden with a clever transition. The preceding poem, "To my Honour'd Kinsman," features a "Sylvan-Chace" (51) undertaken by the self-sufficient, rustic John Driden; the following tale, "Sigismonda and Guiscardo" (from Boccaccio) is a study of a passionate woman who is driven to suicide because her father has killed, and dismembered, her lover. "Meleager and Atalanta" fits neatly between the two, because it begins with a hunt, the hunt of the Caledonian boar, and ends with another passionate woman driven to suicide, Althea. Given Dryden's affection for Ovid's treatment of women tormented by violent passion, I think that Althea's struggle is the poem's central issue, the one thing that would have especially engaged Dryden.[33]

Yet whatever the central issue, and whatever the contribution of the tale to the gallery of portraits in passion, Dryden, still following Ovid closely, adds fuel to the anti-heroic fire. "Meleager and Atalanta" is another tale of vengeance, beginning when Oeneus offers libations to all the gods except Diana. Since "Wrath touches ev'n the Gods" (14), an offended Diana sends a boar to ruin the Caledonian harvest and, for that matter, the Caledonians. Within the larger picture of the enactment of Diana's vengeance, we find auxiliary vengeances, always occurring with the same pattern, whereby vengeance once started keeps expanding, effects far exceed causes, and bloodshed abounds. The immediate agent of Diana's wrath is the wild boar, which Meleager kills; he then offers the spoils to Atalanta because of his admiration for her, and because it was she who first wounded the animal. However, the "*Thestyan* Brethren" (222) think *they* deserve "the Prize of War" (225). They "vent their Spleen" (223), and, "inflam'd with Spite" (230), they snatch the gift from Atalanta, at which point Meleager, impatient, sudden, and no less wrathful than Diana, kills them.[34] All this for the sake of a pelt.

Since they are acting, for the sake of a small prize, in the same way that Achilles and Agamemnon are about to act over their spoils of war, these vengeful brothers serve to make the grand Homeric warriors seem all the more petty. Agamemnon and Achilles have larger roles, greater power, more impressive prizes of war, and more pyrotechnics in their wrath, but their selfish behavior is indistinguishable from that of the envious Thestian Brethren. Meleager dispatches them; unfortunately, they happen to be his uncles, which means that Meleager's mother, Althea, must avenge the death of her brothers by killing her own son (she casts a brand into the fire, which she knows will result in Meleager's death). Then, in grief, Althea commits suicide, and Meleager's distraught sisters "beat their Breasts with many a bruizing Blow, / Till they turn'd

38

livid, and corrupt the Snow" (381–82), after which they are turned into birds that continue to mourn (the image of blood against the snow is a Dryden addition).

Although this is all part of Diana's vengeance, we cannot help noticing that Meleager, who avenges an insult, is himself undone, and that Althea, who avenges the murder of her brothers, "punish'd on her self her impious Deed" (374). Victors become victims, and we are left with abundant human suffering, graphically described, and "lofty *Calidon* in Ruines" (364). As the plot summary suggests, "Meleager and Atalanta" provides further examples of people who, just as they think they are in control, are toppled. In the middle of the boar hunt, the male warrior Anceus boasts that men are superior to women:

> Give place, and mark the diff'rence, if you can,
> Between a Woman Warriour, and a Man;
> The Boar is doom'd.
> (169–71)

In the world of *Fables*, one should know better than to say such things. Like Cygnus, and like Achilles himself, characters no sooner boast their prowess than they themselves are cut down. The doomed boar answers Anceus by charging, so that he

> . . . upward rips the Groin of his audacious Foe.
> Ancæus falls; his Bowels from the Wound
> Rush out, and clotter'd Blood distains the Ground.
> (176–78)

When Meleager in his wrath kills his uncles, he puts his finger on the inefficacy of boasts: he reminds them that they will "learn the Diff'rence, at your proper Cost, / Betwixt true Valour, and an empty Boast" (234–35), and they learn soon enough. Yet the very person who teaches them the lesson, who boasts about empty boasts, finds his own boast empty enough as he dies in agony for this vengeful action.

Dryden and Ovid include a few other anti-heroic touches. For one thing, the fabled heroes who chase the boar are an unimpressive lot. Great warriors like Caeneus and Perithous (both of whom appear in book twelve) keep missing the mark. Nestor, at this point still young and vigorous, actually uses his javelin to vault up into a tree, where he cowers, thinking "his monstrous Foe was still too near" (136). Telamon, not one to be fearful, charges, but he clumsily trips on a root, sprawls on the ground, and has to be disentangled by his brother. Seeing such prowess, the great Theseus advises Perithous to fight from afar rather than risk getting gored: "The Strong may fight aloof" (183) he claims, and he tries his skill by throwing his javelin, an "unerring Weapon" (186). It hits an oak tree. While vengeance is taking its unremitting toll, warriors are proving inept and cowardly, and the somewhat comic images of Nestor vaulting into a tree, of Ajax's father helplessly entwined in roots, or of Theseus advising the distant as opposed to the immediate fight that might be dangerous, make warriors seem less than noble, and certainly less than superhuman.

N O T E S

1. Judith Sloman presents the case for anti-heroism most fully in "The Structure of Dryden's *Fables*," Ph.D. diss., University of Minnesota, 1968, where she finds "the overall movement of the *Fables*" to be "a transition from heroic to anti-heroic ideals" (iii). See also her subsequent articles arising from the dissertation: "An Interpretation of Dryden's *Fables*," *Eighteenth-Century Studies* 4 (1970/71):199–211, and "Dryden's Originality in *Sigismonda and Guiscardo*," *Studies in English Literature* 12 (1972):445–57. Michael West, in "Dryden's Ambivalence as a Translator of Heroic Themes," *Huntington Library Quarterly* 36 (1973):347–66, uses *Fables* in passing, along with *Amphitryon* and Dryden's translation of the *Aeneid*, as part of his proof of Dryden's ambivalence toward heroism. J. Peter Verdurmen, in "Dryden's Cymon and Iphigenia at Century's End: Ploughshares into Swords," *Revue des langues vivantes* 44 (1978):285–300, focuses on the last tale and claims that here "Dryden gave final form to his rejection of heroic possibilities" (286). And Derek Hughes, in *Dryden's Heroic Plays* (Lincoln: University of Nebraska Press, 1981), mentions *Fables* briefly as an instance of Dryden's continued fascination with "the limitations of heroism" (150). In note 3 (pp. 168–69), Hughes recounts the history of modern critical attitudes toward Dryden's treatment of heroes, which serves to clear the ground for his own argument that Dryden's anti-heroism is ever apparent, even as early as *The Indian Queen* (1664); others, like West and Verdurmen, maintain that Dryden began by endorsing heroic ideals and grew disillusioned gradually.

2. Judith Sloman states that "*Fables* are Dryden's replacement for the epic he never wrote" ("Structure," 66). In *Dryden: The Poetics of Translation* (Toronto: University of Toronto Press, 1985), 125–46, Sloman revises this into the interesting suggestion that *Fables* is a continuation and in some respects a resolution of the epic issues raised, but left unresolved, in his translation of the *Aeneid*.

3. Dryden probably consulted, but did not rely upon, the translation by Thomas Hobbes (1676), which is even more bathetic than Ogilby's. Dryden in his Preface describes the Hobbes version as a "bald Translation" and adds that

Hobbes studied "Poetry as he did Mathematicks, when it was too late" (Kinsley, 4:1448). For texts of the Chapman and Ogilby translations, I rely upon the following: *Chapman's Homer: The Iliad, the Odyssey, and the Lesser Homerica*, trans. George Chapman, ed. Allardyce Nicoll, Bollingen Series, 41, 2 vols. (New York: Pantheon Books, 1956) [*Iliad* appears in vol. 1], and *Homer His Iliads translated, Adorn'd with Sculpture, and Illustrated with Annotations*, trans. John Ogilby (London: James Flesher, 1669). For convenience, I also rely upon Richard Lattimore's familiar modern translation, *The Iliad of Homer*, trans. Lattimore (1951; rpt. Chicago: University of Chicago Press, 1963). It would be presumptuous of me to compare Dryden's translation with the Homeric Greek, since I am totally ignorant of Greek. It also might be beside the point, because, although it is clear Dryden consulted Chapman and Ogilby, it is not clear what Greek text he used, or whether he used one at all. Mark Van Doren, in *John Dryden: A Study of His Poetry* (1920: rpt. Bloomington: Indiana University Press, 1963), claims that "in translating" the first book of the *Iliad*, "Dryden did not use the original Greek" (216). J. McG. Bottkol, in "Dryden's Latin Scholarship," *Modern Philology* 40 (1943):241–54, the prime source for information about Dryden's classical texts, maintains that "Dryden evidently knew much less Greek than Latin" (253n), and finds that he is unable to disprove Van Doren's contention (Bottkol, 243). Subsequent scholars, like James Kinsley, in his annotations of Dryden's Homer, and William Frost, in his *Dryden and the Art of Translation* (1955; rpt. Hamden, CT: Archon Books, 1969), remain silent about Dryden's knowledge of Greek and about his source texts.

4. William Frost, discussing Dryden's first book of the *Iliad* in the Introduction to *The Twickenham Edition of the Poems of Alexander Pope*, vol. 7 (*Pope's Iliad*), ed. Maynard Mack (New Haven: Yale University Press, 1967), uses the adjectives "slapstick" and "anti-heroic" (cxl) and maintains that Dryden's translation served to carry "the burlesque tradition of Homer translation" (cxxv) forward into Pope's age, a tradition that Pope had to reject in his ennobled version of Homer. Similarly, Michael West, in "Dryden's Ambivalence," claims that Dryden is "constantly verging on travesty" (362). On the other hand, H. A. Mason, in *To Homer through Pope: An Introduction to Homer's 'Iliad' and Pope's Translation* (New York: Barnes & Noble, 1972), feels that Dryden's version captures the spirit of the *Iliad* and offers the key to understanding Homer's work as "highly disreputable and profoundly ambiguous" (40). Mason's view seems to me eccentric, perhaps an overreaction against the majority of translators who impart high seriousness or added nobility to Homer's comic and rustic bits.

5. Despite the fact that he is translating Homer, Dryden, like Chapman and Ogilby, uses Roman names for the gods, a practice I will adhere to whenever possible.

6. Ogilby's translation merely has Achilles "dismay'd," primarily to rhyme with "said" (p. 11); Lattimore's translation reads "Achilles in amazement turned about" (line 199). Quoting parallel passages in Dryden, Ogilby, Chapman, and a modern translation such as Lattimore's would be cumbersome, to say the least; for the reader's convenience, I will cite Chapman, because Dryden seems to have followed him the most, borrowing particular phrases and often expanding upon

one of Chapman's own additions. I will provide Ogilby or Lattimore, usually in footnotes, only when I think there are significant differences.

7. The *OED* gives, as its first definition, "Having one's faculties deadened or dulled: in a state of stupor, stupefied, stunned," and adds that this is "very common in Dryden."

8. Lattimore's translation of this passage reveals where Chapman has inserted "politique" and how that adds an implication of public responsibility not in the original:

> These then putting out went over the ways of the water
> while Atreus' son told his people to wash off their defilement.
> And they washed it away and threw the washings into the salt sea.
> Then they accomplished perfect hecatombs to Apollo,
> of bulls and goats along the beach of the barren salt sea.
> The savour of the burning swept in circles up to the bright sky.
> Thus these were busy about the army. But Agamemnon
> did not give up his anger and the first threat he made to Achilleus.
>
> (Lattimore, lines 312–19)

Ogilby's version of the same passage has rites being duly observed, without any implication about Agamemnon's motives for ordering the ceremony:

> Great *Agamemnon* gave the Priests command
> To purifie the Camp; and so they doe,
> And all their Soil into the Ocean throw.
> Next, Bulls and Goats they on the Altar lay,
> And compleat Hecatombs to *Phoebus* pay.
> In Clouds of curled Smoak the favour flies
> From Sea-wash'd margines to the arched Skies.
> Thus duely were the sacred Rites perform'd.
> But yet incensed *Agamemnon* storm'd
> As much as ever, and thus, undismaid.
>
> (Ogilby, p. 17)

Side by side, these samples demonstrate how it is that Dryden leaned on Chapman: e.g., Dryden's "With perfect Hecatombs the God they grac'd" obviously owes a debt to Chapman's "the angrie God they grac't / With perfect Hecatombs." One can also see how Dryden probably took Chapman's "politique king" who "made shew" of respects to heaven, and twisted that into Agamemnon the royal hypocrite.

9. Where Chapman uses the phrase "subject-eating king" (Chapman, line 229), and Ogilby the description "Devourer of thy People" (Ogilby, p. 12), Dryden adds "arbitrary Pow'r" (342), another Drydenian leitmotif, to Agamemnon's kingly virtues. Elsewhere, Dryden has Achilles assert that "We bear thee on our Backs, and mount thee on the Throne" (239), and complain that "Thy hook'd rapacious Hands usurp the best" (247), both of which are Dryden insertions. Usurping Agamemnon, who is bent on increasing sovereign sway, on imposing his might, on exercising arbitrary power, sounds suspiciously similar to usurping William of Orange. See Steven N. Zwicker's *Politics and Language in Dryden's Poetry: The Arts of Disguise* (Princeton: Princeton University Press, 1984) for a discussion of Dryden's added or expanded phrases that "are given an explicitly political turn though not necessarily a topical focus" (168).

10. As Michael West, in "Dryden's Ambivalence," observes, "the king emerges as cowardly tyrant, the hero a bullying booby" (361).

11. Dryden's treatment of this scene is consistent with Ogilby's pointed misogynistic marginal comment on the Jove-Juno debate: "It is a feminine quality, to trouble and perplex themselves about seeking out that which being found they cannot in the least redresse, though that by so doing they do but purchase their Husbands ill will, with their own Disquiet, Vexation and Repentance, and sometimes also, what *Jupiter* here threatens his Wife with, Blows" (Ogilby, p. 28).

12. According to Judith Sloman, who does little with the texts available to Dryden but instead compares his translation of Homer to Pope's, Dryden's "treatment of the gods' quarrel" leaves "no doubt in our minds that Jupiter, Juno, and Vulcan are ridiculous." Sloman also points out an interesting parallel when she describes Juno and Jove as "a squabbling, married couple, similar to the Emperor and Nourmahal in Dryden's heroic play, *Aureng-Zebe* (1675), where the highest ranking pair were also the silliest and least controlled" ("Structure," 82).

13. Ogilby's more literal, and much less sonorous, ending reads:

> But *Jove* where his Retirements were apart
> Went, and, surpriz'd by Sleep, laid down his Head,
> Fair *Juno* by him on a golden Bed.
>
> (p. 30)

14. As does Michael West in "Dryden and the Disintegration of Renaissance Heroic Ideals," *Costerus* 7 (1973):193–222, where he describes this as the "culmination" of Dryden's "disillusionment with epic heroism" (212).

15. Robert H. Bell, in "Dryden's 'Aeneid' as English Augustan Epic," *Criticism* 19 (1977):34–50, observes: "This scene helps us understand the limits of Dryden's epic vision, and the reason he could not produce an epic of his own. He was unable to render supernatural powers seriously; consequently, his gods are too mortal and his heroes all-too human" (47).

16. For a thorough account of the circumstances of Ovid's career, see William Brewer, *Ovid's Metamorphoses in European Culture*, included in *Ovid's Metamorphoses*, trans. Brooks More, rev. ed., 2 vols. (Francestown, NH: Marshall Jones, 1978), 135ff.

17. Brooks Otis, in *Ovid as an Epic Poet*, 2nd ed. (Cambridge: Cambridge University Press, 1970) finds Ovid's *Metamorphoses* "intentionally anti-Augustan" (vii). For Ovid, the heroic mythology celebrated by Virgil "is false and human passions and love are true; . . . the connection of Julius and Augustus, of modern Rome, with the saga-world of heroes and gods, apotheosis and miracle, is both unreal and ludicrous" (372).

18. With regard to Dryden's source texts for Ovid, we are on firmer ground, thanks to the pioneering work of J. McG. Bottkol, who argues that Dryden relied upon the explanatory notes in the variorum edition by Borchard Cnipping, *P. Ovidii Nasonis Opera*, 4 vols. (Leyden, 1670), an edition whose Latin text is almost exactly that of the Nicolaus Heinsius 1652 edition (Bottkol, 242–43). For an English trot, Dryden used the popular heroic couplet translation by George Sandys, *Ovids Metamorphosis Englished* (1626). I have been obliged to rely upon later editions: *Publii Ovidii Nasonis Operum*, ed. Nicolaus Heinsius, 3

vols. (Amsterdam: Elzevir, 1676) [*Metamorphoses* appears in vol. 2]; and *Ovids Metamorphosis Englished*, trans. George Sandys, 3rd ed. (London: Andrew Hebb, 1638). I have compared Dryden against both the Heinsius and Sandys texts. Again, referring to multiple texts in my own discussion would be cumbersome; I reserve such commentary for those instances where I detect significant differences between versions.

19. Judith Sloman, in commenting that Dryden's treatment of "old men in *Fables*" is often "coloured by Dryden's various confessions about himself," notes that Nestor serves as a Dryden alter ego, and that this parallel between Nestor's treatment of Hercules and Dryden's of William also entails a self-critical revelation, with Dryden in effect confessing to "his obstinate resentment of his enemies" (*Dryden: The Poetics*, 192).

20. This is Michael West's observation, in "Dryden's Ambivalence" (360). Brooks Otis, speaking of Ovid, describes "the effect of the more ingenious death-scenes" as "on the whole grotesque, not humorous" (283), but I wonder whether, in Dryden's version at least, the result might be both grotesque and humorous.

21. Heinsius, p. 219 [Loeb, line 240]. The Heinsius text lacks lineation; hence, I will refer to the Heinsius by page, but will also provide the Loeb line number for those wishing to consult a convenient modern text.

22. This also holds true for human warriors in the story outside the story; as Sloman points out ("Structure," 213), Dryden, in describing the fight with Cygnus, likens Achilles to a bull provoked by the sight of blood, charging into the circus (136–41). Ovid uses the same metaphor ("quam Circo taurus," Heinsius, p. 215 [Loeb, line 102]).

23. Heinsius, p. 219 [Loeb, line 249].

24. Ovid uses the same cheese-making metaphor, starting with "concretum . . . lac" (curdled milk), pushed through "vimine querno" (oaken twigs; Heinsius, p. 223 [Loeb, lines 436–37]). Dryden's selection of words owes something to Sandys's translation of the latter phrase as "draining colendars" (line 437).

25. Dryden emphasizes the boast by rendering "tamen indestrictus abibo" (yet I will emerge unharmed, Heinsius, p. 215 [Loeb, line 92]) into the more defiant "Secure of Death, I shou'd contemn thy Dart," and by moving the line from the middle of Cygnus's speech to a climactic position near the end.

26. For a detailed account of the deficiencies in Ajax's argument, see Brewer, 1401–31.

27. Heinsius, p. 228 [Loeb, line 3].

28. Otis, speaking of Ovid, thinks "Ulysses' speech is that of a very clever lawyer who knows every trick of his craft" (284); Sloman ("Structure," 215) and West ("Dryden's Ambivalence," 360), two proponents of Dryden's anti-heroism, agree that the Ovid-Dryden Ulysses is a hypocrite. One might again note that the innuendo about pretending to wipe away tears is in Ovid as well as in Dryden: "(manuque simul veluti lacrymantia tersit / Lumina)" (Heinsius, p. 231 [Loeb, lines 132–33]), which Sandys translates as "(With that appeares to weepe, and wipes his eyes)" (line 133).

29. William Myers, in *Dryden* (London: Hutchinson, 1973), remarks that Ulysses "adroitly deploys the arts of the rhetorician to involve the entire Greek army in the guilt of his own unprincipled political guile" (186).

30. Since "Ajax is an athletic brute," and "Ulysses is manipulative and in-

humanly cold," Judith Sloman suggests that "one may end in rejecting both" (*Dryden: The Poetics*, 152), which is precisely what Michael West does when he sees Dryden's selection of this episode as offering him "a wonderful opportunity to denigrate the heroic world" ("Dryden's Ambivalence," 360).

31. These three fables are also an appropriate starting point because, as Dryden explains in his Preface, they were the first tales he translated, in the order in which I have discussed them (Kinsley, 4:1444).

32. Judith Sloman, in *Dryden: The Poetics* (186–206), comments upon the contrasts and connections between feasts throughout *Fables*, ranging from disrupted feasts like these to more productive feasts (symposia), such as Kinsman Driden's generous feeding of his relations, and the ceremonious banquet in "The Flower and the Leaf." Sloman also observes that since Nestor's narrative containing the story of the Lapithae and centaurs itself begins at a feast celebrating the victories of the day, we have in effect an anti-symposium within a symposium (193).

33. In his letter to Robert Howard that prefaces *Annus Mirabilis* (1667), Dryden singles out three of Ovid's characters for special praise: Althea, Myrrha (both of whom appear in *Fables*), and Biblis. Ovid has "touch'd those tender strokes more delicately then Virgil could" (*Works*, 1:54) in his portrait of Dido.

34. Neither Ovid nor Sandys says much about the two envious brothers' behavior, except that they "cry aloud with streacht-out armes" (Sandys, line 433, translating "tendentes brachia voce," Heinsius, p. 147 [Loeb, line 432]); Dryden adds "vent their Spleen" and "inflam'd with Spite," just as he added kindling and boiling when describing the behavior of Ajax at the beginning of "The Speeches of Ajax and Ulysses."

Chapter Three

PARTIAL IDEALS

ON THE OTHER HAND...

*T*HOSE critics who have attributed anti-heroism to *Fables* have often done so on the basis of anti-heroism detected elsewhere in Dryden, usually in his plays, or in an interpretation of his life: as he grew older, he grew disillusioned, especially after his loss of the laureate, so one might expect that "Dryden Agonistes," as Michael West calls him, would, in his last major work, reject former values.[1] Old men get bitter sometimes. But it is easy to find what you look for, because you will not find what you are not looking for, and one could question whether the anti-heroism usually discovered in *Fables* is an imposition, particularly since those who assume it is there seldom examine *Fables* at any length.[2] By going over the evidence I hope I have put that question to rest; anti-heroism runs rampant, and the critics are right. In addition, one can make a case for Dryden's purposefully crafting an anti-epic in miniature, starting with Homer, which Dryden alters toward the burlesque, moving on to the anti-heroic Ovid, which Dryden translates "straight" so as to finish the Trojan War in a rousing grotesque, harping on the same issues in other tales, and ending the collection with a final, gruesome inversion of the story of love and arms, "Cymon and Iphigenia."

I think it important to see just how strong the anti-heroic is, how pervasive the evidence, because one can make an equally valid case for *Fables* being pro-heroic. By this I do not mean that we will find war and gore glorified. No. Generally speaking, war is hell. But so far, the examples discussed stress the purposelessness of the entire enterprise. Pain and devastation result from the most trivial of motives: the ruin of Caledon and Meleager's family comes because of an oversight by Oeneus, or because of an argument over who best deserves a boar's pelt; the Greeks suffer or succeed because of a domestic squabble between small-minded gods. War is not based on noble love, but on lust misconstrued: kingdoms are embroiled in endless war over Cymon's infatuation with a woman not worth the having; bodies are impaled and defaced because of a drunken centaur's lust. Pain, bloodshed, and destruction are seldom worth the price, and the motives as Dryden presents them only make the participants look petty and ignoble.

However, there is another pattern here as well: if the heroic tradition degrades its participants, it also can be ennobling. If passion leads to slaughter (or, in Theodore's case, dreams of slaughter), Dryden can at times reverse the pattern and show bloodshed leading to ennobling passion. In the middle of the battle of the centaurs and the Lapithae, Dryden has an episode (fifty-three lines, expanded from Ovid's thirty-six) that, far from belittling its actors, exalts them. It concerns the love of two worthy centaurs, Cyllarus, a work of art, and Hylonome, "Excelling all the Nymphs of double Race" (541), and this is love, not uncontrollable passion: "fair *Hylonome*, possess'd his Mind / . . . At once both loving, and confessing Love" (539, 543). Cyllarus emerges as a noble, perfectly formed young lover; where he is human, "the Beast was equal to the Man" (531), which serves as a commentary on the many humans whom Dryden depicts as equal to beasts. Dryden describes the innocent pleasures of these lovers, emphasizing Cyllarus' youth and beauty, making Hylonome a romantic heroine who bedecks herself with "Roses, Violets, and Lillies mix'd / And Sprigs of flowing Rosemary betwixt" (546–47). Both enter the battle, and Cyllarus is killed in a death scene that differs in tone from the other gory deaths:

> Uncertain from what Hand, a flying Dart
> At *Cyllarus* was sent; which pierc'd his Heart.
> The Javelin drawn from out the mortal Wound,
> He faints with staggring Steps; and seeks the Ground.
> (560–63)

He is not vomiting into his cup or tripping over his bowels, and although the death is as random as the others, he is at least killed decorously with a javelin rather than accidentally by a piece of furniture. Hylonome, in her grief, seizes the weapon that has killed Cyllarus, plunges it into her breast, and dies in the arms of her lover:

In madness of her Grief, she seiz'd the Dart
New-drawn, and reeking from her Lover's Heart;
To her bare Bosom the sharp Point apply'd;
And wounded fell; and falling by his Side,
Embrac'd him in her Arms; and thus embracing, dy'd.
(572–76)

This sentimental vignette, dripping with pathos, ill accords with the rest of the tale, a noble sacrifice for love, like Dido's, amidst senseless and comic slaughter.[3] To be sure, this episode amplifies the dire consequences of the fight, but at the same time, it presents us with something noble and worthy from the heroic world right in the middle of a tale that debunks heroism.

Along the same lines, we discover that Dryden's translation of "The Speeches of Ajax and Ulysses" ends with a curious twist, curious, that is, if we are committed to seeing *Fables* as entirely anti-heroic. After Ulysses wins the argument, Dryden presents us with a separate section, "The Death of *Ajax*," wherein Ajax, the "dull Soul . . . with stupid Eyes" (452), the "Fool" (475) who cannot even understand the shield he is arguing for, Ajax who has just been denigrated by Ulysses at great length, becomes an object of sympathy:

He who cou'd often, and alone withstand
The Foe, the Fire, and *Jove*'s own partial Hand,
Now cannot his unmaster'd Grief sustain,
But yields to Rage, to Madness, and Disdain;
Then snatching out his Fauchion, Thou, said He,
Art mine; *Ulysses* lays no claim to Thee.
O often try'd, and ever trusty Sword,
Now do thy last kind Office to thy Lord:
'Tis *Ajax*, who requests thy Aid, to show
None but himself, himself cou'd overthrow:
He said, and with so good a Will to die
Did to his Breast the fatal Point apply,
It found his Heart, a way till then unknown,
Where never Weapon enter'd, but his own.
No Hands cou'd force it thence, so fix'd it stood
Till out it rush'd, expell'd by Streams of spouting Blood.
(593–608)

What Ulysses called "that monst'rous Bulk" (532) is now he who could "alone withstand / The Foe, the Fire, and *Jove*'s own partial Hand." In claiming that "None but himself, himself cou'd overthrow," Ajax sounds

48

like one of Dryden's full-fledged earlier heroes, Montezuma in *The In-dian Emperour* (1665), who also hoped to regain his reputation and self-sufficiency by committing suicide, announcing: "But I'm a King while this [his sword] is in my Hand" (V.ii.234).

Whatever Ajax's limitations, all of which Ulysses has harped upon, this was a noble warrior. "Eloquence" has "o'er brutal Force prevail'd" (592), but the victory has proved costly, and one might say that Ajax snatches the final victory from the "smooth Tongue" (18) of Ulysses. As we finish this episode, Dryden emphasizes the loss of genuine heroic qualities—courage, strength—a loss likened to the accidental death of Hyacinth, a youth of great promise mourned by Apollo:

> The fruitful Blood produc'd a Flow'r, which grew
> On a green Stem; and of a Purple Hue:
> Like his, whom unaware *Apollo* slew:
> Inscrib'd in both, the Letters are the same,
> But those express the Grief, and these the Name.
> (609–13)

There is nothing comic, satirical, or denigrating here. Like the truly loving centaurs, Ajax dies from a wound straight to the heart, the most sentimental of all locations. The purple markings on the hyacinth form the characters AIAI, a cry of woe, and AIAΣ, the name of Ajax, and Dryden ends with this image whereby nature herself will eternally mourn the loss of this hero.

I might add that this is from book thirteen of the *Metamorphoses*, and Dryden does not translate the whole book. Ovid goes on from the death of Ajax to more brutality. Troy and Priam fall, in one short sentence, and Ovid gradually moves into the story of Hecuba. Her husband Priam, and her son Hector are dead; her daughter Cassandra is dragged off by her hair; her grandson Astyanax is hurled from a tower. Her son Polydorus had been left with the Thracian king, Polymestor, for safe keeping; un-fortunately, a treasure had been left as well, and Polymestor, greedy for the treasure, slits the throat of his young charge and hurls the corpse from a cliff into the sea. Hecuba's daughter Polyxena, once beloved by Achilles, remains, but Achilles rises from the grave and demands her sacrifice. Having lost most of her family, all of her kingdom, and even her remaining daughter, Hecuba is desolate, her only vestige of hope the

49

son she thinks has been protected by Polymestor. As she goes to fetch water to wash Polyxena's body, the corpse of her other hope, Polydorus, washes up at Hecuba's feet.

Nor does it end there, for wrathful Hecuba, pretending she is offering gold she had hoarded for her son, seeks audience with her son's treacherous protector, Polymestor. She takes the opportunity to gouge out his eyes with her fingernails, and she even continues to gouge out the empty sockets. Grief, wrath, and vengeance have turned her into an uncontrollable beast, and she dies like a dog, literally—stoned by the Thracians as she barks. On it grinds in a familiar pattern: loss, pain, murder in colorful variety, treachery, greed, unrelenting and bloody vengeance, with another human rendered bestial along the way. Had Dryden continued the translation of book thirteen, he would have had more grist for the antiheroic mill. Instead, Dryden ends his translation with the death of Ajax, ends by stressing the loss of greatness implicit in the death of a hero, a hero he has just debunked. The flower that celebrates Ajax is a far cry from the mad queen turned barking dog.

PALAMON AND ARCITE[4]

The heroic values we glimpse in these tales appear even more prominently in Dryden's translation of "The Knight's Tale," which in his Preface Dryden describes as a "Noble Poem . . . of the *Epique* kind, and perhaps not much inferiour to the *Ilias* or the *AEneis*" (Kinsley, 4:1460).[5] Love and deeds of arms, which serve to wreak so much havoc elsewhere, appear here, but in a different light, golden rather than blood red:

> In Days of old, there liv'd, of mighty Fame
> A valiant Prince; and *Theseus* was his Name:
> A Chief, who more in Feats of Arms excell'd
> The Rising nor the Setting Sun beheld.
> Of *Athens* he was Lord; much Land he won,
> And added Foreign Countrys to his Crown:
> In *Scythia* with the Warriour Queen he strove,
> Whom first by Force he conquer'd, then by Love.
> (1:1−8)

This does not depart markedly from Chaucer, but Dryden ever so slightly alters the emphasis. Chaucer's Theseus, "with his wysdom and his chivalrie" (865), is a blend of wise leader and strong warrior (combining the commonplace heroic attributes of *sapientia et fortitudo*); he is "lord and governour" in one line, neatly rhymed and balanced against "swich a conquerour" in the next (861–62). But Dryden omits "governour" and "wysdom," and lingers on the remaining half of the character, turning Chaucer's "worthy duc" (1742) into "the stern *Athenian* Prince" (2:302), and also adding phrases describing his "warlike Pomp," his "proud Array" (1:14), and his "imperious Tone" (2:255). Dryden even sharpens Chaucer's casual account of Theseus' desire to hunt—"That for to hunten is so desirus" (1674)—into the more vicious "In *Theseus* this appears; whose youthful Joy / Was Beasts of Chase in Forests to destroy" (2:222–23).

Like power-mongering Agamemnon and most of the other rulers we encounter in *Fables*, Theseus provides Dryden with an opportunity to comment sardonically on what he took to be the typical dangers of royal power. We get an idea as to where Dryden may be aiming his remarks from his earlier mention of Theseus, in the first poem of *Fables*, "To the Dutchess of Ormond"; Dryden is glancing forward to the next poem, suggesting parallels between the Ormonds and the Chaucerian characters to follow:

> Had *Chaucer* liv'd that Angel-Face to view,
> Sure he had drawn his *Emily* from You:
> Or had You liv'd, to judge the doubtful Right,
> Your Noble *Palamon* had been the Knight:
> And Conqu'ring *Theseus* from his Side had sent
> Your Gen'rous Lord, to guide the *Theban* Government
> (32–37)

The duchess is a potential Emily, the duke a potential Palamon, and since William III had appointed the duke as his emissary, sent from William's side to guide the Irish, William becomes a potential Theseus. Already he is "Conqu'ring *Theseus*," and Dryden's subsequent treatment of Chaucer's prince, by lingering on the warlike side of his character, amounts to criticism of certain traits Dryden most deplored in William, who, in Dryden's eyes, was too much the conqueror, ever too eager to plunge England into war, and who, as it happens, also had a passion for destroying beasts of chase in forests.

And yet despite his tyrannical and warlike instincts, Dryden's Theseus is subject to other more promising influences; if he serves to embody certain traits that Dryden found dangerous in any king, including his own, Theseus does not remain conquering Theseus, but grows into something better. In Chaucer's opening, Theseus brings home Hippolyta as his conquered queen—"He conquered al the regne of Femenye, . . . / And wedded the queene Ypolita" (866, 868). Dryden, however, adds something, perhaps thinking of Shakespeare's Theseus, who won Hippolyta with his sword but now would wed her in another key. Dryden's Hippolyta is "first by Force . . . conquer'd, then by Love." This is another key entirely. In the anti-heroic tales, love and war interact destructively, but here they cooperate, and Theseus seems to be capable of transcending his warlike character, of modulating from force to love, an idea Dryden develops. The next lines show Theseus "with victorie" and "his hoost in armes hym bisyde" (872, 874), which Dryden renders as:

> He brought in Triumph back the beauteous Dame,
> With whom her Sister, fair *Emilia*, came.
> With Honour to his Home let *Theseus* ride,
> With Love to Friend, and Fortune for his Guide,
> And his victorious Army at his Side.
> (1:9–13)

Dryden retains the triumph and the victorious army, but victory marches side by side with new virtues, honor and love.

We appreciate the value of this combination of traits all the more when we discover that "With Love to Friend, and Fortune for his Guide," a line added by Dryden, appears later in the *Fables* in a much different context. In "Cymon and Iphigenia," one of the more brutal anti-heroic tales, Cymon tries to persuade Lysymachus to join him and seize the objects of their desires:

> Two Brothers are our Foes; *Ormisda* mine,
> As much declar'd, as *Pasimond* is thine:
> To Morrow must their common Vows be ty'd;
> With Love to Friend and Fortune for our Guide,
> Let both resolve to die, or each redeem a Bride.
>   Right I have none, nor hast thou much to plead;
> 'Tis Force when done must justify the Deed.
> (515–21)

The might is right argument wins the day, and both men turn the wedding into a double rape, murdering the bridegrooms, starting a war. Love, the motive, justifies force, which leads to the destruction of marriages and the ruin of two nations. In the case of Theseus, however, the process is reversed; force, changed to love, appears at the reconciliation of nations and leads to a stable social form, marriage.

Having established this productive combination of virtues in Theseus, Dryden extends it throughout his translation of "The Knight's Tale," ever presenting us with a Theseus whose warlike instincts are tempered by feelings from the heart, whose forcefulness makes way for emotion, as it does in line twelve. We see this process when Theseus finds Arcite and Palamon "bath'd in Blood" (2:199) fighting over Emily. One has been banished from the country under penalty of death should he return. The other has escaped from prison. Both legally deserve death, and that is Theseus' first instinct, to sentence both to die. But instead, he arranges the tournament, bends, and he does so only after responding to the softening influence of his queen. All this is in the original, but Dryden if anything sharpens Theseus' vengeful instinct, and heightens as well the emotional force working to turn that forcefulness into constructive action. Upon finding the two former prisoners fighting, Theseus, with an "imperious Tone pursues his Threat; / . . . How dares your Pride presume against my Laws," he says (2:255, 257). This challenge, the imperious tone, and the mention of the law, are all Dryden additions. After hearing Palamon ask that both of them be put to death, Theseus readily agrees:

> To this reply'd the stern *Athenian* Prince,
> And sow'rly smild, In owning your Offence
> You judge your self; and I but keep Record
> In place of Law, while you pronounce the Word.
> Take your Desert, the Death you have decreed;
> I seal your Doom, and ratifie the Deed.
> By *Mars*, the Patron of my Arms, you die.
> (2:302–8)

Dryden's Nestor had reminded Agamemnon that "Sanctions of Law from Thee derive their Source" ("The First Book of Homer's Ilias," 399), an idea that Dryden's Theseus, who mentions the law twice, seems determined to demonstrate, relying initially on Mars to help seal and ratify his sentence. But if Mars impels Theseus one way, the queen, along with the other women in the company, weeps "For tender Pity" (2:312) and implores:

> See their wide streaming Wounds; they neither came
> From Pride of Empire, nor desire of Fame:
> Kings fight for Kingdoms, Madmen for Applause;
> But Love for Love alone; that crowns the Lover's Cause.
>
> (2:320–23)

Not only is the appeal itself an emotional one, dampened by tears, but the appeal is based on the laws of love.[6] The last three lines, added by Dryden, make a distinction between kings and lovers, which is an appropriate distinction considering that the women are addressing a triumphant king, convincing him to act differently from the ways kings (and madmen) usually act.

When Dryden's Theseus relents, he acknowledges that power of love, and although Dryden's translation is fairly close to the original at this point, the implications differ. Theseus

> thoghte wel that every man
> Wol helpe hymself in love, if that he kan,
> And eek delivere hymself out of prisoun.
> . . . .
> "The god of love, a, benedicite!
> How myghty and how greet a lord is he!
> Ayeyns his myght ther gayneth none obstacles.
> He may be cleped a god for his myracles,
> For he kan maken, at his owene gyse,
> Of everich herte as that hym list divyse."
>
> (1767–69, 1785–90)

Dryden's version of these lines runs:

> The Pris'ner freed himself by Natures Laws:
> Both free, he sought his Right: The Man he freed
> Was perjur'd, but his Love excus'd the Deed.
> . . . .
> . . . . The Pow'r of Love,
> In Earth, and Seas, and Air, and Heav'n above,
> Rules, unresisted, with an awful Nod;
> By daily Miracles declar'd a God:
> He blinds the Wise, gives Eye-sight to the Blind;
> And moulds and stamps anew the Lover's Mind.
>
> (2:337–39, 350–55)

For Chaucer's Theseus, these knights are the victims of love and cannot help themselves; he accepts love as a mighty force, like chance, that cannot be controlled, that can make "Of everich herte as that hym list divyse." The other Theseus sees love as a powerful force that *should not* be controlled, a force that, instead of buffeting people despite themselves, "moulds and stamps anew the Lover's Mind," which sounds much more promising. Whereas Chaucer's worthy duke excuses the knights because he sees how idiotically men behave under the influence of love, Dryden's Theseus takes love differently. For him, the law-breaking is justified by the greater law of love: "Love excus'd the Deed."

By contrast, another character in *Fables* makes the same argument: "The Faults of Love by Love are justifi'd" (281), says Guiscardo in defense of his secret marriage, above his station, to Sigismonda. There, the figure in power, Tancred, rather than being persuaded by the argument, orders that the young man be strangled and that his heart be "Torn from his Breast" (595). Love is no excuse here. Tancred applies force to crush love, and, in a passage Dryden added to this Boccaccio tale, that force is specifically military might; those who do Tancred's mutilating are mercenary soldiers:

> For, (Slaves to Pay)
> What Kings decree, the Soldier must obey:
> Wag'd against Foes; and, when the Wars are o'er,
> Fit only to maintain Despotick Pow'r:
> Dang'rous to Freedom, and desir'd alone
> By Kings, who seek an Arbitrary Throne:
> Such were these Guards.
>
> (596–602)

Tancred's minions look a good deal like William's Standing Army.[7] But the Theseus of "Palamon and Arcite," who initially shares some of Tancred's unattractive qualities, moves in the opposite direction, away from instinctive wrath, militarism, arbitrary power, toward an understanding of the power of love over force.[8]

This has been the pattern for Theseus throughout, beginning with the opening lines that establish a transition from force to love, extending through Theseus' response to the appeals of the mourning women, through the episode above, and into the First Mover speech, which in Dryden's version is more optimistic than in the Chaucerian original. Dryden's translation shifts the stress and tone of the whole, as we notice if we compare the opening lines:

> "The Firste Moevere of the cause above,
> Whan he first made the faire cheyne of love,

Greet was th'effect and heigh was his entente.
Wel wiste he why and what thereof he mente,
For with that faire cheyne of love he bond
The fyr, the eyr, the water, and the lond
In certeyn boundes, that they may nat flee."
(2987–93)

The Cause and Spring of Motion, from above
Hung down on Earth the Golden Chain of Love:
Great was th' Effect, and high was his Intent,
When Peace among the jarring Seeds he sent.
Fire, Flood, and Earth, and Air by this were bound,
And Love, the common Link, the new Creation crown'd.
(3: 1024–29)

Chaucer's version defends a God whose ways are inscrutable to all but God himself—"Wel wiste he why and what thereof he mente," a line Dryden omits. Instead, Dryden substitutes "When Peace among the jarring Seeds he sent," which changes the speech from a defense of the loving God whom we should trust despite the apparently "wrecched world" (2995) we see around us, to an appreciation of the peace and stability visible in the world, which attest to the presence of a loving God. Chaucer's Theseus sees the elements as bound, in the sense of limited, "that they may nat flee," but in Dryden, God binds the elements in a "new Creation," a crowning one at that.[9] For Chaucer's Theseus, with death and wretchedness omnipresent, it is best for man "To dyen whan that he is best of name" (3056), while Dryden's sunnier Theseus envisions the same death as a closing of "our happy Life" (3:1092); there is more possibility for accomplishment, and Dryden's Theseus, who recommends "Enjoying while we live the present Hour" (3:1096), adds what might be considered an Epicurean moral, quite different from Chaucer's stoicism:[10]

What then remains, but after past Annoy,
To take the good Vicissitude of Joy?
To thank the gracious Gods for what they give,
Possess our Souls, and while we live, to live?
(3:1111–14)

As Theseus comes to understand the chain of love and operate according to its dictates, he moves away from the stern, tyrannical, warmongering conqueror toward an ideal ruler against which the real monarch can be measured and found wanting.[11] This Theseus is unlike blood-thirsty Tancred. Ultimately, in moving toward compassion and magnanimity, he is unlike William, and Dryden at points slyly suggests the difference between the reformed prince and his own monarch. For example, when Arcite appears to have won over Palamon,

> The People rend the Skies with vast Applause;
> All own the Chief, when Fortune owns the Cause.
> *Arcite* is own'd ev'n by the Gods above,
> And conqu'ring *Mars* insults the Queen of Love.
> So laugh'd he, when the rightful *Titan* fail'd,
> And *Jove*'s usurping Arms in Heav'n prevail'd.
> Laugh'd all the Pow'rs who favour Tyranny;
> And all the Standing Army of the Sky.
> (3:665-72)

Here is Dryden's usual attack upon William's Standing Army, seen as an agent designed to protect the tyrannical power of a usurping monarch, and yet these powers, along with the ever "rude promiscuous Crowd" (3:551), are all on the side of Mars, Arcite's patron god. Theseus, having just refrained from acting according to the dictates of his patron god, Mars, having instead acknowledged the superior "Pow'r of Love" (2:350), is now on the other side of the argument.

This passage, which is not in the original, reveals another of Dryden's major changes in his translation, which occurs in his treatment of Arcite and Palamon. In Chaucer, the two are hard to distinguish; it is giddy chance that picks the winner, not any difference in the merits of the two.[12] When they first appear, dragged from a pile of bodies, they are a perfectly matched set: "Bothe in oon armes, . . . / Of whiche two Arcite highte that oon, / And that oother knyght highte Palamon" (1012-14). For Dryden, however, "These two were Sisters Sons; and *Arcite* one, / Much fam'd in Fields, with valiant *Palamon*" (1:155-56). Arcite is not just "highte" Arcite, but also "Much fam'd in Fields," and a little later, "Known in Arms" (1:367). That is, Dryden's Arcite, who eventually prays to Mars, is first and foremost the warrior, and Palamon, who will pray to Venus, the lover, a distinction Dryden sharpens throughout the tale.

In Dryden, these two warriors have significantly different attitudes toward love, which can be illustrated by considering one key speech by each. Early in the story, when Palamon and Arcite are debating as to who loved Emily first, Arcite comments on the power of love: in Chaucer,

> Wostow nat wel the olde clerkes sawe,
> That "who shal yeve a lovere any lawe?"
> Love is a greater lawe, by my pan,
> Than may be yeve to any ertheley man.
> And therfore positif lawe and swich decree
> Is broken alday for love in ech degree.
> A man moot nedes love, maugree his heed.
> He may nat flee it, thogh he sholde be deed.
> (1163–70)

In Dryden,

> And know'st thou not, no Law is made for Love?
> Law is to Things which to free Choice relate;
> Love is not in our Choice, but in our Fate:
> Laws are but positive: Loves Pow'r we see
> Is Natures Sanction, and her first Decree.
> Each Day we break the Bond of Humane Laws
> For Love, and vindicate the Common Cause.
> Laws for Defence of Civil Rights are plac'd,
> Love throws the Fences down, and makes a general Waste:
> Maids, Widows, Wives, without distinction fall;
> The sweeping Deluge, Love, comes on, and covers all.
> (1:326–36)

Both passages are on the irresistible power of love, but Dryden's Arcite sees love as an anti-social force, one that breaks human laws, which are meant for the defense of civil rights. There is a difference between the original Arcite, confessing that nobody can withstand this powerful and unavoidable force, and the Arcite who sees the destructive consequences and would willingly participate. In effect, his attitude toward love is that of the less articulate anti-heroic characters, like Cymon, Alexander, Eurytus and his fellow centaurs, who topple civil rights and create "general Waste" with gusto.[13]

Dryden's Arcite at points matches these anti-heroes in behavior as well as philosophy. For instance, after he has been exiled from Athens and from the sight of Emily, he suffers:

> So muche sorwe hadde nevere creature
> That is, or shal, whil that the world may dure.
> His slep, his mete, his drynke, is hym biraft,
> That lene he wex and drye as is a shaft.
> (1359–62)

58

Dryden too dwells upon the change in Arcite's physical appearance: his friends do not recognize him; he is pale, his eyeballs "in their hollow Sockets sink" (1 : 526). But Dryden invents a few additional details:

> He rav'd with all the Madness of Despair,
> He roar'd, he beat his Breast, he tore his Hair.
> Dry Sorrow in his stupid Eyes appears,
> For wanting Nourishment, he wanted Tears.
> (1 : 522–25)

Besides "sorwe" and restlessness, Arcite suffers from madness, "The loss of Reason" that "conclude[s] in Rage" (1 : 542). Shades of raving (and stupid) Ajax, of volcanic and uncontrollable Achilles, of ferocious Cymon, intemperate, uncontrolled, bestial. This is love? If so, it is akin to the uncontrollable passion that causes other characters to rave and destroy.

And what of Palamon's attitude toward love? We learn more about this when we overhear him praying in the temple of Venus:

> "Faireste of faire, O lady myn, Venus,
> Doughter to Jove, and spouse of Vulcanus,
> Thou gladere of the mount of Citheron,
> For thilke love thow haddest to Adoon,
> Have pitee of my bittre teeris smerte."
> (2221–25)

Dryden's version is much longer:

> Creator *Venus*, Genial Pow'r of Love,
> The Bliss of Men below, and Gods above,
> Beneath the sliding Sun thou runn'st thy Race,
> Dost fairest shine, and best become thy Place.
> For thee the Winds their Eastern Blasts forbear,
> Thy Month reveals the Spring, and opens all the Year.
> Thee, Goddess, thee the Storms of Winter fly,
> Earth smiles with Flow'rs renewing; laughs the Sky,
> And Birds to Lays of Love their tuneful Notes apply.
> For thee the Lion loaths the Taste of Blood,
> And roaring hunts his Female through the Wood:
> For thee the Bulls rebellow through the Groves,
> And tempt the Stream, and snuff their absent Loves.
> 'Tis thine, whate'er is pleasant, good, or fair:
> All Nature is thy Province, Life thy Care;
> Thou mad'st the World, and dost the World repair.
> Thou Gladder of the Mount of *Cytheron*,
> Increase of *Jove*, Companion of the Sun;

If e'er *Adonis* touch'd thy tender Heart,
Have pity, Goddess, for thou know'st the Smart.
(3:129-48)

Dryden seems to have gotten carried away, right past Chaucer into a paraphrase of the opening lines of Lucretius' *De Rerum Natura*.[14] The Lucretianized Palamon sees love as a genial, generative force, like Spring, complete with "smale foweles [that] maken melodye"; love is capable of turning the lion and the bull away from bloodshed. Such a view accords with that of Theseus, who sees love implicit in the operation of the universe, and who himself is willing to turn from vengeance toward compassion. Indeed, Theseus' First Mover speech is a confirmation of Palamon's view, and a rejection of Arcite's grim and bloodthirsty principles.[15]

While Palamon pledges himself to what he sees as a creative, renewing force, Arcite sticks to his guns, as is clear from another Dryden expansion. Arcite in his prayer to Mars promises that if he wins Emily,

Then shall the War, and stern Debate, and Strife
Immortal, be the Bus'ness of my Life;
And in thy Fane, the dusty Spoils among,
High on the burnish'd Roof, my Banner shall be hung;
Rank'd with my Champions Bucklers, and below
With Arms revers'd, th' Atchievements of my Foe:
And while these Limbs the Vital Spirit feeds,
While Day to Night, and Night to Day succeeds,
Thy smoking Altar shall be fat with Food
Of Incence, and the grateful Steam of Blood.
(3:339-48)[16]

No tuneful birdsongs under a laughing sky for this serious young man. His promise is a commitment worthy of a Cymon or an Achilles.[17] And it is this attitude that "Palamon and Arcite" ultimately rejects. The contest between these knights finally becomes a debate between two world views, the one a hopeful view of a regenerative power in the universe, emanating from love, the other a grim view of the inevitable destruction caused by love. Thus, when Palamon finally wins, it is not just the result of a heavenly coin flip, but the victory of love over war, a confirmation of the order of the universe that Theseus perceives.

Rather than watch an Achilles, an Agamemnon, a Ulysses shrink, we watch a Theseus grow, from conquering warrior, stern Athenian Prince, to a wise ruler who transcends the warlike, acknowledges the greater power of love, and does all he can to instill the laws of love in the figures over whom he rules.[18] It is possible here for warriors to fight justly, as is the case with Theseus' campaign against Creon and "his Tyranny" (1:86, again at the urging of crying women), or with Palamon's combat, not for conquest, but for the principle of a constructive love. Instead of love and arms combining to destroy civilizations, here they combine to create a new order, which Theseus announces as he assigns Emily to Palamon:

> Ordain we then two Sorrows to combine,
> And in one Point th' Extremes of Grief to join;
> That thence resulting Joy may be renew'd,
> As jarring Notes in Harmony conclude.
> Then I propose, that *Palamon* shall be
> In Marriage join'd with beauteous *Emily*;
> For which already I have gain'd th' Assent
> Of my free People in full Parliament.
> (3:1115−22)

We have not only a new order, but also a new Theseus, a ruler of a free people who willingly consults his Parliament. This is a victory for love, with marriages being constructed, for a change, rather than destroyed, but we should remember that the kingdom is also morally stabilized by Theseus' just conquest of Creon, that battle, and honor in battle, are an equal part of the human scene. Deeds of arms are not displaced, but rather acknowledged, properly subservient to love, but still an unavoidable part of civilization and human character.

PARTIAL IDEALS: THE DUCHESS OF ORMOND, AND KINSMAN JOHN DRIDEN

"Palamon and Arcite" comes just after the dedicatory initial poem in the collection, "To the Dutchess of Ormond," and just before "To My Honour'd Kinsman, John Driden." One deals primarily with the beneficent powers of the duchess, the other with the self-sufficiency of Dryden's country cousin, and thus they do not focus on the issue of heroism, at least not in the context of the Trojan war or jousting knights. We are no longer in a mythic past or fictive world, but in Dryden's present, confronting real people. We are no longer in some piece of an epic, but in panegyrics, one an encomium to a family, the other a panegyric to a relative that also celebrates the Epicurean retirement tradition made familiar by Horace. Yet love and deeds of arms are issues here as well, as we have already discovered from the opening lines of the Ormond poem, where Dryden invokes Homer, Virgil, and Chaucer, all of whom sung of love and arms, and goes on to praise the duchess as being a worthy heroine in that tradition: she attests to "What Pow'r the Charms of Beauty had of old" (8) when "such Deeds of Arms were done, / Inspir'd by two fair Eyes, that sparkled like your own" (9–10).

Yet, however powerful her charms, the duchess does not become that kind of heroine; Dryden is going to alter the relationship between love and arms, as he implies when, in comparing Chaucer to Homer and Virgil, he stresses that the English poet "Of Love sung better, and of Arms as well" (6). As is the case with Theseus, love is going to have priority again. The woman who might have inspired deeds of arms instead becomes an embodiment of love as a restorative force, an ideal wife and mother who serves her husband and her country. As "*Ormond*'s Harbinger" (62) she visits an Ireland ravaged by William's wars, and she "Wip'd all the Tears of three Campaigns away" (67). Dryden imagines her second visit to that war-torn country:

> When at Your second Coming You appear,
> (For I foretell that Millenary Year)
> The sharpen'd Share shall vex the Soil no more,
> But Earth unbidden shall produce her Store:
> The Land shall laugh, the circling Ocean smile,
> And Heav'ns Indulgence bless the Holy Isle.
> (80–85)

When she appears, the earth of its own accord will bear harvest. She is Beauty (8), "*Venus* . . . the Promise of the *Sun*" (63), the Dove returning to the Ark (70–71), a Christ figure ("Your second Coming," 80), as Dryden pours forth a cornucopia of allusions to heap praise on his patron's wife.[19] Where in the heroic tradition love and beauty can lead to rape and devastation, the duchess is an example of love and beauty leading to peace, a powerfully restorative peace; instead of inspiring war, love and beauty promise to undo the destruction of war.

Kinsman John Driden is also a peacemaker. Just as Dryden began the Ormond poem by glancing ahead to the characters in "Palamon and Arcite," so does he begin the kinsman poem by hearkening back to the preceding poem, in at least two ways. First, the Chaucer poem ends with

Palamon winning Emily, "the Blessing he so dearly bought" (3:1153), which presumably marks the end of strife and the beginning of happily ever after. Dryden concludes with a couplet (not in Chaucer), reminiscent of tag couplets in Restoration plays, where a moral from the play is addressed to the audience: "So may the Queen of Love long Duty bless, / And all true Lovers find the same Success" (3:1154–55). John Driden's entry marks a continuation of this blessing, although it is now the blessing of a country life rather than of true lovers in a happy marriage:[20]

> How Bless'd is He, who leads a Country Life,
> Unvex'd with anxious Cares, and void of Strife!
> Who studying Peace, and shunning Civil Rage,
> Enjoy'd his Youth, and now enjoys his Age:
> ···
> Just, Good, and Wise, contending Neighbours come,
> From your Award, to wait their final Doom;
> And, Foes before, return in Friendship home.
> (1–4, 7–9)

A second and more substantial link is the parallel between John Driden, the member of Parliament imposing order, and Theseus, who has just achieved order in his society by ordaining the marriage of Palamon and Emily, after consulting Parliament. Dryden's cousin, praised for "Promoting Concord, and composing Strife" (17), accomplishes in his sphere something comparable to the new order, "jarring notes" concluding "in Harmony" (3:1118), that Theseus has brought about in ancient Athens. If Theseus affords Dryden the opportunity of commenting on William, the same can be said of Kinsman Driden, whose power to bring about peace, a "lasting Peace" (15) no less, stands in stark contrast to William's inability to keep England from costly wars, to which Dryden specifically alludes when he advises: "Enough for *Europe* has our *Albion* fought: / Let us enjoy the Peace our Blood has bought" (158–59).[21]

Although both John Driden and the duchess of Ormond are peacemakers, exerting a constructive, civilizing influence, there is a crucial difference between them, outside of the obvious fact that one is a man and the other a woman. One is a bachelor and the other a wife. In Dryden's hands, this becomes more than a matter of circumstance, for he praises the duchess as wife, a "Chast *Penelope*" (158), a good mother providing children to extend the Ormond name and attending to those children, "The Three fair Pledges of Your Happy Love" (164). Then Dryden turns around and praises John Driden for his bachelorhood, unleashing a spirited misogynistic tirade in the process; the kinsman is described as:

> Promoting Concord, and composing Strife,
> Lord of your self, uncumber'd with a Wife;
> Where, for a Year, a Month, perhaps a Night,
> Long Penitence succeeds a short Delight:
> Minds are so hardly match'd, that ev'n the first,
> Though pair'd by Heav'n, in Paradise, were curs'd.
>
> (17–22)

Now marriage is "Two Wrestlers" helping "to pull each other down" (30), and Driden is praised for avoiding marriage: "And better shun the Bait, than struggle in the Snare" (33). Just as Dryden denigrates and admires heroes, so does he take opposing stands toward womankind, warmly praising a Penelope, then cursing another Eve.

In each case, the strength of these characters derives from their marital state: Driden promotes concord *because* he is "uncumber'd with a Wife," and the duchess can achieve a renovation of Ireland because her wifely love is a restorative force. She only does for Ireland what she does for her own family: "Bless'd be the Pow'r which has at once restor'd / The Hopes of lost Succession to Your Lord" (146–47). By providing "future *Ormonds*" (143), the duchess restores the Ormond succession, but of course "lost Succession" also refers to the deposed James II, with whom the Ormond family had long been associated. The current duke's grandfather, James Butler, served both Charles I and Charles II as Lord Lieutenant of Ireland, even following Charles II into exile (Dryden celebrated Butler as Barzillai in "Absalom and Achitophel"). Continuing in that tradition, the current duke had been made Knight of the Garter by James II in 1688, and in that same year accompanied James in his fruitless negotiations with William III.[22] With William's coming to power, the duke of Ormond had to surrender any hopes he had of the proper Stuart succession, but now the duchess can restore those hopes in a modified version, by providing him with an Ormond succession, and by acting as an agent of reconciliation for William, which Dryden hopes will bring a return of "Vertue to Courts" (149). Her wifely love and duty thus extend outward from the private realm into the public sphere.

Though both the kinsman and the duchess are positive examples, both are also incomplete, in different ways. The duchess, for one thing, cannot bring about the lost political succession, and even her ability to restore

Ireland is called into question. After likening her to the Dove, Venus, and Christ, and after predicting the newly fruitful Ireland that her "second Coming" to Ireland would produce, Dryden shifts to the duchess's illness:

> The Vanquish'd Isle our Leisure must attend,
> Till the Fair Blessing we vouchsafe to send;
> Nor can we spare You long, though often we may lend.
> ....
>   Nor dare we trust so soft a Messenger,
> New from her Sickness, to that Northern Air;
> Rest here a while, Your Lustre to restore,
> That they may see You as You shone before.
>   (96–98, 101–4)

Dryden next discourses on her disease, suggesting her fragility by likening her to "Porcelain" that "by being Pure, is apt to break" (121). She may be a restorative force, but she is not strong enough to survive "that Northern Air." She who has the "Pow'r to chase all Poyson" (89) is herself subject to disease, and the very restoration Dryden predicts for Ireland is withheld from Ireland. Beneficial as she is, she lacks sufficient strength.

John Driden, strong as he is, lacks love, a word that, as we have seen, Dryden continually adds to his translation of "The Knight's Tale," and a word that seldom appears in "To my Honour'd Kinsman." Love is mentioned twice in the opening few lines, where Dryden is praising the "Just, Good, and Wise" (7) justice of the peace: "All who deserve his Love, he makes his own; / And, to be lov'd himself, needs only to be known" (5–6). I find this couplet interesting, because it borders on making Driden a loving justice, and yet carefully stays on one side of the border. He is worthy of love, and he "makes his own" those who deserve his love, but he actually is "Just, Good, and Wise," even nobly stubborn (185), "tenacious of the Common Cause" (190) like his grandsire, rather than loving.[23] Above everything else, he is self-sufficient, "uncumber'd with a Wife" (18). What he loves are his country retreat (120) and hunting, and even here he is exercising judicial authority, punishing the "wily Fox" for killing "the Firstlings of the Flocks" (54–55). As healthful exercise, hunting is what makes Driden strong—"Better to hunt in Fields, for Health unbought, / Than fee the Doctor for a nauseous Draught" (92–93)—in contrast to the sickly duchess who requires medical attention and has been lucky enough to find a competent doctor.

Both the duchess and the honored kinsman are ideals, with complementary strengths and offsetting weaknesses.[24] She is loving, a restorative force, but she is also physically weak, unable to effect a restoration of battered Ireland, or of the lost political succession. John Driden is strong, but he lacks warmth; he can stabilize and sustain a judicious order, but he cannot regenerate or restore. Continually, Dryden sees his cousin as somebody who holds things together, rather than one who makes anew:

> A Patriot, both the King and Country serves;
> Prerogative, and Privilege preserves:
> Of Each, our Laws the certain Limit show;
> One must not ebb, nor t'other overflow:
> Betwixt the Prince and Parliament we stand;
> The Barriers of the State on either Hand:
> May neither overflow, for then they drown the Land.
>
> (171–77)

Preserving, standing as a barrier, and later resisting with "noble Stubbornness" (185), all are patriotic virtues, but all act defensively so as to keep power from overflowing.[25] There is no imagery of a new order, of a fruitful Spring, of laughing skies and tuneful birds. Neither the duchess nor the kinsman can turn swords into ploughshares; she is not strong enough, and he can only keep swords from being used as swords.

The loving duchess and the judiciously forceful John Driden stand outside the epic frame, but they have a bearing on the issue of heroism, because the virtues they embody serve to replace the defective central values of the heroic code: instead of heroic love (often merely idiotic passion), we have a regenerative love, a social ideal embedded in biblical allusions; and instead of aggressive deeds of arms, we have strength of a different sort, self-sufficiency and fortitude (which includes the courage to resist deeds of arms), derived from the classical retirement tradition. Dryden has gone beyond the heroic code to other traditions, which include the Christian as well as the classical, to amplify the power and efficacy of love and strength as companion virtues. But the duchess and the honored kinsman are both incomplete; they are at best partial ideals, and if they in some ways replace epic heroes, we also find that replacement snatched away. From another point of view, it appears that it is the heroic world that offers the full ideal, in the character of the completed Theseus who emerges at the end of "Palamon and Arcite." Theseus is a

66

fruitful combination of love and deeds of arms, judicious *and* loving, a warrior-hunter and a husband, who assembles states and promotes marriages, stronger than the duchess, warmer than John Driden. The possibilities span a wide range, from Dryden's honored but limited contemporaries to a chivalric Theseus in Athens of old. Throughout, there is a sense of nostalgia, as in the sympathetic account of Ajax's suicide, a sense of loss or incompleteness, and, most important, a sense that the heroic code has values to offer, values that are at times approached imperfectly from here below.

NOTES

1. Michael West, "Dryden's Ambivalence as a Translator of Heroic Themes," *Huntington Library Quarterly* 36 (1973): 365.
2. This applies to J. Peter Verdurmen, Derek Hughes, and Michael West as well; see Chapter 2, note 1 for a summary of their critical positions.
3. In expanding this episode, Dryden does not so much alter Ovid as flesh out the scene with additional specifics. Thus, when Ovid's Cyllarus receives the mortal wound, Dryden follows the original closely, but adds a description of the centaur staggering and falling (563); where the original Hylonome merely lies down on the spear ("telo . . . incubuit"), Dryden's applies "To her bare Bosom the sharp Point" (574), which Dryden may have borrowed from Sandys's "Even on that steele, which through his bosome past, / She threw her owne." The Ovid text is that of *Publii Ovidii Nasonis Operum*, ed. Nicolaus Heinsius, 3 vols. (Amsterdam: Elzevir, 1676), p. 223 [Loeb, lines 427–28]; the Sandys reference is from *Ovids Metamorphosis Englished*, trans. George Sandys, 3rd ed. (London: Andrew Hebb, 1638), lines 427–28.
4. At the end of *Fables*, Dryden provided texts (from Thomas Speght's 1687 edition) of the Chaucerian tales he "translated." Speght's edition was first published in 1598, then issued in a second edition, with corrections, in 1602, and reprinted in 1687; it was the first text of Chaucer to contain notes, a life, and a glossary. As far as Dryden was concerned, Speght's text was the most complete, the most recent, and the most enduring (it had replaced John Stowe's edition of 1561). The differences between the Dryden-Speght Middle English texts and modern texts are rather slight, mostly a matter of spelling, punctuation, and a dropping of what was then thought to be silent final syllables (e.g., "hadde" becomes "had"). Since Dryden's texts include no lineation and are close to modern texts anyway, I will rely upon John H. Fisher's more conveniently available edition for Chaucer quotations: *The Complete Poetry and Prose of Geoffrey Chaucer*, ed. Fisher (New York: Holt, Rinehart & Winston, 1977).
5. Using Dryden's remark as a starting point, Anne Middleton, in "'The Modern Art of Fortifying: *Palamon and Arcite* as Epicurean Epic," *Chaucer Review* 3 (1968): 124–43, judges this poem as the "last of several attempts to produce a poem of the 'Epique kind'" (124). William Myers, in *Dryden* (Lon-

don: Hutchinson, 1973), senses a heroic strain and an anti-heroic strain as well. Myers concludes that "taken as a whole, therefore, Palamon and Arcite may be a robust, extravagant, authentically heroic performance, but it is infiltrated by an irony which consistently compromises the impressiveness of heroic effort" (177). Insofar as this statement implies a coexistence of these contrary strains, an "authentically heroic performance" compromised, I agree, but Myers, like other critics, having committed himself to anti-heroism, maintains that the irony cancels the heroism, with which I cannot agree. James D. Garrison, in "The Universe of Dryden's *Fables*," *Studies in English Literature* 21 (1981): 409–23, regards "Palamon and Arcite" as a progressive narrative, one of "two narrative paradigms" Dryden presents as "alternate phases of a single cycle" (417; the other phase is the regressive narrative, such as "The First Book of Homer's Ilias"). Garrison's exploration of fire imagery in *Fables*, focusing on its constructive and destructive implications (two phases, again), supports my own argument about the coexistence of heroic and anti-heroic values in *Fables*.

6. As Rachel A. Miller puts it, in "Regal Hunting: Dryden's Influence on *Windsor Forest*," *Eighteenth-Century Studies* 13 (1979/80): 169–88, "thus Venus, the original source of strife, now masters Mars and calms the jarring discord. For the joust, a ceremonial pursuit, is a positive substitute for warfare and the hunt" (175).

7. See Chapter 7 (194ff) for a more thorough account of the Standing Army issue, to which Dryden first alludes in the opening poem, "To the Dutchess of Ormond."

8. Judith Sloman, in "The Structure of Dryden's *Fables*," Ph.D. diss., University of Minnesota, 1968, says that "the power of love has a far different significance in the two versions of 'The Knight's Tale.' Chaucer treats it as folly and madness and Dryden as the very force which harmonizes and beautifies the universe" (102).

9. As Earl Miner, in *Dryden's Poetry* (Bloomington: Indiana University Press, 1967), argues, Chaucer's Theseus premises his speech on the attitude of *contemptus mundi*, but in Dryden the same speech "affirms rather a continuous beneficence of divine purpose through all the orders of creatures" (70).

10. As Anne Middleton argues in "The Modern Art of Fortifying" (141).

11. Earl Miner states that "at the end Theseus has changed from a usurping tyrant to all that an English monarch should be" (*Dryden's Poetry*, 316). William Myers also sees these two sides of Theseus' character: "He is clearly linked with William of Orange in the first phase of the poem; yet by the end he makes a point of consulting the wishes of his parliament, something William was believed to be reluctant to do after Rijswijk; and even if he does ravage Thebes as ruthlessly as William had ravaged Ireland, his war against Creon is in a just cause" (177). Myers does not regard this as growth, but rather as an ambiguity in the character of Theseus.

12. What Paul G. Ruggiers, in *The Art of the Canterbury Tales* (1965; rpt. Madison: University of Wisconsin Press, 1967), refers to as "the equalization of the knights" (157) is a matter of debate, with some critics driving a wedge in the hairline crack that separates Chaucer's Palamon from Arcite. In his *Oppositions in Chaucer* (1973; rpt. Middletown, CT: Wesleyan University Press, 1975), for

instance, Peter Elbow argues that "though the differences are subtle, they are important" (75). Perhaps. It is also important that they are subtle, and, for our purposes, more important that the slight division between Chaucerian characters becomes in Dryden a chasm. William Frost, in *Dryden and the Art of Translation* (1955; rpt. Hamden, CT: Archon Books, 1969), emphasizes that particular Dryden change (73–78).

13. For Rachel Miller, "Dryden's Arcite represents the unjust conqueror—the William who had usurped the Stuart throne, substituted de facto for de jure rule, and who had involved England in 'strife Immortal' " (174). That may be pushing it; it seems to me that Theseus, the monarch, is the main vehicle for anti-Williamite commentary.

14. Dryden had translated the opening lines of *De Rerum*, Book 1 for the miscellany *Sylvae* (1685); both the California Dryden (*Works*, 3:281) and Kinsley (4:2068) note that Dryden's paraphrases also echo Spenser's *Faerie Queen* (IV.x.44, 46).

15. Michael West in passing observes that Dryden has made Palamon "a proper neoclassical hero," although this does not alter West's view that Dryden is anti-heroic ("Dryden's Ambivalence," 358).

16. Chaucer mentions the banner and the arms, briefly: "And in thy temple I wol my baner honge / And alle the armes of my compaignye" (2410–11): all the rest is Dryden.

17. Earl Miner, in "Chaucer in Dryden's *Fables*," from *Studies in Criticism and Aesthetics, 1660–1800: Essays in Honor of Samuel Holt Monk*, ed. Howard Anderson and John S. Shea (Minneapolis: University of Minnesota Press, 1967), 58–72, likens Dryden's Arcite to "a cunning, valiant Achilles, devoted to Mars," and Palamon to "a more sensitive, moral Hector, devoted to Venus" (69).

18. This is how Judith Sloman, in *Dryden: The Poetics of Translation* (Toronto: University of Toronto Press, 1985), regards Theseus, as an unambiguous hero; he is "a morally successful version of both of Virgil's heroes [i.e., Aeneas and Turnus]" (136), and as such represents the completion of what Dryden left incomplete in his translation of Virgil.

19. In his Prologue to John Banks's *The Unhappy Favorite* (1682), Dryden, addressing the king and queen, used the same image of the peace-bringing dove to quite similar ends.

20. Earl Miner notes this link in *Dryden's Poetry* (297).

21. For a thorough account of the political implications and anti-Williamite innuendos throughout the poem, see Alan Roper, *Dryden's Poetic Kingdoms* (London: Routledge & Kegan Paul, 1965), 124–35; Jay Arnold Levine, "John Dryden's Epistle to John Driden," *Journal of English and Germanic Philology* 63 (1964):450–74; and James Anderson Winn (Winn, Chapter 13). As Winn points out, the passage beginning on line 158 alludes to the conquering army of Alexander the Great, establishing an analogy between William and Alexander that Dryden also pursues later in *Fables* in "Alexander's Feast."

22. For a thorough discussion of the politics behind this poem and of the duke's purposes in acting for William, see Alan Roper, *Dryden's Poetic Kingdoms* (115–24). See also Steven N. Zwicker, *Politics and Language in Dryden's Poetry: The Arts of Disguise* (Princeton: Princeton University Press, 1984), who

emphasizes in both the Ormond and Driden poems the significance of lineage, the next generation, restoration and preservation of the family, all as topics that have a bearing on the political succession (163–64).

23. Jay Arnold Levine sees Cousin Driden as "immovable" and "temperate" ("John Dryden's Epistle," 468, 471); Sloman regards him as "explicitly serious, with a Roman austerity" ("Structure," 42).

24. Sloman observes that "femininity and masculinity evoke grace and strength respectively, so that, if the two poems are read together, they present a more complete ideal than either one does alone" ("Structure," 43). In *Dryden: The Poetics*, she refers to them as "balancing opposed forces" (166). I would go a step further and claim that Theseus from the middle tale is the more complete ideal.

25. Also, Levine points out that Driden's virtues "are characterized almost entirely in negative terms connoting withdrawal from activity: 'unvex'd,' 'void,' and 'shunning' " ("John Dryden's Epistle," 472).

Chapter Four

THE CHRISTIAN IDEAL

*B*Y GROUPING "To the Dutchess of Ormond" and "To my Honour'd Kinsman" together with the intervening tale, "Palamon and Arcite," I have been seeking to emphasize the ways in which the duchess and Cousin Driden partially achieve what Theseus embodies, a fruitful combination of courage and love. That the duchess and John Driden are imperfect is not a deficiency in their characters so much as it is a normal consequence of being human. Nobody is perfect, not since the first Fall, and one cannot help but notice Dryden's emphasis, in both poems, on fallen worlds: in one, an Ireland destroyed by the Flood in need of a restorative "second Coming" ("Dutchess," 80), and in the other, an England plagued by disease and bad doctors because

> The Tree of Knowledge, once in *Eden* plac'd,
> Was easie found, but was forbid the Taste:
> O, had our Grandsire walk'd without his Wife,
> He first had sought the better Plant of Life!
> Now, both are lost: Yet, wandring in the dark,
> Physicians for the Tree, have found the Bark [i.e., quinine].
> ("Kinsman," 96–101)

A wasted Ireland, a corrupt England are different realms from the Chaucerian never-never land where "resulting Joy may be renew'd, / As jarring Notes in Harmony conclude" (3 : 1117–8).

I mention these biblical references to remind readers of the abundance of Christian imagery in both poems, which may invite us to consider these two portraits in a different way, not merely as part of the reevaluation of heroic values, as two characters we measure against a Theseus, but as part of something else, something that leads in a different direction. Perhaps this is a completely new order, a Christian value system,

71

glimpsed initially in these two exemplary figures, limited only because they live in a faulty world, and later confirmed by a matching pair of portraits at the end of *Fables*, that of the good parson and the fair maiden lady. It all depends on how one chooses to group the poems; of the twenty-one fables, these four poems—the Ormond and kinsman poems, "The Character of A Good Parson," and "The Monument of A Fair Maiden Lady"—are the only portraits, while the rest of the tales are all narratives of one kind or another.[1] When we observe Dryden beginning this collection with portraits of a historically real woman and man, and ending his collection with portraits of an ideal man and woman, the symmetry is too tidy to resist. Perhaps the duchess and John Driden give us our first glimpse of new ideals, which we find in completed form at the end of *Fables*.[2] The new characters are good Christians again, except that they are very, very good, and they replace the earlier figures because they are not subject to the same limitations. The fair maiden lady is not subject to disease, although one cannot help noticing that she is dead; when she was alive, however, she was scarcely physical at all, but rather a "Celestial Maid" (2), an embodiment of the spiritual:

> So faultless was the Frame, as if the Whole
> Had been an Emanation of the Soul;
> Which her own inward Symmetry reveal'd;
> And like a Picture shone, in Glass Anneal'd.
> (9–12)

She is as faultless as the central figure of Dryden's first poem (1649), Lord Hastings, whose "sublime Soul," together with his starry virtues, "Shone th'row his Body" (27, 36), although the mature Dryden no longer avails himself of metaphysical Archimedean spheres to depict purity. The maiden, in simpler terms, is perfection itself, "All white, a Virgin-Saint" (19), whose love, which has to be as spiritual as she is, is directed entirely heavenward: "So Pious, as she had no time to spare / For human Thoughts, but was confin'd to Pray'r" (28–29). Unlike the duchess, who is loving but weak, both physically and in terms of her power to restore Ireland, the maiden combines "A Female Softness, with a manly Mind" (34).

The good parson also strikes an ideal balance; unlike the honored kinsman, who is strong, tenacious, just, but a trifle cold, the parson is both strong and loving, with Dryden weaving back and forth between the hard and the soft, as a typical passage demonstrates:

> With Eloquence innate his Tongue was arm'd;
> Tho' harsh the Precept, yet the Preacher charm'd.
> . . . .
> He bore his great Commission in his Look:
> But sweetly temper'd Awe; and soften'd all he spoke.
> He preach'd the Joys of Heav'n, and Pains of Hell;
> And warn'd the Sinner with becoming Zeal;
> But on Eternal Mercy lov'd to dwell.
>
> (17–18, 25–29)

A tongue armed with harsh precepts becomes charming; the parson's awesome moral responsibility he tempers sweetly, and Dryden follows with an example of that softened speech, when the parson preaches the joys of heaven, followed immediately by a none-too-soft topic, the pains of hell, urged not just with zeal, but with zeal made attractive. This is reminiscent of the give and take in Dryden's earlier poem to John Oldham (1684), where each instance of praise was mitigated by a hint of criticism, which in turn was undercut by praise, until the young satirist was forgiven for his harsh and rugged verse, which was only "A noble Error, and but seldom made, / When Poets are by too much force betray'd" (17–18). The verse may be rough, but it is noble and forceful, although what is noble is also an error, and what is forceful betrays the poet: back and forth, give and take.

Strong as the parson is, "Charity it self was in his Face" (4), which makes him sound like Absalom in all his innocence, when "*Paradise* was open'd in his face" ("Absalom and Achitophel," 30). The parson's text, which he both embodies and preaches, is "Eternal Mercy" (29), a persuasive text because he administers it with love rather than by threat: he "lov'd to draw" sinners, rather than push them, and, according to Drydenian physics, "Love, like Heat, / Exhales the Soul sublime, to seek her Native Seat" (32–33). The loving parson, who is also "Lov'd by most" (130), is a more complete ideal than the primarily strong kinsman. More complete in another way too, as we learn when we discover that the parson's political position, which follows naturally from his virtues, sounds familiar. At the cost of his benefice, the parson "withstood" a monarch "great in Arms" because "Near tho' he was," he was "yet not the next of Blood" (110–11). This "Saint ... who shone with every Grace" (102) nobly resisted the temptation to acquiesce in the deposition of the rightful monarch, Richard II, quite unlike the ever-thoughtless crowd: "He join'd not in their Choice; because he knew / Worse might, and often did from Change ensue" (123–24). Shades of Dryden, who not only withstood William III, but seemed to take advantage of every available opportunity to rebuke his monarch, including right now, when Dryden expresses yet again his strong disapproval of warlike, usurping kings (106–26). Thus, the parson serves as one of many Dryden alter egos, in this case an elevated embodiment of personal ideals; in a manner of speaking, Dryden is casting himself into the saintlike mold, making the parson both a strong and loving Christian ideal, and an idealized Dryden at the same time.

Forget Theseus. Both the parson and the fair maiden combine love and strength, and *they* may be the ideals against which the loving duchess and the tenacious John Driden are measured. Unlike these earlier characters, the "All white" (19) maiden and the "Spotless" (139) parson are removed from that grubby, post-lapsarian reality into a higher realm, hovering just below the angels. The two final portraits not only balance the initial portraits, but they also give us a progression, and we can see *Fables* moving away from the motley assortment of wrong-headed, selfish, disastrous passions and physical lusts that nonchalantly destroy people and nations, moving towards these ideals of Christian charity, love of God, and self-denial.[3]

If *Fables* is based on these Christian virtues, how can we accommodate this to those instances in the work where Dryden endorses heroic ideals, all from the pagan world? Easily. The key comes both in our choice of tales to group, and in our willingness to make the grouping a progression. Not just some good heroes, some brutal ones, and an occasional good Christian, but some instances of true heroism that gradually prove false as the bodies pile up, followed by a shining Christian ideal, a progress from the dark lands of vengeful brutes to a Christian haven, where such as the good parson and perfect maiden dwell. Perhaps the brutal and savage heroes Dryden debunks are not, as I earlier suggested, redeemed by the selfless, loving centaurs, or by chivalric Palamon, or by the magnanimous and judicious Theseus. The few genuine heroes we encounter we can regard as the exception, like Ajax, sadly lost, representing a code that no longer applies; he is ever honored by the purple flower, but he and his greatness are dead forever. And Theseus may be the ideal prince, but that was long ago and far away, all part of an appealing dream from which we must awake, a fiction we relinquish after we have been dragged through the welter of beasts and warriors. The Dryden who converted to Catholicism in 1685, who wanted to write an epic and never quite did, may now be embracing his new religion with what Judith Sloman calls a new "variety of epic" ("Interpretation," 199), dismissing an old order with mixed feelings—on the one hand seeing clearly the brutality and selfishness such a code entails, and on the other nostalgically remembering the greatness of heroes.

"THE CHRISTIAN IDEAL" MEETS "CYMON AND IPHIGENIA"

I think this interpretation is true, in the same way that calling *Fables* anti-heroic is true—true, but only in part. *Fables* is a work that endorses an attitude or a group of values, but then questions what it seems to promote, as we discovered in our examination of Dryden's anti-heroism. *Fables* does provide us with an anti-heroic strain, which it undoes as well. The same, I think, can be said of this Christian ideal. We half expect it to be there from what we know of Dryden's continued adherence, at his own cost, to his unfashionable religion.[4] And we find it in these exemplary Christian characters who so neatly complete the earlier portraits of good but limited Christians, and who serve as a final comment. And yet, that is not all we find (and these tales are not quite the final comment).

Why weigh the poems on the parson and the maiden so heavily, two of the shortest, and dullest, poems in the anthology? At a mere thirty-six lines, "The Monument of a Fair Maiden Lady" scarcely tips the scales. "The Character of A Good Parson" is longer, but I wonder whether the parson, rather than serving an elevated Christian purpose, does not answer a more mundane and immediate need. Throughout *Fables*, Dryden is concerned to defend his reputation against Jeremy Collier's recent attacks: "I have been wrongfully accus'd," remarks Dryden in the Preface, "and my Sense wire-drawn into Blasphemy or Bawdry . . . by a Religious Lawyer in a late Pleading against the Stage" (Kinsley, 4:1447). Dryden's fullest exploration of the subject occurs in a prefatory "Poeta Loquitur" added to "Cymon and Iphigenia," in which he good-humoredly takes Collier apart, pointing out that it is Collier, not Dryden, who makes the immorality, by "perverting first my Sense" (10), by making "me speak the Things I never thought" (12). That much is direct counterattack, answering Collier "in his own Language, Self-defence," but what better way to answer Collier's charges that Dryden has vilified men of the cloth, which Dryden overtly denies in his Preface (Kinsley, 4: 1453–55), than by following "*Chaucer* in his Character of a Holy Man" and enlarging "on that Subject with some Pleasure" (Kinsley, 4: 1454–55), by creating a portrait of an exemplary parson, who also just happens to be a Dryden alter ego? Is this part of a noble Christian resolution, or merely a palpable hit?[5]

These are questions worth raising, but the biggest question has to do with the idea of seeing *Fables* progressing toward a resolution; why see the collection moving toward these final poems, especially since they are not the final poems? The final poem is "Cymon and Iphigenia," another rousing tale of lust disguised as love, of rape leading to war. *That* is Dryden's last word, and the concluding lines depict no inspiring vision of purity, but rather two countries at perpetual war for ignoble reasons, settling at last into a hypocritical peace that occurs after both sides have exhausted themselves in killing:

> A War ensues, the *Cretans* own their Cause,
> Stiff to defend their hospitable Laws:
> Both Parties lose by turns; and neither wins,
> 'Till Peace propounded by a Truce begins.
> The Kindred of the Slain forgive the Deed,
> But a short Exile must for Show precede;
> The Term expir'd, from *Candia* they remove;
> And happy each at Home, enjoys his Love.
> (633–40)

Two barbarous "Ravishers" (606) who have just besmeared the walls with sprinkled Gore (607–8) will finally win their stolen brides. Not a hint of justice either in this world or the next. And not a hint of Christian charity, patience, or self-sacrifice here, but rather more indiscriminate slaughter; how can we consider the parson and maiden as beacons of hope when the concluding tale returns us to the land of anti-heroic gloom?[6]

The world of Cymon and Iphigenia is beyond the redemptive powers of a pure, dead maiden and of a parson who tends his flock and quietly endures poverty. Yet one cannot help noticing that the chief participants in Dryden's last tale have their foils elsewhere in *Fables*, and one can begin to see groupings and regroupings that a minute will reverse. Consider Iphigenia, whose beauty is the immediate cause of all the fuss. While she sleeps, the "charming Features of her Face" (97), not to mention "comely Limbs" (99) and "Her Bosom," which "to the view was . . . bare" (101), awaken Cymon's interest. Unfortunately for him, she is engaged to Pasimond of Rhodes, but Cymon, not one to mope about in the dejection of the lovelorn, equips himself for war, sets sail, and captures his intended after a fierce battle. As Cymon sails away with his prize, Dryden adds a passage that gives us our first glimpse of the character behind this young Diana with the "celestial Face" (166):

> While to his Arms the blushing Bride he took,
> To seeming Sadness she compos'd her Look;
> As if by Force subjected to his Will,
> Tho' pleas'd, dissembling, and a Woman still.
> ·
> Thus while he spoke he seiz'd the willing Prey,
> As *Paris* bore the *Spartan* Spouse away:
> Faintly she scream'd, and ev'n her Eyes confess'd
> She rather would be thought, than was Distress'd.
> (308–11, 318–21)

She is not exactly an object worthy of his affection, but rather something of a coquette, favoring Cymon when it is to her advantage, then regretting their escape when it appears a storm will destroy their ship. While the storm rages, she blames Cymon—"And lays the Load on his ungovern'd Love" (358)—but she quickly changes her mind:

> Then impotent of Mind, with alter'd Sense,
> She hugg'd th' Offender, and forgave th' Offence,
> Sex to the last.
> (366–68)

Fickle, dissembling, opportunistic, all part of being a woman, apparently, with Dryden turning Boccaccio's neutral character into the kind of woman misogynists particularly enjoy hating.[7]

Yet Dryden has given us, in the character of the duchess of Ormond, another example of "What Pow'r the Charms of Beauty had of old" (8):

> The Waste of Civil Wars, their Towns destroy'd,
> *Pales* unhonour'd, *Ceres* unemploy'd,
> Were all forgot; and one Triumphant Day
> Wip'd all the Tears of three Campaigns away.
> Blood, Rapines, Massacres, were cheaply bought,
> So mighty Recompence Your Beauty brought.
> (64–69)

The duchess has the power to undo what women like Iphigenia inadvertently do. If Iphigenia appears to represent her "Sex to the last," she is counterbalanced by the the duchess, a "Chast *Penelope*" (158), who not only loves her absent husband in the traditionally approved way, but whose love, like her beauty, offers hope for the future.[8] She too represents her "Sex to the last," but in the sense of good wife and mother who makes the succession of the Ormond line possible by producing children, "The Three fair Pledges of Your Happy Love" (164). This is the kind of force needed in a land of Iphigenias; fragile as the duchess may be, she offers a more productive and promising ideal than does the pure maiden whose tomb inspires us to reflect on chastity.

Returning to the world of "Cymon and Iphigenia," consider one of the more active participants in the melee, Lysymachus, the auxiliary ravisher, a remarkable case study of a corrupt, self-serving public servant. He is an elected official, the "annual Magistrate" who currently "rul'd the *Rhodian* State" (437–38), and he has had the misfortune to fall in love with Cassandra, the "destin'd Bride" (434) of another. This sounds familiar, only Lysymachus, unlike Cymon, hesitates before taking action: he has public responsibilities, and he is pledged to uphold the law. Lysymachus reflects on this situation, and before long begins to see how he can use his powerful position to his own personal advantage:

> If Force were us'd,
> The Magistrate his publick Trust abus'd;
> To Justice, liable as Law requir'd;
> For when his Office ceas'd, his Pow'r expir'd:
> While Pow'r remain'd, the Means were in his Hand
> By Force to seize, and then forsake the Land.
> (452–57)

The internal debate does not take long, since "Love never fails to master what he finds" (464), and Lysymachus "proposing to possess, and scape, / Began in Murder, to conclude in Rape" (467–68). Just as Dryden generalizes on the basis of Iphigenia about the dissembling nature of womankind, so does he pause to remark on what Lysymachus tells us about the nature of powerful public officials: "The Great, it seems, are priviledg'd alone / To punish all Injustice but their own" (471–72).

Public servant to the last, as it were. Once we view Lysymachus in this light, it is hard to resist comparing him to that "Just, Good, and Wise" (7) public servant, Driden of Chesterton, respected member of Parliament for Huntingdon, trusted justice of the peace to whom "contending Neighbours come" willingly "to wait their final Doom" (7–8). Driden's decisions lead to "a lasting Peace" (15), not to blood-besmeared walls and nations at war, and Driden is constant to his duty, in part because he is *not* swayed by passion. He is "Promoting Concord, and composing Strife" because he is "Lord of . . . [him]self, uncumber'd with a Wife" (17–18), quite the opposite of Lysymachus, who wreaks havoc all for the sake of a Cassandra. His crime undermines the state, leaving the people helpless, as Dryden explains in detail, expanding considerably on Boccaccio's brief and general allusion to the commotion:

> What should the People do, when left alone?
> The Governor, and Government are gone.
> The publick Wealth to Foreign Parts convey'd;
> Some Troops disbanded, and the rest unpaid.
> *Rhodes* is the Soveraign of the Sea no more;
> Their Ships unrigg'd, and spent their Naval Store.
> (615–20)

But a people served by officials like Driden might avoid such confusion, might instead find stability and strength, for his steadfast performance of his duties, as we have seen, makes him a patriot who shines in "resisting Might" (185), a barrier protecting the state from the dangerous tides of power that threaten to engulf it (171–85). As one of the "Good Senators" (135), Driden opposes William's military expenditures, preferring to rely on "our Native Strength, in time of need" (139);[9] while William pushes for the Standing Army, Driden instead insists that "the Naval Stores" are "the Nations Care, / New Ships to build, and batter'd to repair" (148–49). This is noble stubbornness, a patriotic service to king and country that entails defending the country from its king.[10] Rhodes, whose chaos is visually represented by the image of a defeated navy, with "Ships unrigg'd" and an exhausted "Naval Store" (620), seems to be in specific need of somebody like Driden, whose constructive contribution to his nation is in part conveyed by imagery involving the repairing and building of ships.

Cousin Driden, then, is the kind of official who might save a Rhodes, a more convincing Drydenian ideal, I think, than the perfect parson who shares the kinsman's political views, but who acts differently. The parson too, as we recall, resists a usurping monarch (Henry IV):

This Prince, tho' great in Arms, the Priest withstood:
Near tho' he was, yet not the next of Blood.
Had *Richard* unconstrain'd, resign'd the Throne:
A King can give no more than is his own:
The Title stood entail'd, had *Richard* had a Son.
. . . .
He join'd not in their [the people's] Choice; because he knew
Worse might, and often did from Change ensue.
Much to himself he thought; but little spoke:
And, Undepriv'd, his Benefice forsook.
(110–14, 123–26)

In similar political situations, one character acts to prevent the tides of power from drowning the land, the other thinks to himself and says little. There is nothing wrong with that. But actions speak louder than non-words, and it seems to me that of the two, it is the kinsman who elicits Dryden's strongest support. It seemed that way to Dryden too: "I have not onely drawn the features of my worthy Kinsman," wrote Dryden to Charles Montague, "but have also given my Own opinion, of what an Englishman in Parliament oughto be; & deliver it as a Memorial of my own Principles to all Posterity" (#65, probably written in October 1699, *Letters*, p. 120).

When we group all of these characters and compare them, we discover that the brutal universe of "Cymon and Iphigenia" would better be served, or even saved, not by two perfect Christians remote from the dirty business of life, but by active humans like Cousin Driden and the duchess, by a responsible magistrate who honors his duty, promotes stability, protects a nation, and a woman whose beauty and love inspire a family and promise to restore a country. These are not static examples worthy of emulation, but real people, limited, perhaps, but actively engaged in making civilization civilized.

A MODIFIED CHRISTIAN IDEAL

As we pursue different parallels, different groupings, notice what happens to the whole notion of an "informing ideal." The first three tales of *Fables* establish contrasts and balances, poising the loving duchess and the strong kinsman against a heroic standard, Theseus, who combines qualities they only partially embody. Later, near the end of the anthology, Dryden provides matched sets of portraits, and the perspective changes; now the two earlier characters seem to be contrasted against a Christian ideal, represented by the exemplary characters that " replace" the earlier portraits. The final tale may change the perspective yet again. After weighing Driden and the duchess against an ideal on one side, and another ideal on the other, we discover that perhaps *they* are the ideal; next to these civilizing humans, the pure Christians look rarefied, pale, and impotent, and the characters in "Cymon and Iphigenia," members of a heroic world that Dryden has gradually debased, look all the more selfish, blind, and brutally destructive. As the tales unfold, echoing, contrasting, and commenting upon one another, each informing ideal is subject to revision and reversal, leaving us to ponder where, exactly, Dryden stands.

The standard way around this, I think, is to fall back on *via media* Dryden, whose habitual strategy, whatever the issues may be, is to argue one side of the argument, argue the other, and then settle comfortably in what appears to be the middle of the road. Many Dryden scholars take this mediating process for granted, and we can see why if we shift back to an earlier time (and an earlier Dryden religion), and watch as Dryden steers his course through a series of opposed possibilities. In "Religio Laici" (1682), for example, Dryden argues against the likelihood of the profit-minded, self-aggrandizing Catholic church preserving sacred truths through an oral tradition; given "*Interest, Church,* and *Gain*," such a tradition becomes "*Immortal Lyes*" entailed on "*Ages*" (273–75). Some people have every reason to think they can more readily find sacred truths by reading the Bible themselves, and Dryden argues the case for individual interpretation:

> . . . the *Scriptures,* though not *every where*
> Free from Corruption, or intire, or clear,

81

Are uncorrupt, sufficient, clear, intire,
In *all* things which our needfull *Faith* require.
(297–300)

So much for the direct descent of Christ's word through an uninterrupted apostolic succession; better to read the text oneself. Then, Dryden turns around and argues the case for tradition; truths may well have been soiled as they passed through the unclean hands of the "partial *Papists*" (356), but they are more likely to be torn and galled in the "horney Fists" (404) of "every vulgar hand" (400).

Since both approaches are problematic, the only thing to do is find the center line:

What then remains, but, waving each Extreme,
The Tides of Ignorance, and Pride to stem:
Neither so rich a Treasure to forgo;
Nor proudly seek beyond our pow'r to know?
(427–30)

Dryden relies upon a little tradition, from Anglican divines free from generations of Papist cupidity, and upon a little private judgment. When private judgment and tradition disagree, the best thing to do is trust in the tradition: "In doubtfull questions 'tis the safest way / To learn what unsuspected Ancients say" (435–36). This sounds like the middle, thanks to the process of arguing A, then B, then not-A, then not-B, but it only sounds like the middle. In actuality, the middle turns out to be to the right of center.[11]

Could we not say that Dryden is using a similar strategy, stretching it out across *Fables*? The issues are different, but the process of presenting a viewpoint by negotiating through opposed extremes persists. Dryden gives us one extreme, and then the other, and undercuts each of them; like the true individual interpretation of the Bible and an omniscient church, heroism and Christianity prove to be desirable but untenable ideals. The noble values of a Theseus can no longer exist in a world of Cymons and Iphigenias, which is similar to the world of warmongering William; and the Christian ideals enshrined in the characters of the maiden and parson prove to be irrelevant and ineffective in a world populated by unchaste women and usurping kings. The duchess and the kinsman, nevertheless, display some of the traits found in the best characters from each extreme, from the heroic past, and from an ethereal

Christian realm. These two characters may constitute Dryden's modified, *via media* Christian ideal, standing seemingly between heroism and
pure Christian virtue, but leaning toward Christianity.

This is not to suggest that Dryden was anything less than a firm be-
liever in Catholicism, but his own experience, his age, and his recurrent
illnesses might have produced a different set of expectations and a different mood. The older Dryden may have been less inclined to consider
any ideal transcendent, and he may be expressing a world-weary view of
Christianity rather than passionately endorsing the cause as he once
did.[12] In 1685, the year of his conversion, Dryden published his ode to
Anne Killigrew, a grandly baroque testament to his enthusiasm for his
newfound ideals, which he embodied in this "young Probationer, / And
Candidate of Heav'n" (21–22). Unlike Dryden, who felt he had "Made
prostitute and profligate the Muse" (58), Anne Killigrew remained true
to God's "Heav'nly Gift of Poesy" (57). Her poetry may have been
trivial, but her heart was in the right place, and she is more significant
for her Christian purity than for her minor artistic accomplishments.[13]
And how does this ideal Christian poet fare? At the Last Judgment, when
"the Golden Trump shall sound" (178),

> The Sacred Poets first shall hear the Sound,
>   And formost from the Tomb shall bound:
> For they are cover'd with the lightest Ground
> And streight, with in-born Vigour, on the Wing,
> Like mounting Larkes, to the New Morning sing.
> There Thou, Sweet Saint, before the Quire shalt go,
> As Harbinger of Heav'n, the Way to show,
> The Way which thou so well hast learn'd below.
>   (188–95)

A bold claim for sacred poetry and its power. Not only does this "Sweet
Saint" lead all mankind at the Last Judgment, but she also leads men
here on earth, acting as guiding light to her seafaring brother (in stanza
ix), and acting as a maker reshaping the king himself:

> For not content t' express his Outward Part,
> Her hand call'd out the Image of his Heart,
> His Warlike Mind, his Soul devoid of Fear,
> His High-designing Thoughts, were figur'd there,
> As when, by Magick, Ghosts are made appear.
>   (129–33)

As a painter, she makes James II kinglike, calling forth virtues that are not there until she puts them there. And as a poet, "What Nature, Art, bold Fiction e're durst frame, / Her forming Hand gave Feature to the Name" (123–24). This is one powerful artist, and Dryden does not hesitate to make her a conqueror, who "stretcht her Sway" (92) from poetry to the adjoining realm of painting. When she finally ascends "As Harbinger of Heav'n," she is powerfully different from the duchess, who goes to Ireland as "*Ormond's* Harbinger" (62), promising a restoration that she is too weak to deliver.

In 1685, this "Youngest Virgin-Daughter of the Skies" (1), up there among the seraphim singing her "Celestial Song" (13), was a Christian ideal and a powerful, effective force, instructing kings, as Dryden liked to think he was doing. But in *Fables*, Christian ideals elicit no such enthusiasm, attain no transcendent victory. If the Killigrew ode is a supercharged statement of faith, both in poetry's sacred power and in a Christian ideal, in *Fables* the ideals fail to ascend. The "Celestial Maid" (2) of 1700 is not shown treading the skies heavenward with all mankind in tow, but is rather "In Sickness patient; and in Death resigned" (36). Such a line, the final one in the portrait of the maiden, suggests limitation rather than triumph. Dryden's attitude in *Fables* toward the Christian ideal may be like his attitude toward heroism; he can see and appreciate the greatness, but as a realist, he sees the limitations in both codes of behavior. Neither invariably works, yet both offer some hope. If Dryden does not, after all, make the parson and the maiden the grand resolution, he at least locates good within Christians. Neither the tough kinsman nor the fragile duchess can combine strength with love, but can only represent them partially, one trait apiece. Although that is not perfection, it is the best we have, and the best we can hope to have in a fallen world: a noble but limited *via media* Christian ideal, part of Dryden's resigned and now acquiescent Catholicism.

NON-CHRISTIAN IDEALS: "BAUCIS AND
PHILEMON," "CEYX AND ALCYONE"

There are other tales that shed light, that offer other possible sources of values. We need not consider Christianity as an ideal at all. Could one not argue, just as easily, that "Baucis and Philemon," another tale from Ovid, comprises an informing ideal? Here we discover an idyllic pair, married for years without a trace of "Domestick Strife" (172), quite unlike the squabbling Jove and Juno in Dryden's translation of "The First Book of Homer's Ilias." Whereas, as we have seen, the gods argue over who has the authority in marriage, with male-chauvinist Jove insisting that "no Wife / Has Pow'r to regulate her Husband's Life" (735–36), and shrewish Juno complaining because in this marriage "The Consort never must the Council share" (730), humble Baucis and Philemon are above all that. They are "a happy Pair" (33), living a contented, peaceful life, never arguing, not ever, because they share the responsibility and authority:

> For Master or for Servant here to call,
> Was all alike, where only Two were All.
> Command was none, where equal Love was paid,
> Or rather both commanded, both obey'd.
> (37–40)

The first couplet is more or less straight Ovid, but the second couplet is an addition, and since it emphasizes the issue of marital authority, I cannot help but think that Dryden is asking us specifically to compare this relationship with the heavenly power-struggle. Ovid is merely explaining that this couple is too poor to have any servants, that the only people they had to command, therefore, were one another, but Dryden's passage, instead of merely describing the couple's poverty, defines the central strength of their marriage.[14] Notice that the measure of the heavenly mismatch is a simple, poor, and non-Christian couple.

The magnanimity and selflessness Baucis and Philemon display in marriage extend into the rest of their behavior, and that brings us to the central event of the tale: one day, they offer the hospitality of their "homely Shed" (30) to two travellers who have sought in vain for harbor throughout the countryside. As poor as Baucis and Philemon are, they give their guests the best they have—a warm fire, a comfortable place to sit, and a meal. Although one expects the food to be humble fare, it is a two-course "Feast" (90), a meal that would probably warm the heart of a health-minded Californian: fresh fruit, nuts, berries, figs, dates, plenty of greens, topped off with local wine, "the best the Cottage cou'd afford" (101, a Dryden addition). Lots of natural foods, all served in rustic earthenware. This may be the "Poverty they bore" (35), but there is nothing shabby about it.

The travellers are actually Jove and Hermes in disguise. After the feast, they reveal their identity and enact the traditional vengeance upon the less hospitable households: "The Neighbourhood . . . / Shall justly perish for Impiety" (141–42), Jove announces, but "You stand alone exempted" (143). Baucis and Philemon are told to flee to the mountains, without looking back (a Dryden addition), and when they reach the top, they discover that a flood has destroyed their less generous countrymen. All that remains below is their home on a little island, and before their eyes "Their little Shed" (157) grows into a stately neoclassical temple. Jove then asks them what they desire as a reward; obviously, they are being rewarded for their unhesitating generosity, but Jove understands that this virtue is an inseparable part of their marriage:

> Then thus the Sire of Gods, with Look serene,
> Speak thy Desire, thou only Just of Men;
> And thou, O Woman, only worthy found
> To be with such a Man in Marriage bound.
> (163–66)

They consult with one another privately, a nice domestic touch, and inform Jove of "their joint Request" (169). They desire merely to serve Jove, offering "at your Altars Rites Divine" (170), and to die in the same hour so that neither will have to mourn the other. The god grants their wish; when they finally die, at the same instant, they are transformed into adjacent trees whose roots intertwine. They become a monument to . . . well, not to chastity, like the maiden. And certainly not to celibacy, like the kinsman. And not to anything especially Christian, but rather to the domestic ideal of a faithful, loving marriage.

Nor is "Baucis and Philemon" an isolated example of what might nowadays be called a non-Christian role model.[15] The story of "Ceyx and Alcyone," from book eleven of the *Metamorphoses*, is another tale of conjugal love, a pathetic rather than an idyllic version of the theme. Ceyx is a "pious Prince" (1), honorable, god-fearing, and the gods he fears are the pagan gods who have been venting their wrath on his family. He wants to consult the oracle of Apollo to find out how to appease the gods, and this entails a sea journey, which he tries to conceal from his wife, just as Jove tried to conceal from Juno his granting a favor to Thetis. Neither husband succeeds in keeping a secret from his spouse,

Jove because he has a prying wife who will find out everything and challenge him at any opportunity, Ceyx because he "cou'd . . . not from her he lov'd so well / The fatal Voyage, he resolved, conceal" (6–7). What a refreshing difference, and the marital dispute that ensues is equally appealing, for it shows us a husband and wife deeply concerned with each other's welfare rather than at each other's throat. Alcyone breaks into tears at the very thought of her husband's risks; when she finds she cannot dissuade him from the voyage, she wishes to join him, whatever the cost: "Go not without thy Wife, but let me bear / My part of Danger with an equal share" (49–50). Not to be outdone in concern for his mate, Ceyx rejects her request, "For as he lov'd her equal to his Life, / He wou'd not to the Seas expose his Wife" (56–57). The circumstances are more extreme than anything in the quiet lives of Baucis and Philemon, quiet, that is, until the arrival of the gods, but this too is "equal Love."

Ceyx departs, reluctantly, and as his wife had feared, he encounters a storm, the description of which takes up most of the tale. While members of his crew shriek, or become stupefied with fear, "All *Ceyx* his *Alcyone* employs, / For her he grieves, yet in her absence joys" (188–89). He seems more worried about what she will suffer than he is about his own impending death. At such a moment, "his Consort is his greatest Care" (214), and her name is literally on his lips as he sinks below the waves. Meanwhile, Alcyone prays for him, to no avail. Her prayers are semi-answered. None of the gods deigns to save her husband. Instead, they pass the buck: Juno assigns the responsibility to Iris; Iris visits Sleep; Sleep assigns the chore to his son, Morpheus, who comes to Alcyone in a dream vision, impersonating her dead husband; this gives both Dryden and Ovid a splendid opportunity to indulge in a pathetic scene in which Alcyone embraces what looks like her husband, and the image slips through her arms and vanishes. Later, the body of Ceyx washes up at the feet of a waiting Alcyone—it was one of the things he had prayed for as he sank—and Alcyone in her grief dives into the ocean to join him. This is rather like the story of the loving centaurs, wherein Hylonome "In madness of her Grief" (572) stabs herself with the weapon that has just killed her lover, Cyllarus. That scene ends with a gruesome and terminal embrace, love amidst the carnage, but here, Alcyone and Ceyx are translated into winter birds, so that "Their conjugal Affection still is ty'd, / And still the mournful race is multiply'd" (493–94).[16] Nature blesses their nesting by providing, of course, halcyon winds. Like the intertwined trees, the transformed Ceyx and Alcyone become a monument to "conjugal Affection," except it is an affection cut off in the bud.[17]

Ceyx and Alcyone are lovers of high estate, living in a world of melodrama and intense emotion, while Baucis and Philemon spend uneventful lives filled with planting, harvesting, cooking, setting the kettle on. The prince and his wife express their love with speeches, in prayers, amidst tears, through embraces, while drowning, when dead. The ordinary mortals whose love is second-nature to them, part of their simple, homey, shared lives, quietly express their love by cooperating in domestic chores for their guests: he draws out the bench, she provides cushions, she starts the fire and prepares colewarts picked from his garden, he cooks the bacon, and so on. All told, these characters present an ideal of love across a wide range; it is not the ideal of celibacy or chastity from a Christian code, but love romantic and love domestic, love sentimental and love plain.[18] Impassioned or restrained, overt or implicit, put to severe trial or casually tested, "equal Love" can triumph, and the gods bless both couples by preserving their togetherness, by turning them into symbols of marital devotion, winter birds nesting in a becalmed sea, or intertwining ancient trees. And the gods who perform these miracles are not a Christian God or his only-begotten Son, but Jove and Hermes in the case of the elderly couple, and the unidentified but ever-present "Gods" (490) in the case of the tragic pair.

The same classical world that gives us lust-filled beasts, squabbling deities, and heroes diminished to adolescents by their raging passions, gives us here constructive and transcendent lovers, in high and low versions. Not only do these two tales serve as a contrast to those many anti-heroic instances where passion leads to war, but they also serve as positive examples amidst a host of misguided or star-crossed lovers. Sigismonda's love for Guiscardo, without her father's consent, ends up in death for her lover, suicide for her, misery all around, rather than eternal togetherness. Myrrha's passion for Cinyras, who unfortunately is her father, ends in Myrrha's painful and protracted metamorphosis into a tree, an eternal punishment for her incestuous love that will neither "let her wholly die, nor wholly live" (335). "Sigismonda and Guiscardo" ends with no metamorphosis, just the finality of death and the afterglow of general suffering, while Myrrha's tale ends with a metamorphosis into suffering itself, as the tree that was Myrrha weeps forever. Love goes awry all too often, for heroes, for gods, and for these mere mortals. But Ceyx and Alcyone, Baucis and Philemon, serve as a commentary on all that: not lust misconstrued, not passion that destroys, but love that enriches, love that enlarges, and love that finally transcends human suffering and human mortality itself. Like the Christian duchess, these characters too embody the fidelity and selflessness needed in a land of fickle Iphigenias and rapacious Cymons.

To see *Fables* moving toward a Christian resolution, then, is to overlook other scales of human value, equally viable, equally appealing, that Dryden places alongside the Christian ideals.[19] Viewing those tales side by side often reveals clear parallels that we would otherwise miss were we looking constantly for the road upward to the ethereal Christian realm. We can see the fair maiden, for instance, not as a climactic example of pure virtue, whose "Worth transcended all her Kind" (23), but rather as another version of virtue that transcends, this time into a Christian heaven rather than an animated world of magical birds and trees. And the parson, rather than representing a peak of Christian charity that we attain after trudging through the lowlands, is but another familiar hill in the terrain; the charity that arises out of his Christian calling is strikingly similar to the generosity that grows out of Baucis and Philemon's life of mutual giving:

> Yet, of his [the parson's] little, he had some to spare,
> To feed the Famish'd, and to cloath the Bare:
> For Mortify'd he was, to that degree,
> A poorer than himself, he wou'd not see.
> (50–53)

What the poor parson would willingly do, Baucis and Philemon actually do, demonstrating that Christians do not have a monopoly on Christian charity, any more than the duchess has a monopoly on unselfish and constructive marital love. Even the poor in a heathen land can give selflessly, love one another, and serve as a model of civilized behavior. Baucis and Philemon present another source of virtue and strength, from an alternative tradition; the values here are those of the Golden Age and of the simple, rural life, a tradition celebrated by authors like Theocritus, Euripides, Horace, and, for that matter, by Chaucer in his character of the Christian parson.[20]

Just as Chaucer's Christian portrait contains intimations of classical values, Ovid's tale has biblical elements. As D. W. Hopkins explains, many commentators on Ovid have noticed the obvious biblical parallels in the story of Baucis and Philemon: gods visiting earth in human form, a flood sent to destroy the wicked. If anything, Dryden has sharpened the parallels, by adding Jove's injunction to the old couple—"nor once look backward in your Flight" (146)—which echoes more specifically than Ovid the well-known story of Lot from *Genesis* 19.[21] In the less well-known part of that story, by the way, Lot serves a feast and washes the feet of two angels who visit him, all of which we find in "Baucis and Philemon." This does not, however, render the tale biblical or proto-Christian.[22] Indeed, as we discover in the headnote to "Baucis and Philemon," the purpose of the tale is for the narrator, the aged and wise Lelex (yet another Dryden alter ego), to persuade the atheistic Perithous, "Who laugh'd at all the Gods" and "believ'd in none" (4), to believe in the magical power of the gods to transform people. Not the magical power of Christ to redeem, but the power, specifically, of gods like Jove and Hermes to turn people into trees. If Dryden had meant to Christianize the whole, I doubt he would have allowed this explicitly pagan purpose to remain in his own translation. Rather, I think Dryden is sharpening the biblical analogues to elevate the classical tradition, to emphasize how its myths can contain values similar in kind and quality to those found in biblical beliefs. What emerges is not a world-weary version of Christianity, but rather a broader vision, one that includes classical as well as Christian traditions, for Dryden is finding civilizing human values within the older codes. Generosity is not exclusively a virtue of the Christian parson, nor regenerative marital love exclusively a virtue of the Christian duchess; such virtues belong also to ancient princes and humble peasants "who never *saw* the Light" ("Religio Laici," 183).

Another fable from the collection, "The Flower and the Leaf," has a bearing on this issue (although Dryden thought he was again translating Chaucer, this tale is now commonly regarded as a not particularly distinguished fifteenth-century poem, probably by a woman author). This tale is an allegory, told in the first person by a woman who awakes one Spring night and finds herself wandering into a Spenserian wood where nature arrays itself in catalogues that are rich with specifically named birds, trees, and flowers. In this magical kingdom, the narrator sees two groups of knights and ladies, the first associated with the leaf, the second with the flower. The first group includes "A fair Assembly of the Female Kind" (154), followed by "Kings at Arms a goodly Train, / In proud Array" (240–41), followed by "Nine royal Knights in equal Rank" (254), followed by henchmen in livery, all in an orderly procession. The knights march, engage in jousts, conquer their nameless enemies, after which each lady embraces "her chosen Knight" (311). These participants next join in a vague sort of religious ceremony whereby they all give thanks, apparently to a tree (326–30). Then the second contrasting group, which is about to pay "due Obeisance to the Daisy" (363), appears, "a jolly Band" (339) not very particular about rank or order; their activities consist entirely of playing musical instruments and singing songs. While the knights and ladies of the jolly band frolic, a storm comes rattling down, threatening to spoil their fun. Fortunately the more serious first group, the followers of the leaf (which is more enduring than the transient flower), offer the protection of their tree's "sacred Shade" (330) to the daisy-worshippers. There follows a banquet in which both groups mingle, a happy occasion that serves as a contrast to other banquets in *Fables*, the "Feast" (262) in "Theodore and Honoria," "the Nuptial Feast" (295) in book twelve of the *Metamorphoses*, and that in "Cymon and Iphigenia" (also described as "the Nuptial Feast," 541), all of which, rather than celebrating harmony and peace, are disrupted by destructive, bestial intrusions.

Just when the narrator finds herself "inquisitive to know / The secret Moral of the Mystique Show" (459–60), "Some nymph" (462), a member of the leaf group, conveniently appears to interpret the allegory. She explains that the first group "All Courteous are by Kind; and ever proud / With friendly Offices to help the Good" (496–97). Their queen is the chaste Diana; their knights are of two sorts, first the "Victorious Names" who "in Deeds of Arms excell'd" (518–19), and second, "Knights of Love, who never broke their Vow" (522). The followers of the leaf also include

> Those lawrell'd Chiefs [who] were Men of mighty Fame;
> Nine Worthies were they call'd of diff'rent Rites,
> Three Jews, three Pagans, and three Christian Knights.
> These, as you see, ride foremost in the Field,
> As they the foremost Rank of Honour held,
> And all in Deeds of Chivalry excell'd.

Their Temples wreath'd with Leafs, that still renew;
For deathless Lawrel is the Victor's due.
(534–41)

The second group, however, far from being noble, consists of "inglorious Knights" and "Ladies all untrue" (564), and their sole activity is to "enjoy the present Hour" (569). After hearing this interpretation of the allegory, the narrator is called upon to answer the inevitable question: "Whether the Leaf or Flow'r I would obey?" (603). She responds with the inevitable answer: "I chose the Leaf" (604).

The narrator here is scarcely a character to be compared with other characters in *Fables*. She does not, like the duchess or Kinsman Driden, act in a real world, instead spending all her tale in a "Fairy Show" (481); nor is she an embodiment of a set of virtues, like the honest parson and the chaste maiden lady. Instead, she is a passive observer. Whether she will be chaste maiden, or dutiful wife, is almost beside the point; she is as yet unformed—she has no cares, and she explains that she has never experienced love (24–25). She is merely the recipient of the "Secret meaning of this moral Show" (599), who has yet to accomplish anything, but who is learning which path to follow. What counts is not the bland character, but the virtues represented within the allegory, and that whole crowded set is little more than an orderly, Spenserian arrangement of the values we find elsewhere in *Fables*: the strength and victoriousness we have seen in Theseus, also renowned for deeds of arms; the generosity and willingness to do good that we witness in "Baucis and Philemon" and in the character of the parson; the "spotless" (510) purity of Diana that we also find in the fair maiden lady, herself a "Virgin-Saint"; the loyalty of the knights and ladies to one another that we discover in good husbands like Philemon and Ceyx, and good wives like the duchess, Baucis, and Alcyone.

Dryden has taken a different approach, treading the high allegorical road, but the virtues along the way are well-worn. What I would stress is the plurality of codes from which the values emerge; in the passage quoted above on the Nine Worthies, that is what Dryden himself emphasizes. In the original (I quote from the Speght text Dryden himself includes at the end of *Fables* [1700]), the explicating dame tells the curious narrator:

Sith youre desire is good and debonaire,
Tho nine crowned be very exemplaire,
Of all honour longing to chiualry,
And those certaine be called the nine worthy.

   Which ye may se riding all before,
That in her time did many a noble dede,
And for their worthines ful oft haue bore
The crowne of laurer [*sic*] leaues on their hede.
                    (p. 635)

Here, where the meaning of the allegory unfolds, Dryden could easily have heightened the Christian elements had he wanted to. Instead, he expands upon the exemplary "nine crowned" and creates a balance that suggests an equivalence of different moral codes: Dryden's Nine Worthies are "Three Jews, three Pagans, and three Christian Knights." These, together with other noble knights and a matching set of loyal ladies, all of whom belong to the native strain of the Arthurian Romance, constitute the assemblage of virtues. The sources of civilizing human values, although they certainly include the Christian, are more than just Christian; where Dryden elsewhere invokes the values of the Golden Age, or the virtues in the classical code of heroism, he here also blends various strains into "this moral Show" (599).[23]

   Returning to the two tales from Ovid, we can see at least three different strains at work, one blending the sentimental and pathetic,[24] another relying upon the rustic simplicity of the Golden Age, and the last involving a contemporary Christian family—together, what they comprise is more than sentimental, more than classical, more than Christian. "Ceyx and Alcyone" and "Baucis and Philemon" embody a social ideal, the one a sentimental version of marital love, the other a more mundane version, both supplementing and confirming the values of the Christian duchess, who is praised as a wife and mother, whose offer of hope to a ravaged country is an extension of her loving service in marriage. Yet, while we recognize that these characters owe their strength, virtue, nobility, to loving marriages, we must also acknowledge the example of "To my Honour'd Kinsman," wherein marriage is depicted as "Two Wrestlers" struggling "to pull each other down" (30). We are back where we started.

   Naturally, in praising his bachelor cousin, Dryden takes pains to stress the advantages of the single life; it is highly unlikely that Dryden's own attitude toward marriage accords with what we hear in the poem. Nonetheless, what we hear in the poem stands in marked contrast to what we hear elsewhere. Cousin John Driden owes his strength, his self-sufficiency, his judicial fairness, his patriotic service, to celibacy, not the parson's celibacy based on selfless dedication to God, but rather a celibacy based on hatred of womankind. Look again at the description of Cousin Driden as

> Promoting Concord, and composing Strife;
> Lord of your self, uncumber'd with a Wife;
> Where, for a Year, a Month, perhaps a Night,
> Long Penitence succeeds a short Delight:
> Minds are so hardly match'd, that ev'n the first,
> Though pair'd by Heav'n, in Paradise, were curs'd.
> For Man and Woman, though in one they grow,
> Yet, first or last, return again to Two.
> (17–24)

That is quite different from Baucis and Philemon, "long marry'd, and a happy Pair" (33) rather than long penitent; first or last, this happy pair returns again to one. Their sufficiency and generosity come about because "Command was none, where equal Love was paid, / Or rather both commanded, both obey'd" (39–40).

I repeat these two by now familiar quotations because they neatly summarize my point: whatever *Fables* gives, it also takes away; whatever critical construction Dryden invites us to make, we also find *Fables* unmaking. The strong marriage of Baucis and Philemon, which makes them self-sufficient, is undone by the patriotic celibate, John Driden, whose strength comes from his independence of womankind. But that, in turn, is undone by the story of would-be celibate Pygmalion, who

> Abhorr'd all Womankind, but most a Wife:
> So single chose to live, and shunn'd to wed,
> Well pleas'd to want a Consort of his Bed.
> (2–4)

Pygmalion, "fearing Idleness" (5), takes up sculpting, which in Dryden's version sounds like occupational therapy, something Pygmalion does with his spare time because his bed is empty.[25] As everybody knows, he falls helplessly in love with the ivory maid he sculpts, thereby becoming a slave to the very passion he had disdained. There is nothing at all noble, Platonic, or even dignified about Pygmalion's mad adoration; what interests him is lips, breasts, limbs, and a "naked Body" (30), which this hater of womankind embraces, repeatedly. For once, raw passion, the same passion that inspires Cymon to rape and slaughter, has happy consequences: not war and the destruction of cities, but "Fruitfulness" (97), as Venus transforms Pygmalion's statue into a willing sexual partner and blesses their bed with a son, "a lovely Boy" (99) named Paphos, "who grown to Manhood, wall'd / The City *Paphos*, for the Founder call'd" (100–1).[26] Here, sexual love appears to be healthy, constructive, and fun.[27] Furthermore, passion seems to be an irresistible force, one that entraps Pygmalion even as he is trying to remain celibate. Avoiding womankind, which kinsman Driden does to his own advantage, seems impossible for the determined, woman-hating Pygmalion, who finds his joy in succumbing to an unavoidable and productive passion.[28]

Strength comes from marriage, then, or Christian celibacy, or contempt of womankind, and contempt of womankind leads to self-sufficiency or, in Pygmalion, to helplessness when he finds himself head over heels in love with a block of ivory that will eventually bear his children. The sources of human strength keep shifting, and civilizing virtues arise out of different traditions, from the heroic and classical to the Christian, sometimes arising majestically, sometimes pathetically, sometimes with ringing success, and at other times emerging only to collapse into pathetic failure. Even passion, which is usually destructive, can lead to "Fruitfulness" and a new walled city.

Little wonder that appreciative critics rely on adjectives like "comprehensive," and "spacious" to describe *Fables*.[29] There are so many ideals and values jostling about. Little wonder that earlier Dryden critics rely upon the less favorable adjective " inconsistent." I would stress neither "comprehensiveness," which is static, nor "inconsistency," which is reductive. Rather, I would emphasize the strategy behind *Fables*, the doing and undoing, which is one of the reasons for pursuing the elusive "informing ideal" at such lengths, and through such mazes. It is not just a matter of jarring contradictions that cancel each other out, but rather a case of Dryden establishing an ideal, and then calling it into question. Dryden invokes values implicit in the classical tradition, and reveals their limitations; endorses values implicit in the Christian ideals, and suggests their incompleteness; depicts the inevitable vicious consequences of passion, and suggests the productive, even noble possibilities, the strengths built on love, the limitations implicit in that love, and the strengths and limitations implicit in celibate life as well. As the syntax of that last sentence suggests, this is a complex and inconclusive process. But it is that very process, establishing and subverting, doing and undoing, that may be the "informing ideal" of *Fables*.

NOTES

1. Earl Miner, in "Forms and Motives of Narrative Poetry," from *Writers and Their Background: John Dryden*, ed. Miner (Athens: Ohio University Press, 1972), 234–66, classifies the tales in *Fables* as fabula, historia, and argumentum, all varieties of narrative according to Roman treatises on rhetoric (260).

2. Judith Sloman, in "The Structure of Dryden's *Fables*," Ph.D. diss., University of Minnesota, 1968, maintains that "the end of the *Fables* balances the beginning, since Dryden embodies the new ideals in another male-female couple, who partially replace the Duchess and John Driden" (192). See also Sloman's "An Interpretation of Dryden's *Fables*," *Eighteenth-Century Studies* 4 (1970/71): 199–211, especially 208–10. In *Dryden: The Poetics of Translation* (Toronto: University of Toronto Press, 1985), Sloman repeats the argument, but also qualifies it: "because Dryden has placed his paired poems symmetrically, one pair at each end (almost) of *Fables*, it is hard to decide whether the two pairs are meant to be read as equally important, or if the second pair, about a more spiritualized couple, is meant to replace the first" (218).

3. This is essentially Judith Sloman's argument: she finds that the parson and the maiden "reject secular aspirations and center the ideal in the spiritual world instead of a human representative of it, so that earthly change and mortality cannot affect its value" ("Interpretation," 208). And she considers the entire *Fables* "a variety of epic, but one whose main action is to undermine the motives behind the violent actions of classical epic and to substitute the Christian virtues of charity and patience" (199).

4. Expectation seems to be behind Miner's comment that in *Fables*, "the ultimate values remain as Christian as ever" ("Forms and Motives," 264).

5. Palpable and pointed, since the parson's virtues also serve as satiric commentary on Collier's shortcomings. Dryden praises the ever-merciful parson who uses the gift of "Eloquence innate" (17) with tenderness; he "sweetly temper'd Awe; and soften'd all he spoke" (26). This is a marked contrast to the manner in which the intemperate Collier, who "has not forgotten the old Rule, of calumniating strongly" (Preface, Kinsley, 4:1447), uses his eloquence.

6. Judith Sloman, coming upon "Cymon and Iphigenia" after arguing for Dryden's Christian ideal, admits that "though Dryden has formulated ideals that seem immutable and valid, there seems little evidence that they have any effect on the real world" ("Structure," 211). So much for *that* immutable ideal. In *Dryden: The Poetics*, Sloman retreats noticeably from her earlier position. She no longer weighs the poems to the parson and maiden so heavily, in part because she finds that "the first pair are greater poems" (218); furthermore, she weighs

more heavily the effect of the final tale. Now, the movement "towards positive spiritual values" is only "an apparent shift" (167): "if the frame had been unbroken, *Fables* would have closed with a couple standing for purity and religion, balancing or even supplanting the couple at the beginning who are urged to change the world. As it is, Dryden ends with political realities and a doubtful future" (166; see also 202).

7. Boccaccio's Iphigenia complains about being seized and blames Cymon for going against the will of the gods, but Boccaccio does not otherwise comment on her state of mind; where Dryden makes her fickle, Boccaccio allows her to remain a reluctant and annoyed hostage.

8. Iphigenia is also counterbalanced by the real Iphigenia, Agamemnon's daughter, who is mentioned in "The Speeches of Ajax and Ulysses," as Judith Sloman perceptively points out. Cymon's Iphigenia displays a "remarkable willingness to be sacrificed to men and to let men sacrifice themselves for her," which makes her a "debased version" of the Iphigenia who was literally sacrificed for the Greeks (*Dryden: The Poetics*, 145).

9. Although the solid factual information about Cousin Driden's political activity is thin, Jay Arnold Levine, in "John Dryden's Epistle to John Driden," *Journal of English and Germanic Philology* 63 (1964): 450–74, reasonably infers that Driden was opposed to the Standing Army yet loyal to William. This is what Dryden implies in his own correspondence (especially #65, *Letters*, p. 120), and it is at least implied by Kinsman Driden's membership in the parliaments of 1690, 1698, and 1700, which opposed William and his ministry, and by his absence from the Parliament of 1695, which supported William (Levine, 453). It is further implied by the kinsman poem itself, which Dryden sent to his cousin for approval; Driden would scarcely have approved being described as resisting might and not lending money to the king in peacetime (184–94) had he not felt this to be an accurate characterization of his position.

10. Apparently, Dryden's original version of this passage criticized William more directly, but his kinsman, upon seeing a draft of the poem, took exception to the satire, and Dryden omitted the offending passage, allowing his praise of the navy to serve as an indirect criticism of William's desire for the Standing Army (Kinsley, 4:2071).

11. This is but one possible pair of extremes among many in "Religio Laici," but whatever the pair, critics often follow Dryden to the middle of the road. For Phillip Harth, in *Contexts of Dryden's Thought* (Chicago: University of Chicago Press, 1968), the final resting point is an "Anglican *via media*" (224) between Deism and Catholicism. Sanford Budick, who studies the poem's imagery in *Dryden and the Abyss of Light: A Study of 'Religio Laici' and 'The Hind and the Panther'* (New Haven: Yale University Press, 1970), sees the poem as "a dialectic of ideas" heading toward a "final equilibrium" (93) in which "the opposing forces . . . continue to produce the ground of reason which has elements of both initial dialectical extremes" (104). Using a similar metaphor, G. Douglas Atkins, in *The Faith of John Dryden* (Lexington: University of Kentucky Press, 1980), sees Dryden "demarcating a middle ground" (74) between fideism and rationalism, adopting a stance "reminiscent of the Horatian *via media*" (73). One may well question whether the issues Budick and Atkins raise are valid or are modern impositions; however, what interests me here is not the validity of the

interpretation, but rather the critics' habit of looking for divisions around a center. The one notable exception to this approach is that of Ruth Salvaggio, in *Dryden's Dualities*, English Literary Monograph Series, 29 (Victoria, British Columbia: University of Victoria Press, 1983). She explores the various opposed views, called "doublings," and claims that there is no *via media*; rather, each side cancels the other out, leaving us in irresolution. I am not quite satisfied with either explanation, because the middle road is seldom in the middle, and oppositions, to my mind, seldom merely cancel out one another.

12. See Thomas H. Fujimura, in "'Autobiography' in Dryden's Later Work," *Restoration* 8 (1984): 17–29, for an account of Dryden's altered view toward Christian piety in the face of his own "bitter experience" (20) after 1688. Dryden's personal shift of tone might reflect the general change of English Catholic attitudes during the period; although the Catholics began the century with a missionary zeal to convert and with millenarian expectations, they gradually abandoned that position and, by 1700, desired instead to be tolerated and accepted as a minority religion. See John Bossy, *The English Catholic Community, 1570–1850* (New York: Oxford University Press, 1976).

13. David M. Vieth, in "Irony in Dryden's Ode to Anne Killigrew," *Studies in Philology* 62 (1965): 91–100, was the first to point out that there are really two Anne Killigrews in this poem, the minor talent whom Dryden criticizes and even parodies, and the ideal of Christian poetry, which Dryden endorses. This accounts for the many places in the poem where praise can also be read as criticism. Vieth insists, correctly I believe, that one must respond to both, whereas other critics have tended to see this either as a richly idealistic poem or a satiric attack. See, for instance, Robert Daly's "Dryden's Ode to Anne Killigrew and the Communal Work of Poets," *Texas Studies in Literature and Language* 18 (1976): 184–97.

14. Ovid reads "Nec refert, dominos, illic, famulosne requiras; / Tota domus, duo sunt: idem parentque jubentque," which George Sandys translates as "None Master, nor none servant, could you call, / They who command, obey, for two were all." Dryden borrows the rhyme, and some of the words, from Sandys, but the next couplet that introduces "equal Love" as the reason for this behavior is pure Dryden. The Ovid text cited is from *Publii Ovidii Nasonis Operum*, ed. Nicolaus Heinsius, 3 vols. (Amsterdam: Elzevir, 1676), p. 152 [Loeb, lines 635–36]); the Sandys reference is from *Ovids Metamorphosis Englished*, trans. George Sandys, 3rd ed. (London: Andrew Hebb, 1638), lines 639–40.

15. Sloman argues that "Baucis and Philemon" confirms Dryden's Christian purposes, for this pair is the exception that proves the rule. The rule in this case is the rest of humanity, unredeemed by Christianity, that is obliterated in the flood, which for Sloman implies the need of Christian redemption in this dark world ("Structure," 177). I find this unconvincing, largely because it seems to me an elaborate way of circumventing the obvious fact that the model characters in this tale are pagan.

16. Dryden's "conjugal Affection" amounts to a slight warming of what, in Ovid, is described as an alliance or partnership, "conjugiale . . . fœdus" (Heinsius, p. 212 [Loeb, lines 743–44]); Sandys renders this as "nuptiall faiths" (Sandys, line 744).

17. In *Ovid as an Epic Poet*, 2nd ed. (Cambridge: Cambridge University

Press, 1970), Brooks Otis devotes an entire chapter, Chapter 7 (231–77), to Ovid's story of Ceyx and Alcyone, which he regards as a "mighty epic" (231) that serves as the climax of a group of tales on love.

18. Michael West, in "Dryden's Ambivalence as a Translator of Heroic Themes," *Huntington Library Quarterly* 36 (1973): 347–66, does not discuss these two tales specifically, but in arguing for anti-heroism in *Fables*, he detects "incipient sentimentality" (365), soon to emerge in the novels of the next generation.

19. The California Dryden, in making the case that the "mingling of Biblical and classical elements" was commonplace, cites Samuel Johnson's predictable judgment, that Dryden was not "serious enough to keep heathen fables out of his religion" (*Works*, 3:304). Although few modern critics would make such an assertion, there remains a habit of taking the Christian elements of Dryden's poetry seriously while tacitly regarding the heathen material as metaphoric, decorative, part of his art rather than of his life. Without for a moment denying that Dryden became a devout Catholic and that his religious beliefs play a significant role in his poetry, I suggest that we have sometimes been too eager, by habit, to Christianize that poetry at the expense of other equally pertinent systems of value. Thomas H. Fujimura, in "John Dryden and the Myth of the Golden Age," *Papers on Language and Literature* 11 (1975): 149–67, implies the same thing, praising the many scholarly enterprises devoted to Dryden's use of Christian myth (150–51), and remarking: "but of Dryden's use of pagan myth we have no extensive study" (151).

20. For specific examples from these classical authors, see the commentary by Wilmon Brewer in the Brooks More translation of *Ovid's Metamorphoses*, rev. ed., 2 vols. (Francestown, NH: Marshall Jones, 1978), 847–50. For Dryden's reliance on this tradition, see Thomas H. Fujimura's "John Dryden and the Myth of the Golden Age."

21. See D. W. Hopkins, "Dryden's 'Baucis and Philemon,'" *Comparative Literature* 28 (1976): 135–43. Hopkins too sees Dryden blending "Christian ideas of a god made flesh and dwelling among us with the pagan story, importing an element from his own culture, to bring out the eternally valid truths he sees in Ovid's Latin poem, truths as valid for his own Christian era as for the pagan times in which Ovid wrote" (141).

22. I disagree with Earl Miner, who, in *Dryden's Poetry* (Bloomington: Indiana University Press, 1967), implies that Christian elements necessarily make *Fables* Christian; Miner finds that the Olympian deities in *Fables* "are either simply pagan and false, or humanistic equivalents for the Christian God" (303). It seems to me that the pagan gods can be equivalents and still be pagan.

23. Despite her advocacy of *Fables* as Christian epic, Sloman admits that in "The Flower and the Leaf," "the classical, Biblical and Christian past may all provide models for the present and future" ("Structure," 195).

24. For a complete account of this emerging and changing tradition of pathetic love in this supposedly Age of Reason poet, see Jean H. Hagstrum's *Sex and Sensibility: Ideal and Erotic Love from Milton to Mozart* (Chicago: University of Chicago Press, 1980), especially Chapter 3 (50–71), which deals with Dryden.

25. Ovid introduces Pygmalion's turning to sculpture with a simple "mean-

while" ("interea," Heinsius, p. 183 [Loeb, line 247]), but Dryden adds the explanation that Pygmalion, having no consort, sculpted in order to avoid idleness, which makes the sculpting look more obviously like a sublimation of Pygmalion's thwarted sexual desires.

26. Dryden's Latin text reads: "Illa Paphon genuit: de quo tenet insula nomen" (Heinsius, p. 184 [Loeb, line 297]). Because of the "quo" (the Loeb edition reads "qua") and because "Paphon" appears to be a masculine Greek noun, Sandys translates the female Paphos into a male, and Dryden follows. Notice also that Dryden changes the island ("insula," which Sandys renders as "Isle," line 298) into a walled city, probably because he recognized Paphos as the name of the city on Cyprus. Thus, Dryden's change may actually be a correction, since Ovid's "insula" is wrong (Ovid may have used "insula" simply because "urbs" does not scan). Whatever the reasons for the change, such an alteration conveniently makes the constructive ending of "Pygmalion" more specifically relevant to civilization, one of Dryden's recurrent concerns throughout *Fables*.

27. As Jean H. Hagstrum points out in *Sex and Sensibility*, Dryden enjoys and heightens the overt sexuality he found in Ovid and Boccaccio (51–58). In "Pygmalion," Dryden not only retains the juicy bits, but also adds an occasional erotic detail of his own, especially when Pygmalion touches and kisses his statue.

28. As William Myers, in *Dryden* (London: Hutchinson, 1973), observes, Pygmalion's "assault on his statue puts celibacy like Sir John Driden's in an odd light" (181).

29. As does Earl Miner, in *Dryden's Poetry* (287–323, especially 318–19).

Chapter Five

TURNING POINTS

SIGISMONDA AND GUISCARDO

$\mathcal{T}$ H E twenty-one individual tales in *Fables* have, if anything, received less critical attention than *Fables* itself. Of these tales, "To my Honour'd Kinsman" and "Alexander's Feast" are the two most likely to be familiar to readers, both because they are frequently anthologized, and because they have received the lion's share of the criticism (cub's share, really). One cannot help noticing, however, that interpretations of these poems seldom regard them as parts of a larger structure but rather as separate entities. This approach is justified, since these *are* self-sufficient, original poems, both of them occasional—the one an encomium to a relative, the other an ode to St. Cecilia's Day first published in 1697 and subsequently included in *Fables*—but the question of how these poems contribute to *Fables*, or how *Fables* contributes to them, remains.[1] Scholars have also, on occasion, examined the translated tales, in articles on Dryden's version of Chaucer, or Ovid, or Boccaccio; these essays are valuable in their own right, but since they are primarily concerned with comparative studies—e.g., Dryden vs. Chaucer—they too usually confine themselves to the individual tale, rather than look at the whole collection.[2]

Focusing on individual tales will, I think, reveal that what happens across *Fables* as a whole, what happens across different groups, also at times happens within a given poem; values are established and subverted, ideals offered and withdrawn. We can see this in "Sigismonda and Guiscardo," which makes a convenient starting point, since it is the one translated tale that has received persistent critical treatment as a Dryden poem rather than as a version of Boccaccio. Critics have noticed Sigismonda primarily because she is the kind of character that fascinated Dryden throughout his career: she is a study of ennobling, transcendent passion, a heroine in the Cleopatra, Almeyda, and Dido mold.[3] As I hope to demonstrate, the critical responses to this poem testify to the give-and-take strategy, for the debate centers upon whether or not Sigismonda makes a convincing heroine; the key moment occurs at that turning point in the tale where the values of this new Cleopatra emerge most powerfully, or, to other minds, where those values are undercut most conspicuously and shown to be false.

Instead of turning outward to other Dryden works for studies in passionate heroines, we can turn inward to the rest of *Fables*, where we find that Sigismonda is also a more fully developed version of Hylonome, the centaur nymph who dies in the arms of her centaur lover, and of Alcyone, who dives into the sea to join her drowned husband. Sigismonda too takes her own life for love, dying not exactly in her lover's embrace, since he has been eviscerated and is in no condition to embrace anyone, but dying while clutching his heart, which has been delivered to her in a gem-studded, golden goblet. If Hylonome's death, and that of Alcyone, are impassioned and melodramatic, Sigismonda kissing the heart of her Guiscardo, addressing it, filling the goblet with her tears, poisoning herself, and dying with his heart held "Close to her Heart" (714), extends melodrama to baroque excessiveness.

These are all sentimental heroines, but Sigismonda rises above the rest, not just by the gruesome nature of her final act of love, but also by her sudden eloquence and self-possession when she confronts her fate. Hylonome, upon discovering the lifeless body of her centaur lover, Cyllarus, "fills the Fields with undistinguish'd Cries," so that "At least her Words, were in her Clamour drown'd" (569–70). Alcyone, no less distraught, recognizes "Her Husband's Corps; at this she loudly shrieks, / 'Tis he, 'tis he, she cries, and tears her Cheeks" (464–65), and after saying two more lines, plunges headlong into the ocean. Not so for Sigismonda. When her cruel father, Tancred, discovers her daughter's lover and threatens to have him killed, Sigismonda, like her grief-stricken sisters, "Felt all the Pangs of Sorrow in her Breast" (371), but she refuses to indulge in "Cries, and Tears" (373), let alone shrieks. This in itself makes her appear stronger than her father, who, as he threatens her, "pour'd a Flood / Of Tears, to make his last Expression good" (366–67).

Sigismonda's response is better. While the other star-tossed women are distraught, out of control, hysterical, pushed to desperate acts by their violent passion and intense grief, Sigismonda pushes back, discovering within herself a strength of character and self-control that did not seem to be there moments before:

> But in-born Worth, that Fortune can controul,
> New strung, and stiffer bent her softer Soul;
> The *Heroine* assum'd the Womans Place,
> Confirm'd her Mind, and fortifi'd her Face.
>
> (374–77)

Far from being impulsive, Sigismonda is deliberate; far from being driven beyond control, she is fiercely, even coolly, controlled; and far from being speechless, she talks, and talks, and talks, defending herself forcefully and rationally. She begins by standing up to her demanding father:

> *Tancred*, I neither am dispos'd to make
> Request for Life, nor offer'd Life to take:
> Much less deny the Deed; but least of all
> Beneath pretended Justice weakly fall.
> My Words to sacred Truth shall be confin'd,
> My Deeds shall shew the Greatness of my Mind.
>
> (390–95)

She continues in this vein for nearly two hundred lines, during which she defends her act as lawful, defends Guiscardo as worthy, argues for intrinsic merit being more important than rank ("And he whose Mind / Is Vertuous, is alone of Noble Kind. / Though poor in Fortune, of Celestial Race," 519–21). She even reminds Tancred that he himself had acknowledged Guiscardo's merits, which is what first gained Guiscardo Sigismonda's respect. And she gives her cruel father, who does not manage to get a word in edgewise during her oration, a lesson in justice as well as kingly behavior: "Nor did her Father fail to find, / In all she spoke, the Greatness of her Mind" (582–83). She rivals the eloquent Ulysses in her gift for finding every possible logical argument to justify her behavior.

Impressed as Tancred may be by his daughter's greatness of mind, he has Guiscardo killed anyway, and then has the young man's heart delivered to his daughter, along with this witty message: "Thy Father sends thee this, to cheer thy Breast, / And glad thy Sight with what thou lov'st the best" (615–16). Greatness of mind apparently does not run in the family. Sigismonda, not yet knowing that Tancred has killed Guiscardo, rationally anticipates that her argument will have no effect on so cruel a father: she "weigh'd / The Consequence of what her Sire had said" (619–20), and, "Fix'd on her Fate" (621), she prepares poison for herself. When she knows the worst, even then she remains calm and controlled:

> Then smil'd severe; nor with a troubl'd Look,
> Or trembling Hand, the Fun'ral Present took;
> Ev'n kept her Count'nance, when the Lid remov'd,
> Disclos'd the Heart, unfortunately lov'd.
> (627–30)

Nor is she speechless. "She sternly on the Bearer fix'd her Eyes" (634), and then she delivers a final message to Tancred explaining "this last Act of Love" (646) she is about to commit. After a soliloquy, she does indeed weep, but it is weeping "free from Female Noise, / Such as the Majesty of Grief destroys" (685–86). She had told Tancred that she would be "Fix'd, like a Man to die" (579), and she remains true to her word, ending her life with the same composure, quite literally, composing her body on the "Genial Bed" (711) after taking the poison she has prepared. No sudden, screaming jump over a convenient cliff for Sigismonda. Rather than being rendered helpless and hysterical by grief, both of which suggest frailty and elicit pity, Sigismonda is made heroic by the occasion.

Boccaccio's Ghismonda is noble enough as she stands, but Dryden actually fortifies his version of the heroine. In the original, Ghismonda and Guiscardo are lovers only, and it is their illicit love that Tancredi wishes to punish. But Dryden, significantly, marries the lovers, which removes one of Tancred's principal objections; his insistence that "My Justice, and thy Crime, requires thy Fate" (359) rings hollow when there is no crime. True, Sigismonda has married without her father's consent, so he has some reason to object, although not sufficient reason to rant and demand death. Dryden, however, removes even that reason, or rather, has Sigismonda argue it away; she married her first husband in compliance with her father's wishes, and now that she is a widow, the obligation to await her father's selection of a husband disappears: "That Bond dissolv'd," Sigismonda asserts, "the next is freely mine" (411), for parents do not have "pow'r ev'n second Vows to tie" (413). Even if they had, Tancred's "little Care to mend my Widow'd Nights" (414) by providing Sigismonda with another husband has forced her, she claims, "to recourse of Marriage-Rites, / To fill an empty Side" (415–16). Where the original Tancredi can with some justice claim his daughter has debased herself by taking an illicit lover, the new Tancred is accused of not providing for his daughter, and there he stands, objecting to a lawful match, sanctioned by a holy priest.

Dryden has even more powerful ways of weakening Tancred's position, and one can easily anticipate what Dryden might make of a cruel father who also happens to be a prince; yes, Tancred becomes yet another tyrant exerting despotic power over an unwilling people. We discover this early in Dryden's translation, when we learn of Sigismonda's first marriage, arranged by her father with some reluctance. In John Florio's 1620 translation, which was one of Dryden's sources, Tancredi "so choisely loved and esteemed" his daughter

> and so farre extended his over-curious respect of her, as he would seldome admit her to be forth of his sight; neither would he suffer her to marry, although she had outstept (by divers yeeres) the age meete for marriage. Neverthelesse, at length, he matched her with the Sonne to the Duke of Capua.
> (Florio, 2:142).[4]

What Florio renders as "over-curious respect" should raise some eyebrows; in the Italian, the key phrase is "teneramente amata" (*Decameron*, 283), with "amata" (beloved), not quite the right word to use for a daughter (McWilliam renders this as "passionately fond of this daughter," 332). Dryden, however, drives the point home and adds another reason for Tancred's arranging the marriage:

> At length, as Publick Decency requir'd,
> And all his Vassals eagerly desir'd,
> With Mind averse, he rather underwent
> His Peoples Will, than gave his own Consent:
> So was she torn, as from a Lover's Side,
> And made almost in his despite a Bride.
> (19–24)

Dryden's Tancred, like the original Tancredi, is not merely dilatory about marrying off his daughter, but averse to parting with her. But Dryden adds the idea of public pressure; his Tancred agrees to the match only because his unruly vassals pressure him into it. We get a clear sense of Tancred's attitude toward "His Peoples Will," and a clear idea that this would-be lover has an affection for his daughter that is not entirely paternal. Perhaps that is why "Publick Decency" eagerly desires a marriage. This could merely refer to the people's discomfort at watching their prince's only daughter remain single past the proper age for marriage; however, it also implies that the father-daughter relationship has become a shock to public decency, and a marriage would come as a welcome relief. At any event, what in Boccaccio remains a possible motive behind arranging the marriage, implied by the circumstances more than by the description, in Dryden emerges more explicitly, so much so that even vassals recognize it and protest. No wonder Tancred gets upset about Guiscardo later on. Not only is the young man a rival for the affections of Sigismonda, but he is also one of those damned vassals; later, in a line added by Dryden, Tancred in anger refers to Guiscardo as "A Man so smelling of the Peoples Lee" (317).

Throughout, Dryden colors his Tancred political, not just at those many points where he offhandedly adds the word "tyrant," but also in unexpected places. When discussing the murder of Guiscardo, obviously an ideal opportunity to display Tancred's cruelty most dramatically, Dryden makes Tancred's vicious behavior seem a natural consequence of his being a Williamite king. The "Slaves to Pay" (596) who are instructed to strangle Guiscardo and cut out his heart, and who sound suspiciously like William's Dutch Guards, are "Fit only to maintain Despotick Pow'r . . . / and desir'd alone / By Kings, who seek an Arbitrary Throne" (599–601). Tancred would use these guards against his daughter as readily as he would use them against any of his freedom-loving subjects. No longer is Tancred's unjust behavior confined to a few innocents in his all-too-immediate family; rather, it is the evil of "Despotick Pow'r" that threatens all freedom and undermines the state itself. Dryden takes Boccaccio's murderous king, and heavily puts the accent on "king" whenever an opportunity presents itself. Even in scenic description, Dryden manages to squeeze in a comment or two reminding us of Tancred's kingly behavior. For instance, the long-forgotten cave in which Sigismonda surreptitiously meets her lover takes on a new significance in Dryden's hands:

> a Cave was dug with vast Expence,
> The Work it seem'd of some suspicious Prince,
> Who, when abusing Pow'r with lawless Might,

From Publick Justice would secure his Flight.
The Passage made by many a winding Way,
Reach'd ev'n the Room in which the Tyrant lay.
(103–8)[5]

Although Tancred may not be the "suspicious Prince" who actually built this escape, he is the suspicious prince who knows the function of this "safe Retreat" (112), who keeps it a secret from all but his daughter, and who one day might use this "Tyrants Den" (119) for just the kind of emergency described above.

All of these additions not only enlarge the evil that is Tancred, but they also add a new dimension to Sigismonda's argument; one cannot help but notice that her longer speeches are laced with added political commentary. When, for instance, she argues that her lover's worth exists despite his lowly rank, in a speech echoing that of the crone in "The Wife of Bath Her Tale," Sigismonda points out that

His Poverty augments thy Crime the more;
Upbraids thy Justice with the scant Regard
Of Worth: Whom Princes praise, they shou'd reward.
Are these the Kings intrusted by the Crowd
With Wealth, to be dispens'd for Common Good?
The People sweat not for their King's Delight,
T' enrich a Pimp, or raise a Parasite;
Theirs is the Toil; and he who well has serv'd
His Country, has his Countrys Wealth deserv'd.
(548–56)

The first three lines are from Boccaccio, but the rest is pure Dryden. This goes beyond defending Guiscardo, and turns into an attack on Tancred's injustice together with helpful instructions on how it is kings are supposed to handle public trust. These are strong words, and mostly Dryden's rather than Boccaccio's; they shift the argument slightly, for they make Guiscardo not merely a poor but worthy man, but also a man who has served his country better than certain monarchs Sigismonda could mention.

By making Tancred's cruelty an extension of his behavior as a selfish, suspicious, vindictive, arbitrary prince, Dryden gives the contrast between father and daughter a new look. Sigismonda and Guiscardo are more than tragic lovers showing their mettle in response to cruelty and injustice. They are also patriots resisting a despotic monarch, and as such, they take their place alongside characters like the parson and Kins-

107

man John Driden. We will not find exact parallels here, for Sigismonda is more concerned for herself than for her people or principle; she is not, like the parson, a non-juring clergyman, nor, like Kinsman Driden, a barrier of state resisting the king by voting against him in Parliament. But the praise accorded such "Patriots" fits Dryden's Sigismonda; if ever there were "noble Stubbornness resisting Might" (185), which is said of Kinsman Driden, it is here in a Sigismonda who stiffens her soul, "Confirm'd her Mind, and fortifi'd her Face" (377) to confront a "sullen Tyrant" (288, an added Dryden epithet). Dryden's expansions of the political innuendo add to Sigismonda's "Greatness of . . . Mind" (395); she becomes another version of the noble patriot, confronting and withstanding another despotic, Williamite villain, only this is a high-wrought, melodramatic variation of the theme, where the character pursues noble stubbornness to the death.

As was the case with Dryden's version of Homer, the extensive additions allow us to talk with some confidence not just about what is conveniently there in Dryden's source material, but about what he *put* there. He is making black blacker, and white whiter, weakening Tancred's case and strengthening Sigismonda's, and one could as easily have added other Dryden insertions, expansions, twists, or modifications that follow suit. Boccaccio's Tancredi, a man shocked by his daughter's crime into inhumanly cruel actions, becomes in Dryden a tyrant from the start (he is first called tyrant in line 3).[6] He becomes in Dryden an evil force misruling a kingdom, exerting "pretended Justice" (393, a Dryden addition) to punish a non-crime. The already heroic Ghismonda becomes stronger still, both by being on the side of the patriots who dare confront a bad king, and by rising above the softer soul of womanhood to Amazonian courage and strength.

But that is only part of the story. What *Fables* gives us, it also takes away. What we found true of Dryden's anti-heroism, of his models of conjugal fidelity, of his Christian ideals, is equally true of his ennobled Sigismonda; all are established yet undercut. If we continue the examination, focusing still on Dryden's amplifications, we discover that not only does Dryden make white whiter, but he also simultaneously makes it gray. There is no denying the force of Dryden's additions and shifts, which cumulatively assert a familiar Dryden ideal, a heroine in the Cleopatra mold who is meant to elicit admiration and respect. Yet, if Dryden makes his Sigismonda even more the heroine than Ghismonda, Dryden also makes her less a heroine; he fortifies her case, and he undermines it, sometimes in the very act of adding lines that strengthen his heroine, so that our growing acceptance of Sigismonda as heroine is constantly challenged.

Let us return to one of Dryden's most obvious changes, when he adds a priest who marries Sigismonda to Guiscardo, thereby transforming a sinful liaison into a lawful union. As I have argued, this change of plot obviously adds ammunition to Sigismonda's argument by removing her "crime" and replacing it with a holy marriage. However, the marriage itself, which we witness, raises serious questions about the holy matrimony Sigismonda is soon to defend. With the priest standing in wait, an anxious Guiscardo appears. He has made his way from the cave through the connecting passage into Sigismonda's room. He knocks:

> The longing Lady heard, and turn'd the Key;
> At once invaded him with all her Charms,
> And the first Step he made, was in her Arms:
> The Leathern Out-side, boistrous as it was,
> Gave way, and bent beneath her strict Embrace:
> On either Side the Kisses flew so thick,
> That neither he nor she had Breath to speak.
> The holy Man amaz'd at what he saw,
> Made haste to sanctifie the Bliss by Law;
> And mutter'd fast the Matrimony o're,
> For fear committed Sin should get before.
> (156–66)

This is marriage in the nick of time. The lovers do not, on the whole, seem to be thinking primarily in terms of honorable marriage; as a matter of fact, they do not appear to be *thinking* at all. The difference between bliss "sanctifie[d] . . . by Law" and "committed Sin" is a matter of seconds, and it is only thanks to a speedy priest that the lovers make it to the legal side of the line, after which

> they took their full Delight;
> 'Twas restless Rage, and Tempest all the Night:
> For greedy Love each Moment would employ,
> And grudg'd the shortest Pauses of their Joy.
> (173–76)

With the actual circumstances of the marriage in mind, how do we regard Sigismonda's subsequent defense of her action?

> For, too well I knew
> What Honour was, and Honour had his Due:

109

Before the Holy Priest my Vows were ty'd,
So came I not a Strumpet, but a Bride.
(404–7)

Her argument is technically correct, but her own interpretation of her intentions does not match the intentions we have seen in action, which would more accurately be called desires, pure and lustful. It is worth weighing the two above passages side by side, one wherein Sigismonda indulges greedily, the other in which she claims that she always had honor on her mind. What she actually has in mind is enough to upset the poor harried priest who has been summoned to unite the two lovers:

His Work perform'd, he left the Pair alone,
Because he knew he could not go too soon;
His Presence odious, when his Task was done.
What Thoughts he had, beseems not me to say;
Though some surmise he went to fast and pray,
And needed both, to drive the tempting Thoughts away.
(167–72)

The priest is shocked and, although it beseems not Dryden to say it, aroused by the scene of passion (Dryden may again be poking fun at Jeremy Collier, an all too easily shocked priest who, in Dryden's view, spends too much time pondering over pornography). Instead of two lovers being sanctified by a priest, we have a priest nearly corrupted by two overtly erotic lovers who begrudge his presence, such is their haste to get on with the serious business of "full Delight."

Comparison to the original at this point is instructive; everything pertaining to the priest and marriage is, as I have said, a Dryden addition, but what about the behavior of Sigismonda and Guiscardo when they are alone? In the original version, the encounter is described briefly: "After giving each other a rapturous greeting, they made their way into her chamber, where they spent a goodly portion of the day in transports of bliss" (McWilliam, 334).[7] Boccaccio does not spell out the precise details, but there is little doubt what constitutes a transport of bliss, and one can easily recognize in the passage the source of Dryden's "full Delight" ("con grandissimo piacere"). Florio's version tones down the implicit sexuality of the occasion, in ways that would have made the Victorians happy: instead of raptures or transports, Sigismonda's joys seem to consist of stimulating conversation: when she finds "her amorous friend. Guiscardo," she greets him by

saluting [him] with a chaste and modest kisse; causing him to ascend up the stayres with her into her Chamber. This long desired, and now obtained meeting, caused the two deerely affected Lovers, in kinde discourse of amorous argument (without incivill or rude demeanor) to spend there the most part of that day, to their hearts joy and mutuall contentment.
(Florio, 2:145).

As one can see from comparing versions, what Florio tones down, Dryden tones up, making sexuality more explicit, giving us not just "rapturous greeting," but an embrace that bends Guiscardo's "Leathern Outside"(159)—Sigismonda is clearly the aggressor—and kisses flying "so thick, / That neither he nor she had Breath to speak" (161–62).[8]

The breathless Sigismonda appears different to us than she does to, well, Sigismonda. Constantly, there is a pull between what we see and what she sees, to such an extent that we find ourselves smiling at her self-deception, offered in the ringing, persuasive tones of a victimized woman, a wronged daughter, a stubborn patriot. When she describes the process of her growing affections for Guiscardo, she elicits sympathy; few would side with the sullen Tancred who will soon mete out a punishment ill befitting the non-crime:

> Nor took I *Guiscard* by blind Fancy led,
> Or hasty Choice, as many Women wed;
> But with delib'rate Care, and ripen'd Thought,
> At leisure first design'd, before I wrought:
> On him I rested, after long Debate,
> And not without consid'ring, fix'd my Fate.
> (465–70)

Yet one is tempted to laugh, especially if one has in mind an image of the deliberate care with which the two loudly collapsed upon the bed:

> Attending *Guiscard*, in his Leathern Frock,
> Stood ready, with his thrice-repeated Knock:
> . . . .
> The Door unlock'd, to known Delight they haste,
> And panting in each others Arms, embrac'd;
> Rush to the conscious Bed, a mutual Freight,
> And heedless press it with their wonted Weight,
> The sudden Bound awak'd the sleeping Sire.
> (225–26, 229–33)

This is their second encounter alone, somewhat more graphic (and noisier) than in Boccaccio: "They then went to bed in the usual way; but whilst they were playing and cavorting together, Tancredi chanced to

wake up, and heard and saw what Guiscardo and his daughter were doing" (McWilliam, 335).[9] Deliberation, leisurely design, long debate,
careful consideration have not been conspicuous parts of Sigismonda's
behavior. To be precise, one should say she is as deliberate as she has to
be to get the lover that she sexually craves, and while she may again be
technically correct—she did not sleep with just anybody—she is making
herself sound a great deal more controlled than her actions prove her
to be.

As far as Sigismonda is concerned, her deliberate choice was based on
Guiscardo's obvious merits, which persuaded her judgment to bestow
her love on this man "whose Mind / Is Vertuous" (519–20). She challenges her father to

> measure all thy Court,
> By inward Vertue, not external Port,
> And find whom justly to prefer above
> The Man on whom my Judgment plac'd my Love:
> So shalt thou see his Parts, and Person shine;
> And thus compar'd, the rest a base degen'rate Line.
> (523–28)

Again, place her explanation alongside the available facts. Who is this
paragon whose intrinsic worth appealed to Sigismonda's discriminating
judgment when she "measured" all the court? Guiscardo, in Boccaccio
and Dryden, remains a blank, a null. He responds to Sigismonda's lust,
receives a note from her (hidden in a hollow cane) telling him "The
Time, the Place, the Manner how to meet" (92), follows her directions,
gets caught, and has but one short speech. As far as we know, he is one
of "the Train of Courtiers" who is "With all the Gifts of bounteous
Nature crown'd" (47–48), but what sort of gifts were these that persuaded Sigismonda's discriminating judgment?

When we consider Sigismonda's actual "decision" to wed Guiscardo,
who, by the way, has little to say in the matter one way or the other, we
discover that, since her first husband died,

> Youth, Health, and Ease, and most an amorous Mind,
> To second Nuptials had her Thoughts inclin'd:
> And former Joys had left a secret Sting behind.
> ·
> Resolv'd at last to lose no longer Time,
> And yet to please her self without a Crime,

She cast her Eyes around the Court, to find
A worthy Subject suiting to her Mind.
(34–36, 41–44)

When she finds him, "ev'ry Day increas'd / The raging Fire that burn'd within her Breast" (57–58). The line about the absence of former joys, as well as the line about raging fire, are both Dryden additions.[10] Guiscardo may well be a "worthy Subject suiting to her Mind," but this is an ambiguous piece of praise; one wonders what kind of worth it is that suits an amorous mind. Does the quiet and passive Guiscardo shine with "inward Vertue" (524), as Sigismonda declares, or is he merely a subject worthy of her pressing desires, whose crowning natural gifts are his attractiveness, his virility, his "blooming Age" (51), and his readiness to do good service, in leather, upon request? And whatever Guiscardo may be, what do we make of the noble Sigismonda? It is difficult to believe that the woman we see casting her eyes about for a second husband to fulfill secret longings is acting with the reasonable, controlled, deliberate "Judgement" she assigns to herself. Throughout, what Sigismonda says is a version of the truth rather than an outright falsehood, but it is a version that becomes difficult to accept, given our awareness of Sigismonda's actual behavior; however nobly heroic Sigismonda sounds, her character also resonates spurious lower frequencies.

Separating the two Sigismondas allows us to examine the ways in which Dryden has added material to both sides of her character; if Dryden has made Tancred blacker while making Sigismonda whiter, pushing the extremes further apart, he has also pushed Sigismonda further apart, reducing her motivation to the sexual (not that Dryden disdains this) while elevating her claims for nobility. The issue of Sigismonda's character is not static. It is not merely that we have an amorous woman with a roving eye on the one hand, and a courageous patriot with greatness of mind on the other, but that Dryden portrays the two Sigismondas continually, and thus the struggle to accommodate her actions to her claims is constant. Furthermore, it is this struggle that appears in much of the critical commentary on this poem. As different as the various interpretations are, they often have this much in common: whatever the approach, and whatever the opinion of Dryden's tale, trying to reconcile the two sides of Sigismonda becomes the crucial issue.

We can see this in Wordsworth's reaction to the poem; his remarks occur in a letter where he encourages Sir Walter Scott in his plan to edit Dryden, and then comments on the limitations of this poet he calls "not . . . any great favourite of mine." Most of Wordsworth's commentary is general, but he pauses to speak about "Sigismonda and Guiscardo" specifically, and to recommend that Scott include the original Boccaccio poems in his edition, or at least

> such extracts as would shew when Dryden had most strikingly improved upon or fallen below his original. I think his translations from Boccace are the best at least the most poetical of his Poems. . . . I think Dryden has much injured the story by the marriage, and degraded Sigismonda's character by it. He has also to the best of my remembrance degraded her character still more by making her love absolute sensuality and appetite, (Dryden had no other notion of the passion). With all these defects, and some other very gross ones it is a noble Poem.[11]

However casual this response, and whatever it may be lacking in the thoughtful analytic technique of later commentators, it compensates by having a certain freshness and immediacy. Wordsworth is not arguing; he is reacting. And for Wordsworth, the crux of the story is the marriage, not the fact of the marriage, but the nature of the scene itself, a marriage that "degraded Sigismonda's character." Tancred and the priest are not the only people shocked by Sigismonda's behavior.

It is easy to dismiss such a reaction as stuffiness, or nineteenth-century self-conscious morality, or gentlemanly embarrassment in the face of erotic acts bumptiously described by a major poet (if we wish to spread the vitriol around, we could attribute the shock to repression). Instead of dismissing those remarks, we should first recognize how weighty they were; they influenced Scott, whose commentary on "Sigismonda and Guiscardo" in his *Life of Dryden* echoes Wordsworth.[12] Much later, even Mark Van Doren, whose appreciation of Dryden helped rescue the poet from oblivion, quoted this very passage with the comment that "Wordsworth's criticism can hardly be improved upon."[13] What intrigues me about Wordsworth's response, however, is not its perfection, but the implicit logic behind it and the way in which it locates the problem in the marriage scene, which seems to be, for Wordsworth, what Desdemona's handkerchief was for Thomas Rymer.

Dryden's tale pulls Wordsworth in two directions, and we find Wordsworth praising the "improved" and "most poetical" while lamenting the "fallen" and "degraded." It is not merely the erotic behavior of Sigismonda that offends Wordsworth; had this been merely an obscene tale bristling with prurience, he most likely would have dismissed it outright as Restoration immorality, beneath contempt. Rather, Wordsworth is offended at Dryden's taking away from Sigismonda what Wordsworth thinks she should have: what bothers him is not the sensuality, but the fact that love is *made* "absolute sensuality and appetite," not the basely motivated character of Sigismonda, but the fact that her character has been "degraded." Caught between the two Sigismondas, Wordsworth finds himself endorsing the exalted one, the woman who defended her honorable love, whose passion was elevated and convincing, who made this the "noble Poem" Wordsworth would admire. Unfortunately, she is a far cry from the Sigismonda who jumps eagerly and noisily into bed with her lover, and Wordsworth rejects that side of Sigismonda to preserve the other.

Modern commentators on the tale have refrained from shotgun blasts from the hip, but even in their careful and appreciative arguments, they wrestle with the same issue. There are basically two schools of thought, one for each Sigismonda. For some, the sensual Sigismonda wins out, and the apparent heroism is nothing more than a sham, wherein the would-be heroine reveals her narrowness in the very act of attempting to achieve nobility. In this view, the character of Sigismonda, unable to understand how little claim she has to what she claims she has, becomes not a study in passion but an object of satire.[14] For others, it is the heroine who wins, the noble soul of part two who replaces the limited woman of part one. If that is the case, the disparity between actions and claims can be explained away by arguing for a progress, a transition that occurs at that "hinge-moment" when Sigismonda "changes at once from a woman of uninhibited sensuality to one of Heroic Mind" (Emrys Jones, 284–85).[15] This crucial hinge-moment may be worth pondering again:

> But in-born Worth, that Fortune can controul,
> New strung, and stiffer bent her softer Soul;
> The *Heroine* assum'd the Womans Place,
> Confirm'd her Mind, and fortifi'd her Face.
> (374–77)

One day she is greedily rushing her lover to bed, and the next day she is a heroine? (Actually, in terms of plot, it is the day after next.) I would say yes, and no; Dryden says that the heroine took charge, so the change is there, explicitly described, but it is so swift, without preparation, without continuity, that we have every reason to wonder how the heroine could possibly assume the woman's place. It is a more remarkable transformation than the other Ovidian metamorphoses, which, drastic as they are, represent continuities: Baucis and Philemon's fidelity persisting in intertwined trees; Ceyx and Alcyone's selfless love enduring in a pair of nesting birds; Myrrha's suffering continuing in a myrrh tree forever weeping.

We have, then, a Sigismonda who transcends her limitations, or whose limitations subvert her claims to spirituality, and a Dryden who celebrates a noble woman, or whose gross errors prevent him from endorsing that nobility, unless he is a satirist criticizing a pretense to nobility, perhaps because he wishes to endorse a Christian ethic.[16] Each reader not only endures the struggle with the two Sigismondas, but sees it through to some kind of civilizing ideal, in what Sigismonda is, or what she should have been if Dryden were less prurient, or what she could have been had she been a beneficiary of "divine truth as revealed in Christ's lifetime" (Sloman, "An Interpretation," 200).[17] The resolutions differ; what remains the same is the process of trying to reconcile the irreconcilable. It is the nature of Sigismonda to be both persuasive heroine and limited human being incapable of the heroism with which she convinces us. It is the nature of the tale to establish ideals but also measure them, to weave a noble portrait and unravel it as well.

CYMON AND IPHIGENIA

The final tale, also from Boccaccio, is worth special attention, just because it is the final tale. All possible progressions end here, and when readers reach "Cymon and Iphigenia," as I mentioned earlier, they all too often discover that the ending is more a demolishing than a completion.[18] If we regard the parson and good maiden as the Christian redemption from the pagan world of brutal heroism and destructive passion, what do we make of a final tale that returns us to the world of violent, corruptible, self-serving warrior-rapists? The various tentative ideals we occasionally glimpse in the brutal, blood-dimmed world do not survive into "Cymon and Iphigenia."[19] Instead of conjugal devotion, practiced by the duchess, and by Baucis and Philemon, we have a double rape and multiple murders. Instead of the self-sacrificing love of a Sigismonda or Alcyone, we have a self-serving Iphigenia, a dissembler who loves her Cymon when it is convenient (although she pretends indifference), and blames him for their plight when he rescues her from her betrothed and sails off into a dangerous storm. Instead of a social ideal, such as the honorable John Driden, justice of the peace, we have the public official Lysymachus who uses his power to free Cymon from prison, then plan, then execute the rape. After all, what is power for?

Although *Fables* gives us a good Theseus, at least at the end of "Palamon and Arcite," and a good justice of the peace, both of whom establish order, the final tale reminds us that "The Great, it seems, are priviledg'd alone / To punish all Injustice but their own" (471–72, a Dryden addition). This, said of Lysymachus, and aimed as well at William III, brings us back down from the world of noble Theseus, and the tale reminds us that practically speaking, in the world at large, justice is usually in the dangerous hands of the unjust, the selfish, the unworthy. And although *Fables* gives us melodramatic lovers, domestic couples free from strife, and those who remain pure and love God, the last tale reminds us that love, potentially a constructive ideal, is more likely to be a destructive passion, lust misconstrued, leading to rape, pillage, war. We have come all the way from the burlesque first book of the *Iliad*, with its raging killer-heroes and squabbling gods, through partial ideals, potential redemptions from gloom,[20] only to conclude grandly with a tale of Cymon, a "slavering Cudden" (179) who delicately expresses his love by seizing "the willing Prey, / As *Paris* bore the *Spartan* Spouse away" (318–19). By mentioning Paris (the simile does not appear in the Boccaccio original), Dryden reminds us that we are back where we started. Yet again.

Such a coda can only be disconcerting to those who would find a progression in *Fables*.[21] What kind of capacious and expansive mind ends his anthology with a return to the world of debased humans and reduced values? If, as Earl Miner comments, *Fables* presents the search for "the good life" in all its variety,[22] one might ask what kind of search, what kind of good life it is that ends on this note:

> The Hall is heap'd with Corps; the sprinkled Gore
> Besmears the Walls, and floats the Marble Floor.

Dispers'd at length the drunken Squadron flies,
The Victors to their Vessel bear the Prize;
And hear behind loud Groans, and lamentable Cries.
(607–11)

I would argue that the final tale repeats the challenge that *Fables* consistently provides, for it is a further example of undoing, unravelling, taking apart possible progressions, undoing what we feel ought to be done up. Although it is the final tale, it is also another tale, not just the last word, but also more of the same words, which establish and subvert, offer and deny. And not only does "Cymon and Iphigenia" qualify or undercut the preceding tales, but it also undoes itself.

Within this crushing return to another Helen and another Troy, this new version of a nuptial feast ending in a miscellany of carnage, we discover another strain, especially in the first third of the poem (which incidentally contains the largest amount of added Dryden material). The opening, far from being merely the beginning of this anti-heroic story of Cymon and his destructive lust, is actually the opposite of that story. Cymon begins as Galesius, a "goodly Youth to view" (50) but unfortunately possessed of "a heavy, dull, degenerate Mind" (53). He is so uncivilizable that all attempts at educating him merely leave him "flound'ring in the Mud" (64). He grows into "the publick Shame" (65), earns his new name, Cymon, "which signifies a Brute" (67),[23] and gets banished to the country by a father who would rather not have to face his own son the clown. This is fine with Cymon, whose "rustick Mind" (74) seems especially suited to farm life. Then, one day, while he is walking along, whistling "as he went, for want of Thought" (85), he sees the sleeping Iphigenia. As he falls, precipitately, in love, we notice that there is nothing terribly elevated about his passion. This is love at first sight, and at sight only; he and Iphigenia scarcely speak to each other, partially because Cymon with his "Clown Accent, and his Country-Tone" (116) is scarcely able to speak in the first place. It is not Iphigenia's character or intrinsic merit, both of which we later discover to be slight, that engages Cymon's idiot mind; what strikes him is her beauty, particularly her naked parts, "Her comely Limbs" (99) and "Her Bosom" which "to the view was only bare" (101). (Boccaccio mentions these and other physical features in a list; Dryden, however, chooses to devote five lines to Iphigenia's bosom.)

This is the same raw physical passion we discover when Pygmalion caresses his statue, the same sexual desire that we see, or rather hear, when Sigismonda is alone with Guiscardo. It is the kind of passion that another resident of the country, Kinsman Driden, successfully avoids; had he not been able to "shun the Bait" (33), he would not have achieved self-sufficiency, and we have more than enough examples of what the alternative, "struggl[ing] in the Snare" (33), entails. Yet, however base and basic Cymon's passion, and however destructive, "Love" also becomes, for him, a powerful, generative force:

> Through the rude Chaos thus the running Light
> Shot the first Ray that pierc'd the Native Night:
> Then Day and Darkness in the Mass were mix'd,
> Till gather'd in a Globe, the Beams were fix'd:
> Last shon the Sun who radiant in his Sphere
> Illumin'd Heav'n, and Earth, and rowl'd around the Year.
> So Reason in this Brutal Soul began:
> Love made him first suspect he was a Man;
> Love made him doubt his broad barbarian Sound,
> By Love his want of Words, and Wit he found:
> That sense of want prepar'd the future way
> To Knowledge, and disclos'd the promise of a Day.
> (117–28)

The entire passage, not to be found in Boccaccio, is a set piece on Creation borrowed from the song of Silenus in Virgil's sixth eclogue (which Dryden had translated earlier, and which Pope was later to invert in book four of *The Dunciad*). Love, clearly, recreates Cymon, remaking the dark chaos that is the rude, unformed Cymon, illuminating his brutal darkness with the light of reason. Cymon is living proof, or we might say newly created proof, of the regenerative power of love to which Palamon paid tribute in his prayer to "Creator *Venus*" who "mad'st the World, and dost the World repair" (3: 129, 145). As we have seen, what distinguishes Palamon from Arcite is a different attitude toward love, with Palamon considering it a renewing force, like Spring, while Arcite grimly regards love as inevitably destructive. Now, the very character who is about to demonstrate the validity of Arcite's bloody principles begins by enacting Palamon's beliefs; this rustic Paris who will soon prove passion destructive first proves it to be *con*structive.

Love is instructive as well; Cymon is not only remade on the spot, but also reformed "by degrees" (147):

> What not his Father's Care, nor Tutor's Art
> Cou'd plant with Pains in his unpolish'd Heart,
> The best Instructor Love at once inspir'd,
> As barren Grounds to Fruitfulness are fir'd:
> Love taught him Shame, and Shame with Love at Strife
> Soon taught the sweet Civilities of Life.
> (129–34)

The "Man-Beast" (147), under the influence of this new instructor, begins a deliberate course of self-improvement; he forsakes his country clownage, returns to his father's house, dresses himself in "rich Attire" (211) more appropriate to his rank, and

> His Body thus adorn'd, he next design'd
> With lib'ral Arts to cultivate his Mind:
> He sought a Tutor of his own accord,
> And study'd Lessons he before abhorr'd.
>   Thus the Man-Child advanc'd, and learn'd so fast,
> That in short time his Equals he surpass'd:
> (212–17)

Dryden had used a similar metaphor in "Threnodia Augustalis" (1685), describing Charles II as a "Royal Husbandman" (356) ploughing, sowing, and manuring an "uncultivated" (352) England. In the above passage, the uncultivated soil is Cymon himself, and the image has an added, clever twist, since the word "cultivate," in its agricultural sense, signifies the limited best that Cymon could have done on his country farm, and now refers to his elevation above the rustic life. He who was pleased to raise corn and cattle is himself growing, and the process of transformation is both sudden and gradual. While those other man-beasts, the centaurs, move toward the brutal, Cymon is moving in the other direction. I quote the passages to emphasize that this progress of love refining Cymon toward "sweet Civilities" is no sidelong innuendo, but rather deliberate and sustained.

Moreover, and this makes the ultimate consequences of Cymon's passion all the more disturbing, Dryden has introduced the tale of Cymon with a "Poeta Loquitur," which endorses the story of Cymon's upward spiritual mobility. This, as I mentioned, is where Dryden answers Collier's charges, accusing "the severe Divine" (4) of over-reading, and thereby putting into Dryden's poetry more obscenity than ever Dryden put there: "What needs he Paraphrase on what we mean? / We are at worst but Wanton; he's Obscene" (21–22). The following tale, Dryden suggests, will edify, perhaps better than "A Tale of only dry Instruction" (26). Love in Dryden's poetry is not the wanton, obscene passion that Collier finds it to be:

> Nor Love is always of a vicious Kind,
> But oft to virtuous Acts inflames the Mind.
> Awakes the s! ;epy Vigour of the Soul,
> And brushing o'er, adds Motion to the Pool.
> Love, studious how to please, improves our Parts,
> With polish'd Manners, and adorns with Arts.
> Love first invented Verse, and form'd the Rhime,
> The Motion measur'd, harmoniz'd the Chime;
> To lib'ral Acts inlarg'd the narrow-Soul'd:
> Soften'd the Fierce, and made the Coward Bold:
> The World when wast, he Peopled with increase,
> And warring Nations reconcil'd in Peace.
> *Ormond*, the first, and all the Fair may find
> In this one Legend to their Fame design'd,
> When Beauty fires the Blood, how Love exalts the Mind.
> (27–41)

By setting the "Poeta Loquitur" in his own time (he has just been roaming the Platonic realms where the fair maiden dwells), and by speaking as an "I" at war with Collier, Dryden gives the impression that "Cymon and Iphigenia," far from being an escape into fancy, is a poem of some personal importance. Indeed, we are led to take it as the last word in the debate with Collier, as Dryden's demonstration that he can understand and write about love that leads to "virtuous Acts." Dryden also connects love's creative power with that of poetry, suggesting that love's power to improve, polish, and adorn inspires the poet-artist: "Love first invented Verse," Dryden claims, and then attributes to love the capacity to make rhymes, create harmonies, enlarge narrow souls, all of which are as much part of the power of Dryden's muse as they are parts of love's power. Making the coward bold and softening the fierce is also what Timotheus, the "poet-musician-rhetorician-hero,"[24] does with his at times dangerously manipulative voice that "Cou'd swell the Soul to rage, or kindle soft Desire" (160). Finally, in offering the tale as a tribute to the duchess of Ormond, whom he had celebrated in the opening poem, Dryden implies that he is about to pull everything together; as the duchess offered to restore a devastated Ireland so that "Earth unbidden shall produce her Store" (83), so will beautiful Iphigenia remake and cultivate the "barren Grounds" of Cymon "to Fruitfulness" (132). The legend that follows will supposedly confirm the auspicious, generative power of beauty and love, which is also the harmonizing power of poetry, and the restorative power of the Christian duchess.

What kind of tribute is this to the duchess of Ormond "and all the Fair" that ultimately celebrates the power of beauty to produce "Blood, Rapines, Massacres" ("Ormond," 68)? Why announce the "moral" of the final tale and invest it with such substantial authority, only to undercut it? One might be tempted to see this as Dryden losing control, trying unsuccessfully to impose order on material that is about to wriggle out from under its ostensible purpose, but the distinction between love's power to enlarge and its power to diminish is too sustained, too sharp, too controlled to allow us to dismiss the contradiction as authorial sloppiness. Dryden could certainly have smoothed out the conflict between love's contrary influences, or edited his source, or chosen another final tale if he merely wanted to exalt love; he could have skipped the "Poeta Loquitur" if he merely wanted to recapitulate his anti-heroic theme. Instead, Dryden, if anything, sharpens love's extremes, by amplifying the passages that describe Cymon's re-creation at one end of the story, and by increasing the details of the gore and criminality at the other. We are left with a tale that charts the Progress of Love, as promised in the "Poeta Loquitur," and then with equal vigor charts the Regress.

That Dryden wishes to have it both ways is, I think, slyly implied in the "Poeta Loquitur." Even though he is to celebrate love enlarging the narrow-souled, he is also stressing that love "oft to virtuous Acts inflames the Mind" (28), and certainly "inflames," with its suggestion of destructiveness and wildness, is a peculiar word to use for the operation that leads the mind upward to virtuous acts. An inflamed mind is what possesses Achilles, what reduces Ajax to madness, rage, and suicide; the flames of vengeful passion are what possess Althea to destroy her own son by casting a brand in the fire. In the tale to follow, of course, Cymon will both move toward virtuous behavior, good manners, knowledge surpassing his equals, and then onward to "too much Fire" (235) and "excess of Passion" (238). The hint of fire imagery at the outset, right in the middle of this special plea for love's generative power, threatens to consume whatever love may build. One word, "inflame," does not exactly constitute a mighty threat; the passage by and large emphasizes the process of awaking, improving, polishing, inventing, forming, harmonizing, enlarging. Yet the last lines of the "Poeta Loquitur" both summarize these productive powers of love and hint at their undoing: Dryden offers the poem as a legend wherein "all the Fair may find . . . / When Beauty fires the Blood, how Love exalts the Mind" (39, 41). That may well be the central question the tale asks: whether the mind can ultimately transcend the body, whether love can exalt once the blood is fired.

We most likely begin to ask that question when, after following the progress of Cymon, which confirms love's creative power, we watch as Cymon changes, or rather, as Cymon who has already changed, changes back. Cymon has just surpassed his equals and has "His brutal Manners from his Breast exil'd" (218); now comes the fire:

> What then of alter'd *Cymon* shall we say,
> But that the Fire which choak'd in Ashes lay,
> A Load too heavy for his Soul to move,
> Was upward blown below, and brush'd away by Love?
> Love made an active Progress through his Mind,
> The dusky Parts he clear'd, the gross refin'd;
> The drowsy wak'd; and as he went impress'd
> The Maker's Image on the human Beast.
> Thus was the Man amended by Desire,
> And tho' he lov'd perhaps with too much Fire,
> His Father all his Faults with Reason scan'd,
> And lik'd an error of the better Hand;
> Excus'd th' excess of Passion in his Mind,
> By Flames too fierce, perhaps too much refin'd;
> So *Cymon*, since his Sire indulg'd his Will,
> Impetuous lov'd, and would be *Cymon* still.
> (226–41)

The original has Cymon breaking forth from chains, but Dryden has turned this into an alchemical process, which allows him to fan the refining fire of passion into a white heat. Cymon appears to have been reformed right through neutral into the other extreme, one that his father prefers. But too much fire, excess of passion, flames too fierce all render the "alter'd *Cymon* . . . / . . . "*Cymon* still." [25] And, as was the case with the hinge-moment in "Sigismonda and Guiscardo," we are beset with difficulties in accepting a sudden change, or rather, a change that has suddenly become no change. Cymon is altered, but the same. For over two hundred lines we have followed his progress, and we now watch as he exiles brutal manners and brutal folly from his breast to make room for . . . brutality.

Yet the new brutality that emerges from "*Cymon* still" is worse than
could have been expected from the happy-go-lucky cudden with the idiot
laugh who whistled mindlessly as he walked. When Cymon's suit to Iphigenia's father fails, the new (and former) Cymon sounds like Arcite; he
"in secret" (257) pledges to win this woman, by force, if possible:

> The time is come for *Iphigene* to find
> The Miracle she wrought upon my Mind:
> Her Charms have made me Man, her ravish'd Love
> In rank shall place me with the Bless'd above.
> For mine by Love, by Force she shall be mine,
> Or Death, if Force should fail, shall finish my Design.
> (258–63)

The miracle that raises him from bestiality to manhood will, he thinks,
place him among the "Bless'd above," a statement that punctures itself,
for the elevation is based on "ravish'd Love," on force. Then again, we
have already seen in "The First Book of Homer's Ilias" how the "Bless'd
above" behave, so, in a way Cymon does not realize, he is right. He will
be just as destructive and inhumane as the gods. In the end, "how Love
exalts the Mind" does not matter, for "When Beauty fires the Blood,"
passion will win the day, and lose civilization.

The effort to reconcile love's power to reform with its power to de-
form, to reconcile the improved Cymon with the new, brutalized model,
is another version of the attempt to integrate Sigismondas, only the opposing possibilities appear in reverse order. If, in reading of Sigismonda,
we were led to ask how the noble heroine could grow out of the self-
serving, sensual woman, we are now being asked the same question the
other way around: how could the newly civilized Cymon, refined so
"That in short time his Equals he surpass'd" (217), shrink so swiftly and
completely to brutality? Dryden even adds material that encourages us
to compare Cymon to Sigismonda, although once we do, we find it all
the more difficult to reconcile the noble and ignoble sides of human
character. The passage occurs just after Cymon has begun to take action
to secure his Iphigenia. A ship, bound for Rhodes, has set off with Iphigenia, and Cymon has rigged a vessel of his own, equipped it for war,
and set off in hot pursuit. He and his men set an ambush, surprise the
"Rival Bark" (272), board it, fight fiercely, and win the battle, after which
Cymon addresses the defeated crew and makes his claim:

In *Iphigene* I claim my rightful Due,
Rob'd by my Rival, and detain'd by you:
Your *Pasimond* a lawless Bargain drove,
The Parent could not sell the Daughters Love;
Or if he cou'd, my Love disdains the Laws,
And like a King by Conquest gains his Cause.

(296–301)

That a parent cannot decide a daughter's love (an added couplet) is also
part of Sigismonda's argument. She had married a first husband of her
father's choosing, apparently one to her liking because she mentions that
marriage as the source of her current sexual urge, and, in defending her
marrying again without her father's consent, she insists that the choice is
freely hers, even "Had Parents pow'r . . . second Vows to tie" (413).
Marital decisions "Made without our Consent" lack "Pow'r to bind"
(420), with which Cymon would heartily agree.

But what in Sigismonda was a persuasive claim, part of her ennobled
character, is here part of an "ignobled" character. It is not convincing,
because this "furious Lover" (285) acts before he thinks, conquers and
then claims love gives him the right. His dismissal of parental authority
seems like a rationalization, a projection of a self-centered "I am right
and everybody else is wrong" attitude. Even as we consider how self-
serving Cymon sounds next to the Sigismonda who rises in our esteem,
we might recall the other side of Sigismonda that made her ascent to
nobility seem abrupt; her claims to greatness of mind can be taken as
equally self-serving, a word that accurately describes her behavior before
her miraculous transformation.

The two Cymons and the two Sigismondas present the same difficulty,
for they remain irreconcilable, in poems where, if anything, Dryden has
taken pains to push the central oppositions further apart.[26] This play of
oppositions is by no means an empty exercise in which each possibility
cancels out its contrary, but is rather Dryden's purposeful way of expressing a theme, not as fixed conclusion, but as a continuing process. That
process involves a constant questioning of proffered ideals, the heroic
Sigismonda and the cultivated Cymon taking their place with the other
potential ideals *Fables* offers, ranging from the purest of Christians to
heroes of the old epic mold. Do we not discover in each case an ideal
that promises to transform but does not deliver? The new Sigismonda

does not quite redeem the former Sigismonda, and the new Cymon is no sooner new than his transformation falls apart. The gap between the two Cymons, or between the two Sigismondas, is not unlike the gap between the too-limited warriors, and the noble heroes they sometimes, briefly, embody; the gap between the Ajax who "cou'd often, and alone withstand / The Foe, the Fire, and *Jove*'s own partial Hand" ("The Speeches of Ajax and Ulysses," 593–94), and Ajax the stupid, raging brute; the gap between the duchess as the restorative force of love, and the sickly duchess who is too weak to achieve her own ideal.

Throughout this anthology, Dryden relies upon various value systems, Christian, heroic, domestic, sentimental, consistently making appealing and convincing cases for a host of possibilities for civilizable mankind. The possibilities include passionate love, conjugal love, love of principle, love of country, love of God, all of which vie against limitations, failures that Dryden presents persuasively as equal parts of the human scene. All the ideals have their appeal and their temporary successes, but all are constantly under a subversive pressure, so that the ideals are unattainable or inapplicable to life, even as they are precious and necessary. The divided Cymons and Sigismondas are not merely unresolved characters, but further instances of Dryden measuring ideals; what cannot be reconciled is the difference between imperfect human nature and the heroic, noble aspirations that are equally human.

ALEXANDER'S FEAST

The two Boccaccio poems are especially effective examples because the contrary pulls are so clear, and so contrary. Whereas other tales poise a character in one against a character in another, the kinsman vs. the parson, the duchess vs. the kinsman, the duchess vs. Iphigenia, and so on, here each tale poises a character against him or herself. This is but one strategy, and we will not find various Dryden always dividing his characters, and our loyalties, quite so neatly. Yet some of the other individual tales, quite different in tone and content, nonetheless embody a similar process, with the tale progressing toward a resolution that does not arrive, or that arrives only to dissolve unexpectedly into something else.

"Alexander's Feast" is a good example, because it is so strikingly different from the preceding poems. As an occasional poem from 1697, this poem is not really a part of *Fables*, but appears at first glance to be an earlier piece Dryden added perhaps to pad out the volume, something easily inserted into a miscellany because variety can contain most anything without much strain. With Dryden rambling from one author to another, his "Thoughts, such as they are, . . . crowding in so fast upon me, that my only Difficulty is to chuse or to reject" (Kinsley, 4:1446), it is charming to find him borrowing from Dryden as he borrows from Homer, Chaucer, Boccaccio, and Ovid. In assembling his tales into the final arrangement, Dryden sandwiches "Alexander's Feast" between the pseudo-Chaucerian "The Flower and the Leaf" and "The Twelfth Book of Ovid His Metamorphoses," where it fits as well as anything. That is to say, "Alexander's Feast" does not fit as an integral part of a formal structure, or as a step in a progression, but as a piece associated with the rest by virtue of the issues addressed. The poem's setting places us in the familiar territory of deeds of arms, and love (which are also issues in the two surrounding tales). We watch as Alexander celebrates his victory over Persia (1), and part of that celebration is "The Lovely *Thais* by his side" (9), presumably a sexual reward for military victory, the fair courtesan whom "None but the Brave" (13, 14, 15) has just deserved.[27]

"Alexander's Feast; or, the Power of Musique " is not a tale of personal growth, like the stories of Sigismonda and Cymon; as the subtitle suggests, the poem is primarily about music, and naturally, much of the scholarship concerns the musical modes, Dryden's indebtedness to Renaissance theories of music, his treatment of the effects of music, and the like.[28] In addition to being about the power of music, however, this poem is more broadly about power itself and about art, especially when the poem is separated from its original occasion and placed within a collection that frequently touches upon such topics. I think the central figure of Timotheus, the "poet-musician-rhetorician-hero" (Hollander, 412) who sings to Alexander and his court in a variety of modes, raises some obvious, if unsettling, questions. Whenever we meet an artist figure in Dryden, it is at least possible, and in this case rather likely, that the artist is an alter ego, one of the company that includes John Oldham, Anne Killigrew, Godfrey Kneller, William Congreve—all artists to whom Dryden wrote poems that allowed him to examine his own accomplishments. All have talents of varying degrees, special abilities, from the fellow satirist John Oldham who played the same lyre (but with a harsher music), to the only young talent worthy to succeed to Dryden's laurel, William Congreve.[29] What Timotheus has, most conspicuously, is power. In stanza after stanza, he shifts the mood, changes the song, and in general manipulates Alexander, who melts, shouts, weeps, rejoices, and conquers, on cue. The supposedly great Alexander seems little more than a puppet responding to the man who pulls the strings.

Not only does Timotheus make Alexander do things, but he also in a way "makes" Alexander; when the myth-maker sings of Alexander's birth from the union of Jove and the "fair *Olympia*" (30), he endows the emperor with divinity:

> The list'ning Crowd admire the lofty Sound,
> A present Deity, they shout around:
> A present Deity the vaulted Roofs rebound.
> > With ravish'd Ears
> > The Monarch hears,
> > Assumes the God,
> > Affects to nod,
> And seems to shake the Spheres.
> > (34–41)

At the beginning of the poem, Alexander was "*Philip*'s Warlike Son" (2), but Timotheus has created a new myth, given Alexander a new father, Jove, and it is only then that the crowd acknowledges "a present Deity" and that Alexander "Assumes the God." Divinity does not quite fit the real Alexander; the myth is fraudulent. He only "seems to shake the Spheres," but Timotheus has so much control over audience and monarch, that the illusion comes to life and Alexander appears to be "A present Deity." This suspect identification carries with it a delicious irony: Alexander may not be much of a deity, but the Macedonian king who, fired by love of his woman, destroys Persepolis is rather like the Jove who, motivated by passion, rapes Olympia.[30] Jove has "stamp'd an Image of himself," leaving us with another rapacious, Jovian "Sov'raign of the World" (33). The bard Timotheus, then, defines the nature of his king and manages to criticize Alexander in the very act of glorifying him. Such is the poet-rhetorician's power.

One is reminded of the ending of the Anne Killigrew ode, in which

Dryden, having depicted the poetess as a powerful conqueror stretching her sway into the adjacent realm of painting, comments on how her painting remakes the king. Here art does not imitate nature. Rather, it is the other way around, as the artist makes qualities as insubstantial as "Ghosts" (133) a part of James II's character—these qualities, like Alexander's divinity, are there when the artist puts them there. These are grand, baroque claims for the artist, suitable to the hyperbole one finds in Pindaric odes, but there is a crucial difference between Killigrew and Timotheus. Killigrew is pointedly unlike Dryden; she is a sacred poet, an *"Arethusian* Stream" that remained "unsoil'd" (68), and Dryden hopes her purity might serve as compensation, as atonement for the entire "lubrique and adult'rate age" (63) of Restoration drama. She serves as a contrast to Dryden who, in a winningly self-critical tone far removed from the braggadocio of "Alexander's Feast," admits that he has "Made prostitute and profligate the Muse" (58). Killigrew is what poetry could be, what poetry should be. The equally powerful Timotheus, however, is what poetry *is*, not an ideal contrasted against fallen Dryden, but Dryden himself, a poet who dares criticize a usurping monarch. No longer does a sacred poet march onward to heaven leading all mankind at the Last Judgment; in "Alexander's Feast," the mighty artist does the leading right here, right now.

The actual circumstances surrounding the publication of "Alexander's Feast" help explain the grandiose, high-spirited claims.[31] Dryden had just finished his translation of the *Aeneid*, a work that cost him much travail; as he explained in his postscript, "What *Virgil* wrote in the vigour of his Age, in Plenty and at Ease, I have undertaken to *Translate* in my Declining Years: strugling with Wants, oppress'd with Sickness, curb'd in my Genius, lyable to be misconstrued in all I write" (Postscript to the Reader, Kinsley, 3: 1424). After such a major undertaking, Dryden must have been pleased with the enthusiastic reception afforded his *Aeneid* by the public. "Alexander's Feast" comes in the wake of this success, and can be taken both as a buoyant release from the labors of translating Virgil and as a celebration. When the stewards of the St. Cecilia's Day Feast visited Dryden to ask him to write the ode for 1697, their request must have confirmed the success of his translation and marked a moment of personal triumph.[32] What made the success all the sweeter was that, since having done the St. Cecilia's Day ode for 1687, the deposed laureate had watched as lesser talents, including Shadwell, wrote the annual ode. I doubt this would have shaken the confidence of the old poet who, though officially out of favor, was still producing plays, collections of translations, and the like. But it probably was irritating that such as Shadwell, who had been actively sniping at Dryden, should be receiving assignments that had once fallen Dryden's way. When the assignment came his way again, the poet who had recently (1694) complained that "Poetry is curs'd; / For *Tom* the Second [Rymer] reigns like *Tom* the first [Shadwell]" ("To Congreve," 47–48) had been given the rare opportunity to have the last word.

In the figure of Timotheus, Dryden, the "deposed" laureate, in effect reigns again, and he asserts the awesome power of the artist over a monarch.[33] Dryden had developed this idea in his Dedication to the *Aeneid*, where he suggests the parallels between himself and Virgil, between his monarch and Augustus, also a usurping ruler, described by Dryden as a "Conquerour" who, "though of a bad kind, was the very best of it (Kinsley, 3:1014). When Dryden recommends that we "consider" Virgil "as writing his Poem in a time when the Old Form of Government was subverted, and a new one just Established by *Octavius Caesar*: In effect by force of Arms, but seemingly by the Consent of the *Roman* People" (Kinsley, 3:1012), it is difficult to avoid applying this to Dryden, his own time, and his own newly established warlike monarch, whose authority the poet, with teeth gritted, was forced to accept.[34] Dryden offers his version of the epic as, in his understanding, Virgil offered his: "good Counsel, how [Augustus is] to behave himself in his new Monarchy, so as to gain the Affections of his Subjects" (Kinsley, 3:1016), good counsel that is specially privileged because it is offered by a poet. It was Virgil's achievement that he "dextr'ously ... mannag'd both the Prince and People" (Kinsley, 3:1016), and it is Dryden's hope to accomplish the same constructive goal for his king and country.[35]

"Alexander's Feast" becomes a postscript to this argument, but more, it becomes an expansion of the theme of the artist's power, now couched in uncompromising terms. Therein lies the problem. Managing the prince and offering good counsel are one thing, but manipulating is going a step too far. In Timotheus we hear Dryden's "own confident apologia" offered with "a buoyancy of spirit" (Fujimura, "Personal Element," 1019–20), but it is too confident, insufficiently apologetic, and the buoyancy seems like gloating. Can we really accept Timotheus as a Dryden figure when we see him singing of Bacchus, and inducing this sort of reaction from Alexander?

> Sooth'd with the Sound the King grew vain;
>   Fought all his Battails o'er again;
> And thrice He routed all his Foes; and thrice He slew the slain.
>   The Master saw the Madness rise;
>   His glowing Cheeks, his ardent Eyes;
>   And while He heav'n and Earth defy'd,
>   Chang'd his hand, and check'd his Pride.
>   He chose a Mournful Muse
>   Soft Pity to infuse.
>   (66–74)

First, the great Alexander is made to act like the classic nostalgic drunk who rehearses his war stories, thrice; then, a shift of key, and Alexander's boisterousness melts into "Soft Pity" for the cruel Persian ruler whom he has just defeated. The pity is as suspect as the glory, for the despotic Persian ruler whose defeat is the occasion of Timotheus stringing his lyre in the first place is by no stretch of the imagination "*Darius* Great and Good" (75). Not only is Timotheus rather casually flipping his monarch from one emotional extreme to another, from swaggering to slobbering, but he is also inducing "Madness," "glowing Cheeks," the kind of uncontrolled passion that, in a volcanic Achilles, a grim Arcite, a too ardent Cymon, and in the slaughtering centaurs—they too are drunk—is dangerous and contemptible. This is far from good counsel.

The easy manipulation continues, as "The Mighty Master" (93) Timotheus raises his voice to "A lowder yet, and yet a lowder Strain" (124), perhaps to waken Alexander, "The vanquish'd Victor" (115) who is just about to drop off to sleep on the breast of the courtesan Thais. Timotheus' fortissimo strain rouses Alexander to revenge, the very revenge that, in the behavior of Meleager, of his mother Althea, of the Lapithae toward the centaurs, then of the centaurs toward the Lapithae, and then of Neptune toward Achilles, Dryden shows to be unrelenting, inescapable, bloody, and brutal. "Revenge, Revenge, *Timotheus* cries" (131), and, more specifically directing the vengeance, conjures up a grisly scene for his monarch:

> Behold a ghastly Band,
> Each a Torch in his Hand!
> Those are *Grecian* Ghosts, that in Battail were slayn,
> And unbury'd remain
> Inglorious on the Plain.
> Give the Vengeance due
> To the Valiant Crew.
> Behold how they toss their Torches on high,
> How they point to the *Persian* Abodes,
> And glitt'ring Temples of their Hostile Gods!
> (136–45)

It is especially convenient that these vengeance-seeking ghosts know how to point. Alexander, no more deliberate or contemplative than Cymon when given the opportunity to spill some blood, responds immediately:

> And the King seyz'd a Flambeau, with Zeal to destroy;
> *Thais* led the Way,
> To light him to his Prey,
> And, like another *Hellen*, fir'd another *Troy*.
> (147–50)

This is more than leading a leader; it is misleading a leader. Can the Timotheus who inspires the burning of Persepolis be the alter ego of Dryden, the poet who ends *Fables* with a powerful account of what "too much Fire" (235) does to Cymon—induces him to besmear the walls of Rhodes with gore for the sake of *his* Helen?

Again, the answer is yes, and no. I think the identification of Timotheus with Dryden is inescapable, considering the previous exalted claims for the power of the artist, the circumstances surrounding the composition of this poem, the clear parallels, and Dryden's previous use of similar parallels. It is all the more likely given Dryden's practice, throughout *Fables*, of turning princes into William figures.[36] What we see when we encounter the "Royal Hypocrite" (442) Agamemnon, the unprincely Tancred, the conquering Theseus, we can reasonably expect when we encounter an Alexander, especially when Alexander just happens to be a de facto monarch who has recently usurped a throne. In identifying Timotheus as a Dryden figure, however, we encounter a problem. It is not that there are two Timotheuses, exactly. Rather, there is in Timotheus the voice of the powerful artist, which Dryden seems to endorse, and which we have often heard from Dryden the public poet.[37] And there is a voice that goes too far and becomes disconcerting. There is the voice that, in Fujimura's terms, expresses "the vital myth of the poet as a leader of men, the inspirer of all to high goals, the cherisher and creator of cultural and moral values" ("Personal Element," 1021).[38] Dryden presumes to speak to us in this voice whenever he gives advice to William, which sometimes means criticizing the foreigner for his war-like exploits, and at other times means establishing an ideal monarch to be emulated, like the magnanimous Theseus who emerges at the end of "Palamon and Arcite." It is the voice we hear when Timotheus shifts to "*Lydian* measures" and comments on war:

> War, he sung, is Toil and Trouble;
> Honour but an empty Bubble.
>   Never ending, still beginning,
> Fighting still, and still destroying,
>   If the World be worth thy Winning,
> Think, O think, it worth Enjoying.
>   (99–104)

This is an apt summary, readily applicable to the many specific examples of never-ending destruction, from the petty heroes and gods of the first book of the *Iliad*, down to Cymon and company. Indeed, those who argue for *Fables* as Dryden's most complete statement of anti-heroism might agree that Timotheus' words above describe the central purpose behind the anthology.

This same voice, that of a powerful shaper with moral responsibilities, is what we hear at the end of the kinsman poem, when Dryden posits an equivalence between the man of action and the poet:

> Two of a House, few Ages can afford;
> One to perform, another to record.
> Praise-worthy Actions are by thee embrac'd;
> And 'tis my Praise, to make thy Praises last.
> For ev'n when Death dissolves our Humane Frame,
> The Soul returns to Heav'n, from whence it came;
> Earth keeps the Body, Verse preserves the Fame.
>   (203–9)

Not just any verse, but Dryden's verse, this verse. Not only is Kinsman Driden a "Memorial of my own Principles to all Posterity" (#65, probably written in October 1699, *Letters*, p. 120), but he becomes a memorial because of the power of the poet to define, ennoble, and immortalize "Praise-worthy Actions." They are there, and will be there for future generations, because the poet puts them there.

But the same poet who hopes to act as a "cherisher and creator of cultural and moral values," who often addresses us with the understanding that we share his respect for the power of the artist and that we accept his role as guardian of morality and culture, as a leader of leaders, elsewhere warns us against listening to such a powerful voice. Dryden himself, in a line cagily added to "The Cock and the Fox" ("The Nun's Priest's Tale"), comments on the power of Timotheus, in a passage warning about the dangers of flattery:

> Ye Princes rais'd by Poets to the Gods,
> And *Alexander'd* up in lying Odes,
> Believe not ev'ry flatt'ring Knave's report.
> (659–61)

Dryden presumably has in mind the many third-rate panegyrics churned out for the sake of flattering princes, and certainly Alexander was often used as a triumphant model for kingly power.[39] At the same time, Dryden implicates his spokesman Timotheus, who obviously Alexanders up his Alexander, and one might add that in his Dedication to Ormond that opens *Fables*, Dryden himself praises his patron by at one point likening him to Alexander (Kinsley, 4:1443). It is not merely the despicable poetasters who raise up princes. The vital myth may also be a lying ode. We endorse that myth, accept the familiar poet-maker with his awesome power, only to find ourselves leaning in the wrong direction. It is comforting to think that Dryden actually could have managed William III, that he could have "won" after all the years spent struggling against a hostile government. It is encouraging to think that, after all, art is relevant, influential, significant, greater than earth-bound kings, as Timotheus is superior to the "Great" Alexander, whose name does not even appear in the text of this poem. We lean towards accepting and appreciating all that, only to find ourselves off-balance as the leader of leaders whom we admire becomes a vanquisher of victors (115), one who incites the very excesses of passion and uncivilized behavior that condemn the would-be heroes and should-be gods throughout *Fables*.

I think it significant that those critics who discuss the political ramifications of "Alexander's Feast" have difficulty dealing with this image of the power-mongering artist. Those who comment on the parallel between Alexander and William typically stop short of answering the next obvious question: who must be parallel with Timotheus? Even those who find that the poem expresses Dryden's deeply-felt personal values shy away from asking what character embodies those Drydenian values.[40] The one scholar who faces the identification head-on is Thomas H. Fujimura, who accepts Dryden's grandiose claims, and who suggests in a telling comment why it is so many readers are unable to do so: "Of course, it might be argued that Timotheus is irresponsible, and hence is not a wholly suitable analogue for Dryden" ("Personal Element," 1023). Precisely. Timotheus is an analogue, very suitable, even as he is unsuitable. Timotheus cuts both ways, offering a vital myth that has long been a part of Dryden's pantheon, and a dangerous power that Dryden himself warns us against when he refers to such enterprises as lying odes.

The vital myth cannot be reconciled to the lying ode, which is one of the reasons readers have had difficulty dealing with the Timotheus figure. Luckily, the poem heads toward a resolution that seems to offer an out. The unreconciled demands made upon us by the moral/immoral Timotheus, which accumulate and clash for six stanzas, push us all the more toward some resolution. We will find it in the divine Cecilia, for whom the poem is ostensibly written; after all, the full title is: "Alexander's Feast; or, the Power of Musique. An Ode, In Honour of St. Cecilia's Day," and Dryden or Tonson took care to emphasize the occasion by preceding the poem with a separate leaf that reads "Mr. Dryden's Ode in Honour of St. Cecilia's Day. 1697."[41] Furthermore, the running head reads "An Ode on St. *Cecilia*'s Day"; all the while that we are hearing of Timotheus and Alexander, Dryden is reminding us, page after page, that this poem belongs to somebody else.

The final stanza, then, marks the arrival of the anticipated heroine and promises the solution of all the problems surrounding Timotheus and his power:

> Thus, long ago
> 'Ere heaving Bellows learn'd to blow,
> While Organs yet were mute;
> *Timotheus*, to his breathing Flute,
> And sounding Lyre,

135

Cou'd swell the Soul to rage, or kindle soft Desire.
    At last Divine *Cecilia* came,
    Inventress of the Vocal Frame;
The sweet Enthusiast, from her Sacred Store,
    Enlarg'd the former narrow Bounds,
    And added Length to solemn Sounds,
With Nature's Mother-Wit, and Arts unknown before.
                    (155–66)

This seems to be the climax, where Dryden moves from Timotheus to Cecilia, and where all that Timotheus may lack is here provided by the saint, where all Timotheus represents will be transcended by the heroine of the poem, whose day the poem celebrates. Whether his power is good or bad no longer matters, for Cecilia is here with a more sublime power. The organ, Cecilia's invention, will replace flute and lyre; the sustained notes will outlast the lesser sounds of Timotheus' instruments and will enlarge the "narrow Bounds," both in the sense of enlarging the physical volume of sound itself, and in the sense of enlarging music of the passions by introducing material from the "Sacred Store." A music that is divine, that enlarges, is better than a narrowly bounded music that merely kindles rage or desire. Whatever the limitations of Timotheus as a power-mongering pagan, sacred Cecilia, like the parson and the fair maiden, offers a possible superior ideal; this poem moves toward a similar resolution, escaping from the pagan world where the flames of passion burn all too brightly, into a Christian transcendence in the figure of the saint for whom "Alexander's Feast" was written.[42]

And like the progression toward the parson and the fair maiden, the resolution does not stay long enough to displace uncertainties. What seems to be the climax, in the lines just quoted, is more than a climax, or less than a climax. It is another hinge-moment, fraught with the same difficulties we have encountered at other turning points. The "climax," begun above, continues into these lines, the final lines of the ode:

Let old *Timotheus* yield the Prize,
Or both divide the Crown;
He rais'd a Mortal to the Skies;
    She drew an Angel down.
                (167–70)

This is not the transcendence it seemed to be: no sooner does Timotheus yield the prize to Cecilia than he gets it back, in the next line. In a manner of speaking, Cecilia has been enthroned, then dethroned, made to share the crown with the myth-maker whose power she had just displaced. Her drawing an angel down from heaven is made equivalent to Timotheus' raising Alexander to "A present Deity" (35), and the poem ends with a resolution that dissolves, an upward movement that collapses. Like the upward movement of Sigismonda's character, which is undercut by the rest of her character, and the refining of Cymon, which Cymon himself undoes, here an enlargement of the powers of art from "the former narrow Bounds" is no sooner achieved than the narrow bounds make an immediate and unexpected comeback.

An anonymous reader of 1767 noted that "the great falling-off in the conclusion has been repeatedly observed and censured; the subject of it has no connection with the preceding part of the poem, and the quibble in the last four lines is puerile."[43] Whoever the reader is, his criticism attests to the poem's troublesome resolution; he is obviously persuaded that the poem ought to have a certain conclusion, one that Dryden refuses to give it, and, quite naturally, he censures Dryden for failing to wrap up things neatly (the same reader remarks that Dryden "has evidently counteracted his own design"). Samuel Johnson's better known reaction to the same passage illustrates the same thing, for Johnson too senses that the proper conclusion is transcendence, endorses that conclusion, and then gets irritated when it fails to occur:

> The conclusion is vicious: the musick of Timotheus, which "raised a mortal to the skies," had only a metaphorical power; that of Cecilia, which "drew an angel down," had a real effect; the crown therefore could not reasonably be divided.[44]

But the crown *is* divided, whether or not Johnson approves. Like Wordsworth, who could not accept his own image of the noble Sigismonda being degraded, moralist Johnson cannot accept the sacred Cecilia being made to share the throne. In both cases, the desire to find a satisfying resolution is sufficiently strong that Dryden is taken to task for not providing the fully noble Sigismonda or the fully triumphant Cecilia that these readers think the poems demand.[45]

What we have in Cecilia is another precious, sacred Christian ideal, as desirable as any of the ideal figures who, like the parson and the maiden, offer to enlarge our narrow store. And in Timotheus, we have a figure of awesome power subject to the same limitations, the same corruptibility that afflicts other partial heroes. Were Cecilia to replace Timotheus, it would reconcile the difficulties critics have experienced in dealing with the poet-rhetorician's too-much power, but this does not occur, as Dryden again does what he does with other informing ideals, civilizing virtues that *Fables* offers only to snatch back. It is not Dryden who is to be blamed that St. Cecilia, the pure parson, the purer maiden, all fail to transcend. They are the ideals Dryden affirms, ideals that offer to improve mankind's lot, but Dryden so qualifies what he offers that we find those ideals cannot be accommodated to the human condition. By implication, the ideals that should inspire are at best fragile, and the human condition falls short, as does the loving, regenerative, but too weak duchess, as does the strong, judicial, but too misogynistic Kinsman John Driden. Cecilia should march forward like Anne Killigrew, leading all poets and all mankind heavenward, banners unfurling—*that* was the Christian resolution Johnson so admired.[46] But it cannot happen here in the universe of *Fables*, where we no sooner ascend from the limitations of Timotheus than we return to Timotheus still, still on the throne, jostling with a sacred ideal that elicits our support but that cannot conquer. The difference here is that Dryden, by making his half-hero an artist, includes himself in this large canvas. We face the same problem in dealing with Dryden's alter ego as we face in dealing with noble Sigismonda, who is also all too human, heroic and yet blind to the baser desires that undercut her heroism. We face a similar problem when we encounter Cymon, who can be ennobled only so far before his own limitations overtake him and he falls back into Cymon still. Dryden's grandiose ideal of the power of the artist, which he wrote about, rejoiced in, celebrated throughout his career, is ultimately as imperfect, as limited as the best of his characters, who are also at times the worst of his characters.

It would be tedious to examine each of the tales, one by one, although other tales in the collection, including some of those already examined in previous chapters, would, I think, reveal similar hinge-moments. To take but one instance, consider the introductory poem, "To the Dutchess of Ormond," already discussed in relation to the next two tales ("Palamon and Arcite" and "To my Honour'd Kinsman") and in relation to the later portraits in *Fables* (the parson and the maiden); it too has a hinge-moment.[47] It is perhaps more accurate to say that it has a series of hinge-moments, beginning with a turning point discussed previously, where, after praising the duchess's efficacy in bringing a restoration to war-ravaged Ireland, Dryden drifts into a discussion of her illness, and in the process, withdraws what he offers. The mighty restorative force that Dryden has taken pains to amplify is not strong enough to bring about the restoration the poem celebrates; the Christlike redeemer of Ireland becomes too fragile to make the trip. Furthermore, what is ostensibly a panegyric has just turned into "Your Elegy, which now / Is offer'd for Your Health" (129–30). As the words "Elegy" and "Health" suggest, Dryden is about to shift again; he no sooner mentions that this poem could be an elegy than he pulls back, returning to praise of the physician, Morley, who has restored the duchess—praise that leads toward: "Bless'd be the Pow'r which has at once restor'd / The Hopes of lost Succession to Your Lord" (146–47).

From there, Dryden moves onward, and upward, to the finish, where he again celebrates the now-restored duchess as a mother who, by providing children, will guarantee the endurance of the Ormond line:

> The soft Recesses of Your Hours improve
> The Three fair Pledges of Your Happy Love:
> All other Parts of Pious Duty done,
> You owe your *Ormond* nothing but a Son:
> To fill in future Times his Father's Place,
> And wear the Garter of his Mother's Race.
> (163–68)

We move from images of strength to images of fragility, from a poem celebrating a triumph to a withdrawal of the triumph, which drifts toward elegy, which in turn swings back into an encomium for the Ormond family. However, in mentioning the next generation, the children who are to carry the Ormond name forward, Dryden also mentions the absence of a male heir to fill "his Father's Place." The second half of this poem is a continual flux between optimistic possibilities and pessimistic actualities, and the potential resolutions prove to be as temporary, as fragile, as the duchess's health, as unfulfilled as her restorative trip to that "Vanquish'd Isle" (96), as incomplete as the son who is to continue the Ormond name but who does not exist.

Not all of the tales, of course, work in this fashion, pushing in opposite directions. At times, as we have seen, a tale does indeed head toward a clear, unambiguous resolution. Dryden's translation of "The Knight's Tale" presents such an example; it posits two different attitudes toward love, and ends with Palamon, who embodies love's generative capacities, in a stable social form (married happily ever after), confirmed and protected by the enlarged Theseus who has grown from conqueror to magnanimous king. Arcite and his principles do not make an unexpected comeback, nor does the renewed Theseus find himself sharing the throne with a figure who would call his whole order into question. Yet, as I have tried to demonstrate by grouping this tale with "To the Duchess of Ormond" and "To my Honour'd Kinsman," Dryden's version of "The Knight's Tale" is modified by other tales, continually modified, right up through the end of *Fables*. Whatever force the ideal may have has to be called into question when we finally meet Cymon, who begins by confirming Palamon's principles of generative love, and yet ends up an Arcite, for whom love means war, joining forces with an equally vicious public figure. Within "Palamon and Arcite" things resolve, turning points turn, although across the tales one discovers that Arcite's ways return, and the magnanimous Theseus must yield a share of the throne to the corrupt magistrate, Lysymachus, who demonstrates how cruelly the privileged great behave. In the same manner, the tale of Baucis and Philemon establishes without subversion or ambiguity a domestic ideal of strength arising from conjugal fidelity; the qualification occurs when this tale is viewed alongside the portrait of the kinsman, whose strength is based upon misogyny, or that of the parson, whose strength is based upon his Christian celibacy.

Either way, whether we begin with extensive view surveying the whole terrain, or limit our attention to a smaller patch of ground, we find the land shifting and the footing uncertain. Dryden can endorse values that emerge within a tale or group of tales—an ideal of Christian devotion, or of conjugal love, or of unselfish public service—only to subvert, qualify, or challenge that ideal somewhere else, and Dryden can as easily within a specific tale endorse a character—a heroic Sigismonda, an improved Cymon, a sacred Cecilia—only to undercut or dethrone the ideal the character embodies in the same tale that establishes that ideal in the first place. Moreover, upon discovering that the Christian Cecilia does not quite replace the powerful but inferior pagan rhetorician, that the noble Sigismonda does not quite replace the ignoble Sigismonda, we are naturally tempted to search further among other tales to find whether the heroic potential that Sigismonda represents is confirmed, or denied, elsewhere, whether the sacred Cecilia will ever sit comfortably on that throne. Thus, the individual tales that pull us toward, and away from, clear resolutions also push us centrifugally outward to other tales, which, I think, is one of the reasons appreciative readers often describe *Fables* as comprehensive or capacious. In the universe of *Fables*, Dryden continually invites us to search beyond our powers to know.

NOTES

1. Jay Arnold Levine, in "John Dryden's Epistle to John Driden," *Journal of English and Germanic Philology* 63 (1964): 450–74, considers the poem in the light of English history, of biblical traditions, of classical traditions, of Dryden's dramatic works—considers the poem in many important contexts, but not in the context of the rest of *Fables*. Levine's analysis is supplemented both by J. Douglas Canfield's "The Image of the Circle in Dryden's 'To My Honour'd Kinsman,'" *Papers on Language and Literature* 11 (1975): 168–76, which explores a central image, and by Elizabeth Duthie's "'A Memorial of My Own Principles': Dryden's 'To My Honour'd Kinsman,'" *ELH* 47 (1980): 682–704, which provides more historical and biographical background. Neither scholar treats the tale in the context of the rest of *Fables*. Similarly, "Alexander's Feast" has been treated as commentary on music by James Kinsley in "Dryden and the *Encomium Musicae*," *Review of English Studies* 4 (1953): 263–67, and by Dean T. Mace in "Musical Humanism, the Doctrine of Rhythmus, and the Saint Cecilia Odes of Dryden," *Journal of the Warburg and Courtauld Institutes* 27 (1964): 251–92; as political poem by Bessie Proffitt in "Political Satire in Dryden's *Alexander's Feast*," *Texas Studies in Language and Literature* 11 (1970): 1307–16; as personal revelation by Thomas H. Fujimura in "The Personal Element in Dryden's Poetry," *PMLA* 89 (1974): 1007–23; and as ironic debunking of the "whole mode of baroque glorification" (39) by Robert P. Maccubbin in "The Ironies of Dryden's 'Alexander's Feast; or The Power of Musique': Text and Contexts," *Mosaic* 18, no. 4 (1985): 33–47.

2. See particularly William Frost, *Dryden and the Art of Translation* (1955; rpt. Hamden, CT: Archon Books, 1969); Anne Middleton, "The Modern Art of Fortifying: *Palamon and Arcite* as Epicurean Epic," *Chaucer Review* 3 (1968): 124–43; William Frost, "Dryden's Versions of Ovid," *Comparative Literature* 3 (1974): 193–202; Tom Mason, "Dryden's Version of the *Wife of Bath's Tale*," *Cambridge Quarterly* 6 (1975): 240–56; D. W. Hopkins, "Dryden's 'Baucis and Philemon,'" *Comparative Literature* 28 (1976): 135–43. These are all comparative studies emphasizing differences in viewpoint, oftentimes to the detriment of Dryden. Other comparative studies concern themselves with what makes the translations distinctly Dryden's, especially Earl Miner, "Chaucer in Dryden's *Fables*," from *Studies in Criticism and Aesthetics, 1660–1800: Essays in Honor of*

Turning Points

Samuel Holt Monk, ed. Howard Anderson and John S. Shea (Minneapolis: University of Minnesota Press, 1967), 58–72; Judith Sloman, "Dryden's Originality in *Sigismonda and Guiscardo*," *Studies in English Literature* 12 (1972): 445–57; J. Peter Verdurmen, "Dryden's Cymon and Iphigenia at Century's End: Ploughshares into Swords," *Revue des langues vivantes* 44 (1978): 285–300; and Emrys Jones, "Dryden's Sigismonda," from *English Renaissance Studies: Essays Presented to Dame Helen Gardner in Honour of Her Seventieth Birthday*, ed. John Carey (Oxford: Clarendon Press, 1980), 279–90.

3. The best discussion of Dryden's treatment of the woman of passion, which includes Sigismonda, is that of Jean H. Hagstrum in Chapter 3, "John Dryden: Sensual, Heroic, and 'Pathetic' Love," from *Sex and Sensibility: Ideal and Erotic Love from Milton to Mozart* (Chicago: University of Chicago Press, 1980), 50–71. See also Judith Sloman's *Dryden: The Poetics of Translation* (Toronto: University of Toronto Press, 1985), 141–44, for a suggestive comparison of Sigismonda with Dryden's version of Dido from his translation of the *Aeneid*.

4. According to Kinsley, "Dryden seems to have had before him not only an Italian text, but also the anonymous English version (1620) made partly from the Italian and partly from Antoine le Maçon's French translation of the *Decameron* (1545), and William Chamberlayne's *Pharonnida: A Heroick Poem* (1659), which contains an episode based on Boccaccio's tale" (Kinsley, 4:2072). I have followed Dryden with similar sources in hand, using the 1620 translation, now thought to be by John Florio, from *The Decameron, Preserved to Posterity by Giovanni Boccaccio and Translated into English Anno 1620*, intro. by Edward Hutton, 4 vols. (1909; rpt. New York: AMS Press, 1967). The text for Chamberlayne's "Pharonnida" is quoted from *Minor Poets of the Caroline Period*, ed. George Saintsbury, vol. 1 (1905; rpt. Oxford: Clarendon Press, 1968). For the Italian text, references are to *Giovanni Boccaccio: Decameron, Filocolo, Ameto, Fiammetta*, ed. Enricho Bianchi, Carlo Salinari, and Natalino Sapegno (Milan: Riccardo Ricciardi Editore, [1952]); in presenting a modern translation, I rely on that of *The Decameron*, trans. G. H. McWilliam (1972; rpt. Harmondsworth, England: Penguin Books, 1980).

5. Although this passage has no precedent either in Boccaccio or in the Florio translation, there is a clear precedent in one of Dryden's sources, William Chamberlayne's "Pharonnida" (1659), which contains a long and muddled story of Pharonnida, her lover Argalia, and her father, who disapproves of the match and tries, unsuccessfully, to have Argalia killed. That much of the story is similar to "Sigismonda and Guiscardo," as is the father's speech violently disapproving of Argalia, and Pharonnida's firm response wherein she defends her love. There is no cave where the lovers meet, but later on, the father imprisons his daughter in a tower whose original purpose sounds familiar:

> Seated did lie,
> Within the circuit of Gerenza's wall,
> Though stretched to embrace, a castle, which they call
> The prince's tower—a place whose strength had stood
> Unshook with danger.—When that violent flood
> Of war raged in the land hither were brought

Such, if of noble blood, whose greatness sought
From treacherous plots extension . . .
(3.2.496–503)

6. In Boccaccio, Tancredi is a benevolent ruler, "se egli nello amoroso sangue nella sua vecchiezza non s'avesse le mani bruttate" (*Decameron*, 283)—"except for the fact that in his old age he sullied his hands with the blood of passion" (McWilliam, 332), which Dryden renders as "dipp'd his Hands in Lovers Blood" (6). Boccaccio's Tancredi, however, is not called a tyrant.

7. In the original, "insieme maravigliosa festa si fecero; e nella sua camera insieme venutine, con grandissimo piacere gran parte di quel giorno si dimorarono" (*Decameron*, 284–85).

8. What I have argued to be the case with Dryden's translation of Boccaccio, compared to Florio's translation, Jean H. Hagstrum in *Sex and Sensuality* finds true of Dryden's general treatment of Ovid and of Virgil as well: "If Dryden's sexualization of the decorous Virgil . . . does not surprise, perhaps his intensification of Ovid's already assertive sexuality will. Just as the pagan love poet was more specifically erotic than his Latin predecessors, so Dryden surpassed in sexual meaning earlier English translators, reversing the tendency to tone down the ancient to please modern Christian taste" (52).

9. "E andatisene in su 'l letto, come usati erano, e insieme scherzando e sollazzandosi, avvene che Tancredi si svegliò, e sentì e vide ciò che Guiscardo e la figliuola facevano" (*Decameron*, 285).

10. Boccaccio's Ghismonda falls madly in love, but without the fire imagery, which Florio adds to his translation of the passage: "her affections being but a glowing sparke at the first, grew like a Bavin to take flame" (Florio, 2:143). This may be the source for Dryden's "raging Fire that burn'd within her Breast" (58), but Dryden adds more, thereby considerably fanning the flames: "as the Fire will force its outward way, / Or, in the Prison pent, consume the Prey; / So long her earnest Eyes on his were set" (61–63).

11. Letter to Sir Walter Scott, 7 November 1805, quoted in *Dryden: The Critical Heritage*, ed. James Kinsley and Helen Kinsley (London: Routledge & Kegan Paul, 1971), 323–25. The only other specific Dryden works that Wordsworth mentions, interestingly enough, are other tales from *Fables*, which suggests its central position in Dryden's canon back in the nineteenth century.

12. "It may be doubted, however, whether the simplicity of Boccacio's [*sic*] narrative has not sometimes suffered by the additional decorations of Dryden. The retort of Guiscard to Tancred's charge of ingratitude is more sublime in the Italian original, than as diluted by the English poet into five hexameters [Wordsworth made the same point in his letter to Scott]. A worse fault occurs in the whole colouring of Sigismonda's passion, to which Dryden has given a coarse and indelicate character, which he did not derive from Boccacio." Quoted from Walter Scott, *The Life of John Dryden*, ed. Bernard Kreissman (Lincoln: University of Nebraska Press, 1963), 422. This was originally published in 1808 as the first volume in Scott's edition of Dryden's *Works*; Kreissman's edition is a photo-reproduction of the 1834 text, edited by John Lockhart.

13. Mark Van Doren, *The Poetry of John Dryden* (1920); rev. and retitled

John Dryden: A Study of His Poetry (1946; rpt. Bloomington: Indiana University Press, 1963), 229. Emrys Jones remarks that the marriage scene has been made into a "leering intrusion" by a "whole tradition of criticism" ("Dryden's Sigismonda," 286–87); he quotes Wordsworth and Mark Van Doren, and adds C. S. Lewis into the bargain.

14. Judith Sloman, whose argument I am here summarizing, rejects Sigismonda's nobility because, "in spite of her claims to spiritual grandeur, she has acted all along to satisfy her passions" ("Dryden's Originality," 448). Sloman reconciles the disjunction between claims and actions by resorting to "the irony in the poem," which "lies not just in the fact that these characters are moved by lust, but in the way their efforts at nobility are undercut by their limited knowledge" (451). However, earlier in the same article, Sloman pays tribute to Sigismonda, remarking on her defense of freedom in the face of tyrannical authority, and even justifying her taking the initiative with Guiscardo as an act appropriate to "a person conscious of his or her greatness of soul" (447). Sloman's own positive response to Sigismonda's claims suggests that the irony she here ascribes to Dryden does not work.

15. This is essentially Emrys Jones's argument in "Dryden's Sigismonda." Instead of seeing a clash between fraudulent claims on the one hand and solid reality on the other, Jones regards the character as being divided between two contradictory but equally persuasive motivations, "an aspiration to the noble and magnanimous on the one hand, and on the other a frank, and to many readers disconcerting, delight in coarseness and indecency" (279). Jones reconciles the two in favor of the nobler character, calling this tale an "undoubted success" (279) in the heroic vein.

16. For Judith Sloman, Sigismonda's limitations occur because she is not a Christian. Speaking more generally in "An Interpretation of Dryden's *Fables*," *Eighteenth-Century Studies* 4 (1970/71): 199–211, Sloman maintains that "most of the characters in *Fables*" act "without benefit of divine truth as revealed in Christ's lifetime," but instead act "within a framework of limited truth and passionate response" (200). However, in *Dryden: The Poetics* (especially 141–44), Sloman seems to have shifted toward my own argument, for here she treats this "ambiguous character" (141) more in terms of unresolved opposites, describing the heroine as "a genuine attack on tyranny," who is also "flawed by the dubious impulses that afflict everyone" (143).

17. Other critics who comment on the two sides of Sigismonda include Jean H. Hagstrum in *Sex and Sensibility* and Rachel Trickett in *The Honest Muse: A Study in Augustan Verse* (Oxford: Clarendon Press, 1967). Hagstrum accepts the coexistence of "unabashed sexuality" and "love heroism" (54) as simply a part of Dryden's sensibility, as does Trickett, although Trickett's commentary is diluted Wordsworth; she mentions "Dryden's insensitivity to all but the sensual aspect of love" (70), and, although she does not use the term "gross errors," she blames Dryden for not having a mind sensitive and subtle enough "to reconcile these views of human nature" (71).

18. William Myers, in *Dryden* (London: Hutchinson, 1973), neatly summarizes the effect of the last tale: "But the idealism, the simple loyalty to principle which Dryden has consistently asserted through all the urbanely shifting in-

stabilities of the *Fables*, is finally qualified by this wise, sad, and uncensorious recognition that the sweetness and nobility of natural humanity will always be soiled by the inevitably unprincipled compromises of human life" (189–90). See also my own Chapter 4 (note 6) for Judith Sloman's account of how this final tale undoes the very progression for which she had earlier argued.

19. One commentator who does not search for ideals is J. Peter Verdurmen, who argues for Dryden's increasing anti-heroism toward the end of his career; for Verdurmen, "Cymon and Iphigenia" is an epitome of the anti-heroic, wherein Dryden "gave final form to his rejection of heroic possibilities" ("Dryden's Cymon," 286).

20. Earl Miner, in *Dryden's Poetry* (Bloomington: Indiana University Press, 1967), refers to these as "partial answers" (308).

21. Even to those like Earl Miner, who see comprehensiveness, capaciousness, and variety as virtues in *Fables*, the last tale comes as an inconvenient surprise. In *The Restoration Mode from Milton to Dryden* (Princeton: Princeton University Press, 1974), Miner searches for a lesson in the last fable: "If most of us, and indeed the race itself, cannot subsist on charity and celibacy or chastity, we must expect to enact a comedy with such dark shadows and fervently hope to share in the Parson's text, 'Eternal Mercy'" (553). One can, I think, sense a tension here between Miner's critical commitment and his response to the poem: he seems reluctant to part with the Christian parson, the fair maiden, and the values they represent, even though he recognizes that the last tale returns from the heavenly characters to solid, unidealized, and blood-spattered earth.

22. A recurrent Miner observation: *Dryden's Poetry* (319); "Forms and Motives" (263); *Restoration Mode* (457).

23. "Bestione" (*Decameron*, 354), which Florio translates as "Sot or Foole" (3:4), McWilliam as "simpleton" (406).

24. To use John Hollander's apt term, from *The Untuning of the Sky: Ideas of Music in English Poetry, 1550–1700* (1961; rpt. New York: W. W. Norton, 1970), 412.

25. In the original, "Cimone adunque, quantunque, amando Efigenìa, in alcune cose, sì come i giovani amanti molto spesso fanno, trasandasse" (*Decameron*, 357), which McWilliam translates as "Although, in common with many another young man in love, Cymon was inclined in some ways to carry his love for Iphigenia to extremes" (409). Florio, one of Dryden's sources, renders this as Cymon "failed in some particular things" (3:7). These understatements become, in Dryden, "too much Fire," "excess of Passion," and "Flames too fierce," which are reminiscent of the imagery in a line added to the portrait of Sigismonda, where Dryden describes her interest in Guiscardo as "The raging Fire that burn'd within her Breast" (58).

26. I think it significant to note that, as was the case with "Sigismonda and Guiscardo," some readers, pushing toward a resolution, avoid the problem by choosing one Cymon over the other. Thus, J. Peter Verdurmen, who writes of Dryden's anti-heroism (in "Dryden's Cymon and Iphigenia"), finds that the final Cymon obliterates the refined one, who is primarily there to be toppled, whereas Mark Van Doren praises the ennobled Cymon, as if the degraded one did not exist: "No one remembers the last two-thirds of the poem," says Van Doren,

"but the first hundred and fifty-seven lines are classic" (*Dryden: A Study*, 231). I find it somewhat difficult to accept a reading that relies upon ignoring two-thirds of a poem.

27. John Dawson Carl Buck, in "The Ascetic's Banquet: The Morality of *Alexander's Feast*," *Texas Studies in Literature and Language* 17 (1975): 573–89, refers to this opening scene as "a tableau of unredeemed classical heroism and the sexual rewards appropriate to that heroism" (578).

28. Those dealing with the issue of music in "Alexander's Feast" include: James Kinsley, "Dryden and the *Encomium Musicae*"; Dean T. Mace, "Musical Humanism"; John Hollander, *The Untuning of the Sky*; and Mace again in "A Reply to Mr. H. Neville Davies's 'Dryden and Vossius: A Reconsideration,'" *Journal of the Warburg and Courtauld Institutes* 29 (1966): 296–310.

29. I have dealt with these alter egos and with the way Dryden treats the subject of the poet's power elsewhere, in "Dryden's 'Essay of Dramatick Poesie': The Poet and the World of Affairs," *Studies in English Literature* 22 (1982): 375–93.

30. Robert P. Maccubbin also makes this point in "Ironies" (40).

31. As Thomas H. Fujimura argues in "Personal Element" (especially 1019–22).

32. The source of this information is Dryden's letter to his sons, in which he explains: "I am writeing a Song for St Cecilia's feast, who you know is the Patroness of Musique. This is troublesome, & no way beneficiall: but I coud not deny the Stewards of the feast, who came in a body to me, to desire that kindness" (#47, which Ward dates 3 September 1697, *Letters*, p. 93). Dryden's complaint may be nothing more than an automatic admission of authorial weariness—after all, he perpetually referred to his writing of *Fables* as drudgery. Within a few months, Dryden's attitude toward "Alexander's Feast" demonstrates that the poem was, indeed, beneficial to him: "I am glad to heare from all Hands," Dryden writes to Tonson, "that my Ode is esteemd the best of all my poetry, by all the Town" (#50, December 1697, *Letters*, p. 98). As troublesome as he might have found the task when he accepted the assignment, his subsequent appreciation of the poem, and his decision to reprint it in *Fables*, implies that he may have warmed to the task once he got started, and that he was certainly pleased with it once he had finished.

33. Earl Miner, in *Dryden's Poetry*, remarks that "the governing subject of the poem . . . is the superiority of the artist to the man of action" (267). Similarly, Fujimura maintains that "the major theme" is "the primacy of the artist over the political-military leader" ("Personal Element," 1020). And Judith Sloman, speaking of Timotheus as well as other artist figures, remarks that "Dryden's artist-heroes have supreme control over their art, and through their art over the more conventional figures of power, kings and men of action" (*Dryden: The Poetics*, 220).

34. The parallels are not exact, nor would it be any advantage to Dryden, who was under constant suspicion as a Catholic and Jacobite, to wrench historical fact into overly precise parallels; that would only make the political commentary dangerously overt. However, there *are* parallels, and Dryden manages to use them to make his point safely, by innuendo. One notices, for instance, that Virgil depicts Augustus in the character of Aeneas, and Dryden's description of that par-

allel makes it clear that Aeneas is also a William figure. Aeneas was not Priam's heir, and thus not "in a Lineal Succession" (Kinsley, 3:1016). For a fortuitous near parallel, consider Dryden's comment that "*Æneas*, tho' he Married the Heiress of the Crown, yet claim'd no Title to it during the Life of his Father-in-Law" (Kinsley, 3:1017). This makes Aeneas like William in his claims upon the throne; yet in his reluctance to pursue those claims while his father-in-law (Latinus) is still alive, Aeneas is superior to William, who sits on the throne while *his* father-in-law (James II) is on the run. For other parallels, see Thomas H. Fujimura, "Dryden's Virgil: Translation as Autobiography," *Studies in Philology* 80 (1983): 67–83. Judith Sloman, who regards Dryden's Virgil as "a device to analyze his own situation as a writer forced to live under an alien, but not hopelessly oppressive government" (*Dryden: The Poetics*, 36), also examines parallels (especially 125–46).

35. As Thomas H. Fujimura puts it, "the dedication of the *Aeneid* suggests a parallel between Dryden and Virgil, and an analogy is established between Virgil-Augustus and Dryden-William III" ("Personal Element," 1019–20). One might also note that the plates for the *Aeneid* depict Aeneas with William's hooked, Hanoverian nose, presumably Tonson's idea, done without Dryden's approval, but a clear indication that the audience would have been alert to the political parallels (*Life*, 289). Steven N. Zwicker, in *Politics and Language in Dryden's Poetry: The Arts of Disguise* (Princeton: Princeton University Press, 1984), also examines the parallels between Virgil and Dryden (177–205), although Howard D. Weinbrot's review of this book, in "Recent Studies in the Restoration and Eighteenth Century," *Studies in English Literature* 25 (1985): 671–710, takes Zwicker to task for this identification, remarking that the parallels do not work out consistently (see especially 687–89). I think Weinbrot is demanding too much precision, leaving too little room for the kind of innuendo Dryden habitually employed.

36. We find the same sort of political innuendo directed at William III in other late Dryden poems, such as those to Congreve (1694) and Kneller (1694), both of which will be discussed in Chapter 7. On "Alexander's Feast," Robert P. Maccubbin accumulates evidence from history, theories of music, classical lore about Alexander, art, other St. Cecilia's Day odes, all of which support a reading of the poem as "an allusive soured statement on the militarism of King William," ("Ironies," 37). Then, curiously, Maccubbin retreats, finding the poem too ambiguous for the imposition of "an allegorical politic" (39) he has just made seem inescapable. I am persuaded by Maccubbin's evidence, even though Maccubbin apparently is not.

37. It is the authoritative voice of the poet that, though it may sound extravagant to a modern reader, is a vital part of what Earl Miner, in *The Restoration Mode*, calls the public mode: "Men had been taught to listen to other men out of a conviction that what was said mattered. . . . Above all, knowing that they would be attended to, poets could assert *themselves* before others" (14–15).

38. Whereas Fujimura accepts Timotheus as the voice of Dryden, Buck, in "The Ascetic's Banquet," regards Timotheus as vicious, an object of Dryden's criticism. I think both Fujimura and Buck are right; I would argue that their "disagreement" reflects the basic irreconcilability of the vital and vicious powers of Timotheus.

39. Robert P. Maccubbin, in "Ironies," presents a wealth of evidence demonstrating how often the image of Alexander was used, in poetry, prose, and even the visual arts.

40. Alan Roper, in *Dryden's Poetic Kingdoms* (London: Routledge & Kegan Paul, 1965), notes the parallels between Alexander and William but does not discuss who must be parallel with Timotheus (8–9, 13, 18). Similarly, Earl Miner, in *Dryden's Poetry*, goes as far as to say that *"Alexander's Feast* is one of the several symptoms of Dryden's assertions of his own values, of the dignity of his art, and of his personal integrity during the years after the Revolution which had brought William and Mary (unlawfully in his view) to the throne" (273), but he does not consider which character in the poem asserts those values. Bessie Proffitt, in "Political Satire," seems to get closer to the issue, for she gives the most complete account of the poem as a "well-hidden attack upon William III"; however, she too omits examining the significance of the presumably too well-hidden figure who launches the attack (1307–16). Proffitt does suggest, tentatively, that Timotheus may symbolize Parliament, which to me seems a far-fetched possibility (1315). Robert P. Maccubbin, in "Ironies," gets closer still; he recognizes parallels between Alexander's bard and the poet laureate (any poet laureate? the former poet laureate?), but then immediately drops the issue. Judith Sloman, in *Dryden: The Poetics*, acknowledges that "Timotheus is another of Dryden's masks" (201), at one point referring to him as one of several "idealized images of Dryden himself" (220), but she then pulls back, perhaps because of her simultaneous awareness that Timotheus' "cheerfully amoral art provokes Alexander into behaving ridiculously and at last dangerously" (201). It would seem that criticism is just on the verge of identifying Timotheus with Dryden, and yet the closer the critic gets to the edge, the more sharply he or she pulls back.

41. I am quoting the titles from a first edition of *Fables* (1700), 409, 407. All the tales in *Fables* (1700) feature a separate title leaf; the full title is then repeated above the opening lines of each poem.

42. As Judith Sloman puts it, St. Cecilia "displaces, though only at the very end, the pagan musician Timotheus" (*Dryden: The Poetics*, 201). On the other hand, John Dawson Carl Buck, in "The Ascetic's Banquet," argues that Dryden is here criticizing and limiting Cecilia; "sacred" may mean "accursed," if one takes it ironically, and there may be nothing at all sweet in her being an Enthusiast, since Dryden usually used that word with contempt, e.g., in "Absalom and Achitophel" where Dryden denounces the "old Enthusiastick breed" which "'Gainst Form and Order . . . their Power employ" (529–30). I think Buck, recognizing that Cecilia does not ultimately replace Timotheus, rejects the praise of this saint for the sake of consistency, and by so doing, discounts the process whereby Cecilia is first praised, looks transcendent, and *then* fails to transcend.

43. Quoted by Robert Manson Myers, *Handel, Dryden, and Milton* (London: Bowes & Bowes, 1956), 39.

44. Samuel Johnson, "Dryden," from *Lives of the English Poets*, ed. George Birkbeck Hill, 3 vols. (Oxford: Clarendon Press, 1905), 1:457. See also Walter Scott: "It is true, that the praise of St Cecilia is rather abruptly introduced as a conclusion to the account of the Feast of Alexander" (*The Life of Dryden*, 416). John Dawson Carl Buck seems to echo these earlier views of the poem's great falling off: Buck maintains that "the poem was written against the kind of emo-

tional persuasion employed by Timotheus, and even St. Cecilia herself does not provide an adequate model of the kind of asceticism which Dryden wanted to enforce in his world" ("Ascetic's Banquet," 577). Similarly, Robert P. Maccubbin in "Ironies" wants Cecilia and Christianity to win, so much so that after admitting the lack of transcendence in the "undramatic . . . and seemingly irrelevant" (43) seventh stanza, and after stating that "mere division of honors [between Timotheus and Cecilia] would seem to prevent a thoroughly Christian reading of the concluding stanza" (44), Maccubbin reverses field, dismisses his own response as "mere paradox," and claims that "Dryden's point is that Christianity builds upon, but grows out of and improves upon, the pagan world" (44).

45. Modern critics also comment on the hinge-moment, sometimes explaining Cecilia's not-quite transcendence in ways more flattering to Dryden. Bessie Proffitt, in "Political Satire," claims that "the allusion to St. Cecilia was a necessary feature of the genre within which Dryden was working" (1315), which is also what John Hollander maintains in *The Untuning of the Sky* (396). The evidence supporting this is solid, for other authors of both the official and unofficial Cecilia odes, like Christopher Fishburn, Thomas Fletcher, Shadwell, Samuel Wesley, Thomas Durfey, Nicholas Brady, Addison, Theophilus Parsons, and Thomas Yalden, do indeed allude to St. Cecilia. See William Henry Husk's *An Account of the Musical Celebrations of St. Cecilia's Day* (London: Bell & Daldy, 1857). Unlike the anonymous critic of 1767, Samuel Johnson, and Robert P. Maccubbin, who all side with Cecilia, Proffitt and Hollander are merely siding with Timotheus, accepting his victory.

46. Johnson's high praise of the Killigrew ode in his "Life of Dryden" accords with his censorious attitude toward the conclusion of "Alexander's Feast." Anne Killigrew achieved what Cecilia failed to achieve.

47. For a fuller account of the poem, which I am here summarizing, see my article, "Dryden's Final Poetic Mode: 'To the Dutchess of Ormond' and *Fables*," *The Eighteenth-Century: Theory and Interpretation* 26 (1985): 3–21.

Chapter Six

PHILOSOPHIES OF CHANGE

*I*N HIS analysis of Ovid's *Metamorphoses*, Brooks Otis finds the speech of Pythagoras in book fifteen pivotal and especially revelatory, for Ovid uses it to suggest an "underlying plan or principle of arrangement." The metamorphoses depicted through myth and fable are here supported and explained by a Philosophy of Change, a construct that can "harmonize the apparently contradictory elements of variety and continuity."[1] Thus, Pythagoras' speech, using "the language of science and philosophy" (302) rather than the language of fiction, "embraces the entirety of Ovid's *carmen perpetuum* and represents metamorphosis as the universal key to the secrets of both nature and history" (297–98). Similarly, Charles Muscatine, in dealing with Chaucer, regards "The Nun's Priest's Tale" as a key, although a key of a different shape. In his classic study, *Chaucer and the French Tradition*, Muscatine saves this "supremely Chaucerian" tale until last for it "fittingly serves to cap all of Chaucer's poetry" (243), not because it provides an underlying plan, but rather because it undermines apparent plans: "it offers no conclusion but that sublunary values are comically unstable" (242).[2] That is, this tale demonstrates that the issues and values resonating throughout Chaucer are finally subject to change, which is precisely what Pythagoras' philosophy is all about: "And therefore I conclude, whatever lies / In Earth, or flits in Air, or fills the Skies, / All suffer change" (670–72). Even conclusions.

Dryden's anthology, which leans heavily on Ovid (eight tales) and Chaucer (five tales, counting the pseudo-Chaucerian "Flower and the Leaf"), includes both these tales, and one wonders whether Dryden, ever appreciative of his literary predecessors, might have selected these tales for the same reasons that Otis and Muscatine find them appealing and unusually relevant. They serve as enriching commentary not only on

Ovid and Chaucer, but also on the amalgamated *Fables*, and they appear in strategic places. "The Nun's Priest's Tale," retitled "The Cock and the Fox," occurs right in the middle of *Fables*, the tenth tale of twenty-one; "Of the Pythagorean Philosophy" appears toward the end as a final explanation of the universe, a philosophy that counterbalances the Boethian First Mover speech of Theseus at the beginning. Each tale can be taken as a kind of pause, "The Cock and the Fox" a resting place after the heady business of "The First Book of Homer's Ilias," a descent from the heavens, where the king and queen of the gods have been arguing, to a simple widow's humble homestead, where wife and husband chicken are squabbling. "Of the Pythagorean Philosophy," by being essentially a long, rambling set speech, stops the narrative action of *Fables*, which returns (after the two brief characters of the parson and the maiden) with the action-packed "Cymon and Iphigenia" that both recapitulates a host of motifs, and serves as a coda. It is not position alone that calls attention to these tales, but something also in their nature. However they may serve to change the scene or the pace, they also reach out in every direction; in "The Cock and the Fox" and "Of the Pythagorean Philosophy," scarcely an issue arises, scarcely a character appears, but the echoes abound, and the lofty hills in the landscape of *Fables* resound.

I save consideration of these two tales until this point *not* because I think these are, at long last, the truly central tales; what is central depends on where one chooses to stand and how one chooses to center things. Already, I have discussed various possible interpretations of *Fables* based on "key" tales, or groupings of tales, in an effort to illustrate how variable are the possible keys, and how various the results. Rather, it seems to me that these two tales belong to all groupings; since they are especially dependent on the rest of the anthology, they may prove to be more illuminating now that we have spent some time exploring the surrounding terrain.

THE COCK AND THE FOX

As one might expect from a beast fable, "The Nun's Priest's Tale" parodies and punctures virtually everything. What is remarkable is how well Chaucer's tale serves to summarize and undercut Dryden's collection, sometimes when translated "straight," as is the case when the whole barnyard community shrieks in terror at the capture of Chanticleer:

> Not louder Cries when *Ilium* was in Flames,
> Were sent to Heav'n by woful *Trojan* Dames,
> When *Pyrrhus* toss'd on high his burnish'd Blade,
> And offer'd *Priam* to his Father's Shade,
> Than for the Cock the widow'd Poultry made.
>
> (699–703)

The mock-epic parallels continue, with Dryden using all of Chaucer's Trojan and Roman counterparts of the agitated fowl, including the wife of *Asdrubal*, whose husband was killed by Scipio, and the matrons who "Shriek'd for the downfal in a doleful Cry" (714) when Nero burned Rome. In *Fables*, this is the comic version, or inversion, of all those distraught, high-strung heroines, from the centaur Hylonome, who "fills the Fields with undistinguish'd Cries" (569) for her dying lover, to the sentimentally suffering Sigismonda, who frets little but suffers nobly, to Alcyone, who "loudly shrieks, / ... cries, and tears her Cheeks" (464–65) when her husband drowns, to Althea, who rends the air, and herself, over the death of her son (whom she has just killed). If parts of Sigismonda's story give us a perspective that allows us to question the validity of her noble suffering for the murder of her lover, then here our perspective above the distracted fowls teases us into a different response, inviting us to smile at what, from a closer viewpoint, with a human cast of characters, we find serious and perhaps moving.

Although Dryden can often achieve this effect by allowing Chaucer to do it for him, there are other times when Dryden adds a bit, especially when he sees a golden opportunity, as is the case when he is describing Chanticleer's polygamy. In Chaucer, we discover that

> This gentil cok hadde in his governaunce
> Sevene hennes for to doon al his plesaunce,
> Whiche were his sustres and his paramours,
> And wonder lyk to hym as of colours.
>
> (2865–68)

What in Chaucer is incidental incest becomes in Dryden an issue filled with political connotations:

> This gentle Cock for solace of his Life,
> Six Misses had beside his lawful Wife;
> Scandal that spares no King, tho' ne'er so good,
> Says, they were all of his own Flesh and Blood:
> His Sisters both by Sire, and Mother's side,
> And sure their likeness show'd them near ally'd.

But make the worst, the Monarch did no more,
Than all the *Ptolomeys* had done before:
When Incest is for Int'rest of a Nation,
'Tis made no Sin by Holy Dispensation.
(55–64)

It has not been long since we heard Myrrha arguing for the naturalness
of incest, pointing to animals who do it all the time:

But is it Sin? Or makes my Mind alone
Th' imagin'd Sin? For Nature makes it none.
What Tyrant then these envious Laws began,
Made not for any other Beast, but Man!
The Father-Bull his Daughter may bestride,
The Horse may make his Mother-Mare a Bride;
What Piety forbids the lusty Ram
Or more salacious Goat, to rut their Dam?
The Hen is free to wed the Chick she bore,
And make a Husband, whom she hatch'd before.
("Cinyras and Myrrha," 39–48)

Our answer to her first question—is this a sin?—is likely to be yes, since
her unfortunately graphic references to bulls bestriding their daughters
and salacious goats rutting their dams do not exactly ennoble her passion
for father. But when another version of the argument appears in the very
barnyard where hens *do* wed their chicks—Dryden heightens the echo
by turning Ovid's "ales," that is, birds in general, to hen and chick—we
discover that what was a crime in Myrrha's tale is perfectly natural here,
which, of course, is Myrrha's argument, except it no longer sounds
shocking. When Myrrha attempts to justify incest, it is easy to reject her
argument on the basis of our belief in the hierarchical distinction between animals and man; her method of alternating imagery of bestial
corruption with such civilized concepts as "Laws," "Piety," "Bride,"
"Husband," emphasizes that gap, a gap she unsuccessfully tries to
bridge.[3] Yet the comic version of her argument attempts to build the
same bridge, in the opposite direction, as it were. While Myrrha tries to
surmount the distinction between the upper levels of the Chain of Being
and the lower orders, Dryden here reverses the procedure, by implying
that what is natural for fowls down here is equally natural for princes up
there. Those "envious Laws" that we accept with relief as a barrier to
Myrrha's lust do not, it turns out, exist, not for monarchs like Ptolemy
(or Henry VIII). I doubt that any of this makes incest the more accept-

able, but it is a wry inversion, making the unnatural natural, using human behavior to justify animal behavior rather than the other way around, and it does manage to raise questions about just how separate the human and animal are.

In another added passage, Dryden's Chanticleer explains the relationship between man and beast, as it appears to him:

> All these [i.e., what nature offers] are ours; and I with pleasure see
> Man strutting on two Legs, and aping me!
> An unfledg'd Creature, of a lumpish frame,
> Indew'd with fewer Particles of Flame:
> Our Dame sits couring o'er a Kitchin-fire,
> I draw fresh Air, and Nature's Works admire:
> And ev'n this Day, in more delight abound,
> Than since I was an Egg, I ever found.
> (459–66)

Theseus had used the same image: "So Man, . . . / for Hatching ripe, he breaks the Shell" (3:1066, 1069, a Dryden addition); what for Theseus is the figurative description of the first of man's ages is here reduced to the first stage in the life of a chicken, which might raise the question of just how distinct the human and animal realms are. In a larger sense, Theseus' view of the universe, where "Plants, Beasts, and Man" (3:1048) are part of the whole but are "diff'rent in Degree" (3:1047), is inverted in the above passage, his anthropocentric view of the universe turned into a gallocentric view. But we are likely to discount that, because we recognize that the inversion is Chanticleer's, and it is about to be turned right side up when the proud Chanticleer learns that "*Jove* made not him his Master-piece below" (470). We smilingly assent, because anybody can see through the pride and self-aggrandizement of this tiny creature, who thinks nature operates entirely for him, and who himself is only the property of a humble, impoverished widow. That is, anybody outside Chanticleer's charmed kingdom can see, but that raises the question whether man himself, even Theseus, is perhaps proud in thinking his position in the universe different in kind from that of the inferior animals. From a position outside and above man's little world, man can appear puny, a creature "strutting on two Legs," and there is a certain justice in Chanticleer's ludicrous claims, for he sees us from his viewpoint in the same condescending way that we prefer to see him and his kind from ours.

This much is playful teasing rather than serious challenging; it does not so much subvert ideals and principles established elsewhere as whirl them around in a carnival fun house. The kind of debate between possible values that we witness across Dryden's tales we at times witness within this fable, but issues dissolve into contradictions and ambiguities at such a dazzling speed that Dryden allows us no time to get committed to a position. It is not a matter of two Sigismondas pulling against one another, exactly, but rather of eight or nine competing and contradictory tugs that might entangle us, were we not already knotted up with laughter. I am perhaps drawing too fine a line between the kind of rapid shifting we find here and what we have seen in certain passages elsewhere. We have already pondered over the shifting that occurs at the hinge-moments in such tales as "Sigismonda and Guiscardo," "Cymon and Iphigenia," and "Alexander's Feast," where what has been done starts to become undone. But I do think there is a subtle difference, for similar passages in "The Cock and the Fox" do not so much lead toward a resolution that dissolves as dissolve continuously.[4]

We have already considered how it is Cousin Driden's misogyny complicates the pro-feminist portrait of the duchess, and how, across the tales, we find fickle Iphigenias who confirm the intrinsic evil of womanhood, while good wives such as the duchess, Baucis, Alcyone, and the newly-wed Sigismonda resoundingly deny it (that is, half of Sigismonda denies it). When the same issue appears in "The Cock and the Fox," words like "confirmation" and "denial" seem too solid and definite to describe what happens. The basic issue is implicit in the central debate between Chanticleer and Partlet, which follows hard upon the heavenly debate between Jove and Juno. When Juno begins her diatribe, the question for Jove is: what right does his wife have to challenge his "partial Pow'r" (701): "Ev'n Goddesses are Women: And no wife /Has Pow'r to regulate her Husband's Life" (735–36, a Dryden insertion). Obviously, Partlet's address to her husband parodies what we hear from the contentious gods. She begins by upbraiding him for his cowardly fear of dreams, and she reminds him that she does not want a husband who is a fool, a coward, or a "bragging Coxcomb" (134), which in this case is both a figurative and literal description. She then goes on to give Chanticleer specific advice, as well as her own folksy herbs and digestives to cure him of the troubling dream—"Take my Advice, and when we fly to Ground /

With Laxatives preserve your Body sound" (164–65). One could say that advice like this is also an attempt to regulate the husband's life.

Chanticleer, like Jove, asserts his mastery—Dryden even likens Chanticleer to Jove in line 793—but his insults to his wife are never quite so overt as Jove's. Chanticleer at least addresses the issue his wife raises, on the validity of dreams, disputes it with a dispensary full of classical allusions and exempla instead of just raising the issue of mastery and telling her off, as Jove does to Juno. Chanticleer is no less insulting, however. If anything, he is more insidious, particularly when he shows off his learning, and his wife's ignorance of Latin, by mistranslating "*Mulier est hominis confusio*," thereby sharing a joke with the reader at Partlet's expense. Though he refrains from spelling out the wife's womanly inferiority, the semi-omniscient narrator ("semi" because he keeps saying he cannot explain what he is in the process of explaining) summarizes the misogynistic implications of his tale:

> The Tale I tell is only of a Cock;
> Who had not run the hazard of his Life
> Had he believ'd his Dream, and not his Wife:
> For Women, with a mischief to their Kind,
> Pervert, with bad Advice, our better Mind.
> A Woman's Counsel brought us first to Woe,
> And made her Man his Paradice forego,
> Where at Heart's ease he liv'd; and might have bin
> As free from Sorrow as he was from Sin.
> (552–60)

Apparently, woman *is* hominis confusio. Cousin John Driden might well agree, for his strength and success come from shunning the married state, which Dryden justified with the same basic argument, tracing the problem back to Paradise and that inferior Ur-woman who pulled Adam down and set an example for us all. The above passage is not far away from what we hear in the kinsman poem, where after mentioning Eden, Dryden comments that "had our Grandsire walk'd without his Wife, / He first had sought the better Plant of Life! / Now, both are lost" (98–100).

In the poem to Driden of Chesterton, this attitude is developed and repeatedly confirmed, as in lines 17–35, where marriage is a snare (33), where women are not only weaker than men (28) but also man's undoing.

If, however, we reflect on the misogynistic passage from "The Cock and the Fox" in the context of that tale alone, we discover that the misogyny will not wash. Chanticleer *does* believe his dream rather than his wife, or he would not find it necessary to argue at such length for his own belief in the validity of dreams. He does not succumb to her "Counsel," but rather gives in to his own animal appetites, abandoning his conclusive case so that he can "feel your tender Side" (421), which he does "twenty times e'er prime of Day" (438). Our knowledge of Chanticleer's actual behavior invalidates the narrator's claims about the dangers of women who "Pervert, with bad Advice, our better Mind" (556), for Partlet's advice is rejected and has little to do with Chanticleer's behavior. However, that same knowledge simultaneously confirms the misogynistic line, for it is, after all, the sexual temptation of another Eve that undoes Chanticleer. Almost. While it is true that Chanticleer ignores the foreboding dream, it is ultimately not Partlet's counsel, nor her sexual appeal, that causes Chanticleer's woe. He is perfectly safe up in that tree, until Reynard the Fox flatters him, and then:

> So was he ravish'd with this Flattery:
> So much the more as from a little Elf,
> He had a high Opinion of himself:
> Though sickly, slender, and not large of Limb,
> Concluding all the World was made for him.
> (654–58)

It is his own cockiness that undoes him. At the same time, if it is flattery that ravishes him, the cock who trusts in his masculine superiority has become transformed into an Eve-like creature, about to repeat that first sin on the basis of which Eve earned her dubious right to be considered hominis confusio.

The events of the story, then, eventually undermine the kinsman-like attitude toward womankind, as does the narrator who, shortly after pinning the blame on women's counsel, retracts his statement:

> In other Authors you may find enough,
> But all they say of Dames is idle Stuff.
> Legends of lying Wits together bound,
> The Wife of *Bath* would throw 'em to the Ground:
> These are the Words of Chanticleer, not mine,
> I honour Dames, and think their Sex divine.
> (567–72)

We need not look far to find these other authors who praise women. A few tales later, the Wife of Bath, whom Chaucer does not mention at this point, does just this, by portraying a crone whose counsel saves a despicable knight. For that matter, Alcyone's counsel to her husband is also the right advice: do not go abroad; you could get killed. And as we have seen, *Fables* is replete with tales wherein Dryden honors woman-kind by making women divine, which is true of the duchess, whose second coming might rescue Ireland, and of the fair lady, a "Celestial Maid" (2) and "Virgin-Saint" (19). Within "The Cock and the Fox" itself, the misogynistic attitude that emerges is both justified by the events and disproved by the events, affirmed by the narrator who retracts his affirmation. But like typically wry Chaucerian disclaimers, even the retraction is tainted. Misogyny lingers in the air, like a witness's blurted-out statement that the jury is instructed to ignore; the retraction serves to alert the audience to the possible significance of what it is being told to disregard.

The most succinct instance of multiple inversions occurs when Chanticleer, addressing this same issue, announces a "truth," which, since it comes from a strutting cock in a beast fable, we are likely to take with a grain of salt:

> For true it is, as *in Principio*,
> *Mulier est hominis confusio.*
> Madam, the meaning of this Latin is,
> That Woman is to Man his Soveraign Bliss.
> (417–20)

The joke, obviously, is in the mistranslation, a sudden shift from a statement to its apparent opposite. We read the first sentence as a truth, that is, a truth for Chanticleer, who not only cites this misogynistic credo, but further rubs it in by demonstrating his superior knowledge of Latin at his wife's expense. The second sentence, which we read as a male-chauvinist-cock lie, springs the trap and confirms the anti-feminism . . . except that the male who has just shown off his intellectual superiority immediately abandons his medieval argument and goes right from his lie about women being man's bliss into direct enjoyment of his wife's "tender Side" (421). The lie, then, is not a lie: woman *is* man's bliss, and furthermore, because of this, she may also be his confusion, although it is not so much woman's fault as it is man's fault (so man may be hominis confusio). The statement that announces a truth, which we are likely to treat with suspicion, is both untrue and exactly true, the mistranslation simultaneously askew and accurate.[5] And the contradiction between Latin tag and "mis"-translation is also the contradiction between a wife being man's "Household Curse" (according to Jove) and being a duchess of Ormond, whose beauty and power work to restore family and country, although now the alternatives, rather than stretching across different tales, hit us within a few lines.

As all these passages suggest, this is not so much a matter of establishing a view and later challenging it as it is a process of spinning from one inversion to the next. Nothing holds still long enough for us to get our bearings, although our response is more whimsical detachment than confusion. We are too busy laughing to take this seriously, and that alone distances us. We are not sympathizing with a human character, but scrutinizing a pompous cock who, anthropomorphic though he is, remains a caricature, a conspicuous fiction. We know he is not Jove's "Master-piece below" (470), because we observe him from above, looking down into the barnyard, although Chanticleer would think we were below it looking up.[6] In addition, Dryden slyly pushes us further back by altering his political innuendo. We become accustomed to Dryden's sidelong, head-on, and passing shots aimed at William III and his policies: conquering Theseuses, usurping Alexanders, irresponsible Tancreds, Dutch Guards, and Standing Armies make regular appearances, and we come to expect such commentary. At one point, Partlet's unwilling submission to Chanticleer's feathering is likened to passive obedience (73), which is one of the good parson's virtues, and at another, Dryden warns princes against allowing themselves to be *"Alexander'd* up in lying Odes" (660). In each case, the reference is brief, serving more to echo or undercut other tales than to discuss contemporary events. But when we encounter the longer satirical passages in "The Cock and the Fox," where Dryden delays the narrative and inserts political commentary, we often find that it is curiously removed from Dryden's here and now.

For instance, Dryden takes the *one* line in Chaucer referring to incest, and makes an issue of it, not only to bring Myrrha's incest to mind, but also to remark caustically that incest is not a crime when done "for Int'rest of a Nation" (63). When he alludes to the monarchs who had engaged in such activity, we half expect to find William III behind the allusion, with a fresh crime impaled upon his chest. But William, who was criticized for having a mistress, and accused by his enemies of homosexuality, was not, to my knowledge, accused of incest. Dryden is not alluding to the current monarch at all, but rather to Henry VIII and his marriage to his brother's widow, Catherine of Aragon. Dryden had earlier depicted Henry VIII as "A *Lyon* old, obscene, and furious made / By lust" ("The Hind and the Panther," 1 : 351 – 52). The inserted political comment that seems to depart from the beast fable, that begins to apply the fable to the real world, stretches instead to a distant "reality," to what is past, dead, over. It is almost as if we were reading a tale from another era, and that contributes, I think, to a feeling of detachment. We are watching everything from a different perspective, distanced both from the heroic, tragic, noble worlds of the Greek heroes and antiheroes, of Sigismonda, of Alcyone, and distanced as well from the political present of Kinsman John Driden and the duchess of Ormond. From that detached viewpoint, we do not so much grapple with issues, since we are not attached to them, as notice the speed with which they tumble and shift.

Very little remains fixed and stable amidst the swirl, and Dryden even subjects some sacrosanct Drydenian issues to the maelstrom, particularly one of his favorite issues, that of "the Role of the Poet." This was a topic that engaged him throughout his career, from days when he was ostensibly the official spokesman of the nation, to the later days when, as deposed laureate, he spoke as outcast, trying still to consolidate his authority.[7] Dryden does as much in the opening tale of *Fables*, where he likens himself to Chaucer and hopes to follow in the English line that ultimately descends from Homer and Virgil. That much is invocation, a standard way of naming kindred spirits, not just to breathe life into the poet, but also to pump up his claims upon our attention. Later, however, at the end of the poem to his kinsman, where Dryden announces that "A Poet is not born in ev'ry Race" (202), he shifts to a more personal tone, still exuding authority, but his own rather than that of his literary predecessors. As the poem closes, the poet and the patriot become complementary, balanced, one performing "Praise-worthy Actions" (205), the other "mak[ing] thy Praises last" (206), both a tribute to the family name. Instead of the Public Poet planting the banner of the Great Tradition at the foot of the Ormonds, Dryden *in propria persona* builds a memorial to his namesake that is also a memorial to himself. Like any persona, this one is a pose, a fiction; nonetheless, like the persona of the virtuous satirist that Pope cultivated, Dryden's fiction is a sincere, personal statement too, an image the poet fashions of himself as he would like posterity to believe him to be.

"The Cock and the Fox," however, invites us to question such claims about the poet's sincerity, about his virtuous motivation, and about the efficacy of his verse. In the first place, the eloquent fiction-makers are the flattering fox and Chanticleer, who is undone not just by flattery, but also by his pride in his own voice: it is "while he pain'd himself to raise his Note" that "False *Reynard* rush'd, and caught him by the Throat" (669–70). A good lesson for all of us, but especially, it appears, for proud singers like Dryden. By circumstance at least, Dryden is allowing himself and his own pretensions to be implicated in the parody; that is, Chaucer's tale sticks it to Dryden, whether Dryden likes it or not.

Apparently, Dryden likes it: not content with the suspect role of poets suggested by a story involving two all-too-eloquent beasts, the one evil, the other foolish, Dryden amplifies his material and intensifies the implications. This occurs especially when Reynard praises the singing of Chanticleer's father:

> But since I speak of Singing let me say,
> As with an upright Heart I safely may,
> That, save your self, there breaths not on the Ground,
> One like your Father for a Silver sound.
> So sweetly wou'd he wake the Winter-day,
> That Matrons to the Church mistook their way,
> And thought they heard the merry Organ play.
> (616–22)

In a poetic sense, Dryden the author is Chanticleer's sire, who, in the original, is praised for "discrecioun" and "wisedom" (3309, 3311), but here is depicted as somebody who misleads matrons on their way to church. His music sounds like divine music—the organ being Cecilia's instrument, which enlarges music by imparting to it a "Sacred Store" ("Alexander's Feast," 163)—but it is not divine; it only sounds that way. Although this passage attests to the power of poetry, it also makes that power suspect; it is the power to deceive. As Reynard continues, this possible parallel between Chanticleer's father and Dryden becomes more probable:

in Song, he never had his Peer,
From sweet *Cecilia* down to Chanticleer;
Not *Maro*'s Muse who sung the mighty Man,
Nor *Pindar*'s heav'nly Lyre, nor *Horace* when a Swan.
Your Ancestors proceed from Race divine,
(631–35)

The entire passage is a Dryden addition, one that, by associating Chanticleer's sire with both Cecilia and Virgil, cannot help but bring poet Dryden to mind, since he had written two odes to the former (one being "Alexander's Feast"), and had just "sung the mighty Man" by completing his well-received translation of the *Aeneid*.

Like Chanticleer's mistranslation that turns out to be a true translation as well, the deceptively clear passage above raises questions that twist us into knots. First, if we consider what Reynard is trying to do, we regard this praise as flattery, an attempt to mislead Chanticleer as Chanticleer's father misleads matrons. Second, the misleading praise can be taken as a parody of Dryden's own praise of the duchess of Ormond: she too was of a "Race Divine" ("Ormond," 30), and that announcement, like this one, was preceded by an invocation of previous great authors to add authority to the speaker's praise (1–14). Similarly, Reynard's procedure of beginning his flattery by praising the ancestry of Chanticleer also echoes Dryden's opening remarks in *Fables*, where he begins his Dedication to the duke of Ormond by recalling the duke's "excellent Grandfather" and "Heroick Father," and then spends a paragraph wandering among the generations of illustrious Ormonds, concluding that paragraph with the remark: "That as your Grandfather and Father were cherish'd and adorn'd with Honours by two successive Monarchs, so I have been esteem'd, and patronis'd, by the Grandfather, the Father, and the Son, descended from one of the most Ancient, most Conspicuous, and most Deserving Families in *Europe*" (Kinsley, 4: 1439). The fox, for his own sneaky purposes, is parodying Dryden's procedure of invoking ancestry to compliment an individual, and of assembling a Great Tradition to fortify his praise, a process we find in most of Dryden's poems celebrating individuals: "To Kneller" and "To Congreve" both incorporate that strategy, with Dryden taking pains to name the great artists and poets who establish the cultural values Dryden claims as his own.

Furthermore, this consummate flattering fox undoes his own praise in the act of articulating it, for he has just warned his audience about the deceiving power of song (were Chanticleer less proud, he might have noticed). Finally, and this brings things back full circle, or full spiral, the fox's speech is not just an echo of Dryden's own strategies of praise, but his praise-flattery is also directed at Chanticleer's sire, Dryden himself. I would hesitate to call Chanticleer's father yet another Dryden alter ego, for he is not developed as a character, nor is his plight comparable to Dryden's, as are the plights of Kinsman Driden, the non-juring parson, and the good poet Congreve struggling in an age of Shadwells. But there is enough similarity in the circumstances, and enough in added, suggestive parallels, for us to see that this tale, which mocks Myrrha's claims, undercuts Sigismonda and Alcyone's pretensions to nobility, and deflates Jove's beliefs in masculine superiority, also may amount to a gentle debunking of Dryden's career-long pretensions about his authority and about the virtue of his calling as a poet.

In this universe, inversions are so persistent that they beset a host of familiar issues, including many of Dryden's own beliefs. When the cock gives in to such flattery, it is because "He had a high Opinion of himself" (656), which is also true of Dryden, not one to be terribly modest about his own accomplishments as a poet. The cock's downfall, then, is also the crumbling of Dryden's pride, and the warning that "There's many a *Reynard* lurking in the Court" (662), though it comes as an authorial interjection, also reflects upon the sometime flattering author who makes the interjection. We seem to be in a whirlpool. What then is the role of the poet? Is he an especially privileged authority, or a self-server who "raise[s] his Voice with artful Care" for a trivial reason: "(What will not Beaux attempt to please the Fair?)" (623–24, a Dryden insertion)? Is his praise of the duchess as exalted and genuine as it sounds, or is this an instance of flattering the fair? Is Kinsman Driden preserved in fame, or puffed by a practitioner whose creative impulses can mislead? As the explicit moral at the end of the beast fable reminds us, we should "learn besides of Flatt'rers to beware, / Then most pernicious when they speak too fair" (812–13: the second line is not in Chaucer). Were the duchess of Ormond and Kinsman Driden to hear this kind of advice, how comfortable would they feel with the fair words bestowed upon them? When Chanticleer falls because he trusts in what he hears rather than what his own eyes tell him to avoid, does this not put us on our guard against trusting in the silver-tongued? Of course, he also escapes from the fox's clutches by relying upon his voice, tricking the fox as the fox has tricked him. These creative artists who rely upon their voices are deceivers, or deceived, or both. Yet behind them all is the creative artist Dryden (with Chaucer chuckling alongside); what do we make of the author who builds an elaborate rhetorical structure, this tale, which calls into question elaborate rhetorical structures?[8]

One could as easily ask what is the role of woman, what is the efficacy of dreams, what is the truth about free will and predestination, for all of these issues emerge only to be whirled about in the maelstrom. Not only does "The Cock and the Fox" parody a world of human and superhuman activities, puncturing issues that are elsewhere treated seriously, inverting and reinverting, but in its sheer velocity of changing viewpoints, the tale in effect parodies the whole process of doing and undoing that we experience throughout *Fables*. "The Cock and the Fox" is not a "central tale" because it offers resolutions, but rather because it depicts a universe, a barnyard microcosm, where resolution is not possible, where whatever partial ideals Dryden endorses elsewhere, including ideals concerning the authority and validity of the artist who is creating the story, are subject to change. The result, rather than being disquieting, is exhilarating contradiction, an ironic chaos that playfully keeps the reader off-balance and laughing heartily at the contradictory game.

OF THE PYTHAGOREAN PHILOSOPHY

If "The Cock and the Fox" shows us change in abundance, "Of the Pythagorean Philosophy" presents a Philosophy of Change, which provides the theoretical underpinning for what we experience in Chanticleer's little kingdom. In the second paragraph of his Preface, Dryden calls special attention to this excerpt from Ovid by referring to it as "the Masterpiece of the whole *Metamorphoses*" (Kinsley, 4:1444). In addition, Dryden adds a headnote to his translation in which he describes both "the Moral and Natural Philosophy of *Pythagoras*" as "the most learned and beautiful Parts of the Whole Metamorphoses" (Kinsley, 4:1718). Dryden's appreciation can partially be accounted for by considering the tastes of his day, for Pythagoras, as a forerunner of Plato and supposed source for much of the doctrine in *Timaeus*, had become something of a fashionable philosophical figure. According to Dryden's contemporary, Cambridge Platonist Ralph Cudworth, "*Pythagoras* was the most eminent of all the ancient Philosophers," and one might add that his philosophy was probably most widely known by way of Ovid's popular poetic version.[9] Thus, whatever his feelings about the Cambridge Platonists, Dryden might nonetheless have regarded this section of Ovid as an important work, something sufficiently familiar to present a special challenge for the translator, and something worth being saved for a bravura translation that would appear at a climactic moment toward the end of *Fables*. By praising it as both moral and natural philosophy, Dryden also hints at what else might have attracted him to this particular work; as a traditional piece of pre-Platonic philosophy, the ideas of Pythagoras stretch far back into ancient history. And as a piece of natural philosophy—a term then synonymous with what we would call the new science—Pythagoras' ideas were also very much in vogue. Dryden, who so often relies upon history to assemble values applicable to modern events, has in his hands a work that both reaches back into the distant past and has resonance within the framework of contemporary philosophical and scientific speculations.[10]

Like "The Cock and the Fox," "Of the Pythagorean Philosophy" (from the fifteenth and final book of *Metamorphoses*) is also rich with echoes; the most significant and sustained parallels occur in the central speech of Pythagoras, but before that, we encounter a typically Ovidian frame of stories within stories, leading up to a narrator within a narrator.[11] The frame itself buzzes with echoes, which seem to tumble atop one another. We begin by meeting Numa Pompilius, "A peaceful, pious Prince" (6) who, "To cultivate his Mind" (8), visits Crotona and seeks out the philosopher Pythagoras. It will not be long before we discover that this is what love-struck Cymon attempts when "He sought a Tutor of his own accord" (214) in order "to cultivate his Mind" (213), with Dryden using the very same phrase for both Numa and Cymon (the tutor with whom Cymon studies is a Dryden addition). As we have seen, Cymon's cultivation, rather than improving anything, leads to rape and war; Numa's cultivation, on the other hand, will serve to bless Rome with "soft Arts of Peace" (716) and "To teach religion, Rapine to restrain / Give Laws to Lust, and Sacrifice ordain" (717–18).

We scarcely have time to consider this possible contrast between the ideal lawgiver Numa and the accomplished lawbreaker Cymon before other parallels begin accumulating. While searching for Crotona, Numa meets a "Senior of the Place" (14) who tells him the story of the city's birth, beginning back when it was grazing land (18). One day, as Hercules was travelling through the region, he sought "some hospitable House" (19) and was received by "Good *Croton*," who "entertain'd his Godlike Guest" (20). In gratitude for such treatment, Hercules "bless'd the Place" (22) and promised that a town one day would arise here and take its name from Croton. Neither Ovid nor Dryden goes into detail about the rustic countryside or the entertainment—Dryden covers the entire legend in a mere nine lines—but we nonetheless recognize a familiar pattern, another version of "Baucis and Philemon," where a humble household generously receives a special guest who will reward the hospitality. If Baucis and Philemon become immortalized as ancient trees, a tribute to their conjugal fidelity and generosity, Croton becomes immortalized as the eponym of this town that will ultimately inspire the lawgiver of Rome.

Hercules fulfills his promise by appearing to Myscelos in a dream, instructing him to leave his native country, to seek out the region where the river Aesaris flows, and there found a city and name it after Croton. Myscelos, who perhaps should have listened to the debate in "The Cock and the Fox," is bothered by this dream, like Chanticleer, but attempts to shrug it off, like Partlet. The "same forewarning Dream" (38) returns the next night—it looks as if Chanticleer was right about the significance of dreams—and Myscelos decides to follow the instructions. Unfortunately, it is illegal for Myscelos to leave his native country (34); apparently, it is even illegal to think of leaving, for when word of his plan to depart spreads, he is summarily condemned to death. In the preceding Wife of Bath's tale, we encountered another man in trouble with the law, although the Wife's knight is justly condemned for a crime, whereas Myscelos is unjustly condemned by a law that runs counter to a noble, divinely-sanctioned purpose. Neither sentence sticks: the Wife's knight is conditionally released thanks to the intervention of the queen, and here the law reverses itself as well, for the black stones cast unanimously to condemn Myscelos all magically turn to white, thanks to the intervention of Hercules, which enables Myscelos to go off and found Crotona, as he was told to do.

As in "The Cock and the Fox," the echoes in situations, patterns, and even lines, are numerous and overlapping, but they are not parodic inversions, and they do not challenge what we hear elsewhere. Instead, they serve as reminders, brief variations of familiar motifs, which help to locate this plotless tale in the collection as a whole, and which tease us into making connections. This procedure continues when we finally meet Pythagoras. The philosopher is introduced as "the Man divine" (77), formerly of Samos, "But now Self-banish'd from his Native Shore, / Because he hated Tyrants" (78–79), which brings to mind Dryden's view of himself as noble outcast staunchly and self-consciously resisting his warmongering king. The parallel between poet and philosopher is only a general one, however, for neither former laureate, Dryden, nor the exiled Ovid could exactly consider himself *self*-banished. Nevertheless, they both might be making virtue of necessity by changing the outcast figure to one whose banishment arises from his own virtue rather than from being ousted by political happenstance or a hostile monarch. The parallel between philosopher and author(s) need not be exact, for it is enough that the sympathetically depicted figure who makes this speech is an especially privileged outcast, as Dryden and Ovid would like to think of themselves, privileged by having the virtue to resist tyrants, by having "Strength of Mind" (82), and by having the gift of eloquence. In this capacity, Pythagoras can be measured against the other public speakers of *Fables*: like flattering Reynard, the sweet-voiced (600) Chanticleer, his father before him, and the smooth-tongued Ulysses (18), Pythagoras "charm'd his Audience with his Speech" (98). Like the poet-maker Timotheus, Pythagoras too has a godlike power: we learn that when he talks, "The Crowd with silent Admiration stand / And heard him, as they heard their God's Command" (87–88). It might be fairer to say that the other masters of eloquence are measured against him. In this case, the man whose "interiour Light" (83) enables him to penetrate "Heav'ns mysterious Laws" (89) is neither a flatterer nor a self-serving manipulator of the mob (not that crowds can tell the difference), but rather a model of eloquence in the service of truth. He is a better Timotheus, perhaps, and perhaps an ideal Dryden.

When Pythagoras at last begins to speak, this model of eloquence sounds at first more like a health-food fanatic than a philosopher penetrating the mysteries of the universe. He starts not with any vision of the profound, but with an impassioned speech on the necessity of eating organically grown fruits and vegetables. As we soon discover, his argument for vegetarianism is based on his belief in metempsychosis: you should not kill or eat anything that you might have once known personally (you just can't know who that meat has been). His dietary diatribe eventually expands into the central issue that informs his philosophy— that everything, even death itself, changes. It follows, as a necessary consequence of metempsychosis, that mortals should avoid eating meat, should abstain "from your Fellow's Blood" (101), and this in effect is Pythagoras' primary moral principal. That even his diet reflects his deeply held philosophical beliefs implies an integrity and a consistency of character that make for "Strength of Mind."[12] Pythagoras returns to his central principle in his final verse paragraph, where what first might have seemed like a fussy vegetarian's distaste for blood sports now becomes a humanitarian's weighty moral injunction: "Take not away the Life you cannot give: / For all Things have an equal right to live" (705–6, a couplet added by Dryden). It is that concluding precept which, imparted to Numa Pompilius "And thence transferr'd to *Rome*" (713), will bless that kingdom with peace, and the rhetorician delivering this civilizing message serves as a contrast to the powerful Timotheus whose final words to his ruler inspire a "Zeal to destroy" (147) Persepolis.

Just as the figure of Pythagoras serves as commentary upon other masters of rhetoric, so does his speech echo, summarize, and expand upon episodes we encounter elsewhere. For instance, in discussing eating and killing animals, which he labels "this gust of Blood" (202), Pythagoras makes comments that bring to mind the many accounts of the hunt that run through *Fables*.[13] For vegetarian Pythagoras, hunting is reprehensible, but not merely because animals may be recycled humans. There is something else pernicious about hunting: as sage Pythagoras explains, it is hunting that destroyed the peaceful Golden Age, which, for this fanatical vegetarian, was an age when men "fed on Fruit" (137). Along came the first hunter (presumably Nimrod, though Dryden does not mention him by name), whom Pythagoras describes as

> the Wretch (and curs'd be He)
> That envy'd first our Food's simplicity;
> Th' essay of bloody Feasts on Brutes began,
> And after forg'd the Sword to murther Man.
> (143–46)

This reverses the traditional idea of hunting as a socially acceptable outlet for man's aggressive instincts. On the contrary, in Pythagoras' view hunting may be the first regrettable step that leads to manslaughter, something that potentially conquering Theseuses, who enjoy destroying beasts of chase, might be advised to consider.

Yet as the passage continues, Pythagoras recognizes the necessity of certain kinds of killing:

> Had he [Man] the sharpen'd Steel alone employ'd,
> On Beasts of Prey that other Beasts destroy'd,
> Or Man invaded with their Fangs and Paws,
> This had been justify'd by Nature's Laws,
> And Self-defence: But who did Feasts begin
> Of Flesh, he stretch'd Necessity to Sin.
> To kill Man-killers, Man has lawful Pow'r,
> But not th' extended Licence, to devour.
>
> (147–54)

There are, then, two kinds of hunt—the proper, lawful kind, levied against harmful beasts or man-killers, and the indiscriminate slaughter that can lead to man-killing. In a way, this passage summarizes the many hunts we have encountered, including Theseus' joyful destruction of beasts of chase, which expresses his warlike and potentially dangerous instincts; the boar hunt in "Meleager and Atalanta" that begins with animal slaughter and turns into slaughter of most of the participants; and the vision in "Theodore and Honoria," where the hero, unable to win Honoria, dreams of a hunt in which she is disembowelled, repeatedly. Pythagoras' couplet about one bloody feast leading to another (145–46) could serve as epilogue for these examples, wherein hunting might lead to murder, or does lead to murder, or in Theodore's case, leads to murder within a dream, suggesting the connection of the two within the human mind. At the same time, the rest of the above passage acknowledges an alternative possibility, one that Kinsman Driden fulfills, for his "Sylvan-Chace" (51), not for sport but after the felon fox, a beast-killer (well, sheep-killer), is a beneficial hunt, a health-giving exercise that saves Cousin Driden from corrupt doctors and demonstrates his power of bringing justice to the animal kingdom as well as to the civilized world. It is not that Pythagoras' speech alters our attitude toward these previous hunts; rather, it provides a succinct justification for a variety of hunts, and it establishes the end-points—the evil hunt, the proper hunt—on a scale that encompasses the many discrete examples of hunting we encounter elsewhere.[14]

All these echoes, which trip over one another in the first 150 lines, are more like miscellaneous noise than ringing challenges. Except for the hunt, which is actually part of the larger theme of killing and war, the other echoes are brief, sufficient to remind us that this tale touches upon the rest of *Fables* at many separate points, but not sufficiently developed to alter appreciably what we see, or what Dryden encourages us to endorse, from elsewhere in *Fables*.[15] The more substantial links, however, occur once Pythagoras explains his philosophy, for here we have extended arguments, long sections that not only establish parallels but also keep them in front of us long enough for us to ponder the similarities and differences between what Pythagoras says and what we have heard from other mouths.

In particular, the most striking parallel is between Pythagoras' set speech explaining the universe and the First Mover speech in "Palamon and Arcite." One is at the beginning of *Fables*, the other towards the end, rather like philosophical bookends enclosing the variegated narratives in the middle. The first speech is addressed by a lawgiver, Theseus, who at this point is bringing order to his Athenian world of random death and seeming injustice; the second is addressed *to* a lawgiver, the successor to Romulus, who is about to give laws to Rome and thereby "guide the growing State" (1). When Pythagoras has finished speaking, we learn that

> These Precepts by the *Samian* Sage were taught,
> Which Godlike *Numa* to the *Sabines* brought,
> And thence transferr'd to *Rome*, by Gift his own:
> A willing People, and an offer'd Throne.
> O happy Monarch, sent by Heav'n to bless
> A Salvage Nation with soft Arts of Peace,
> To teach Religion, Rapine to restrain,
> Give Laws to Lust, and Sacrifice ordain:
> Himself a Saint, a Goddess was his Bride,
> And all the Muses o'er his Acts preside.
> (711–20)

Dryden, as usual, has altered his source somewhat. Ovid's Numa also is blessed with the Muses' guidance, and he too trains a warlike people in the arts of peace. But Dryden's is offered a throne by a willing people, which is a telling addition, and he is heaven-sent, rather than recently arrived from Holland.[16] In short, he is not a William, but is, like the Theseus at the end of his First Mover speech, an ideal monarch, something that warlike William should have been, devoted to peace, and endorsed by "all the Muses" (rather than criticized by one particular local muse). As I have argued earlier, Theseus grows during the unfolding of "Palamon and Arcite," shifts away from acting according to "*Mars*, the Patron of my Arms" (2 : 308), and instead engages in the more constructive, peaceful pursuits inspired by "The Pow'r of Love" (2 : 350). In imposing stability and order on his civilization, which is what Numa is about to do, Theseus acts in ways William seldom acted, concluding all "jarring Notes in Harmony" (3 : 1118) rather than invading neighboring kingdoms, and even acting only after gaining "th' Assent / Of my free People in full Parliament" (3 : 1121 – 22), which is not the kind of behavior William III usually indulged in.

Both the reformed Theseus who emerges at the end of "Palamon and Arcite" and the Numa who receives Pythagoras' wise instruction serve as models of princely behavior; they are literally philosopher-kings.[17] For that matter, Numa is not only the monarch William III should have been; this passage, while commenting upon politics of the last few years, also reaches back to earlier times, for we cannot help but notice that Numa is also the monarch Charles II should have been. Indeed, Dryden had likened Charles II to Numa back in 1685 ("Threnodia Augustalis," 465ff.). In the above passage, since Dryden has a willing people offering the throne to Numa, he makes Numa's coming to power sound like the Restoration, when, as Dryden claims in "To My Honour'd Friend, Dr. *Charleton*" (1663), Charles II was "chose again to rule the Land" (52) by his "wondring Subjects" (49). The properly empowered Numa who gives laws to lust, then, also serves as an ideal monarch contrasted against none other than the properly restored David/Charles, whose blatant promiscuity suggests that lust gives laws to him.

Both Theseus and Pythagoras serve as ideals, but although they reinforce one another in some respects, they also differ in significant ways. For one thing, Theseus' eye is kept steadily on the informing First Mover behind change, while Pythagoras sees nothing behind change but change. Pythagoras scarcely mentions God, although He makes a cameo appearance in the passage on Creation, just before Pythagoras begins speaking, where we are told what the crowd is accustomed to hearing Pythagoras talk about:

> he discours'd of Heav'ns mysterious Laws,
> The World's Original, and Nature's Cause;
> And what was God, and why the fleecy Snows
> In silence fell, and rattling Winds arose;
> What shook the stedfast Earth, and whence begun
> The dance of Planets round the radiant Sun;
> If Thunder was the Voice of angry *Jove*,
> Or Clouds with Nitre pregnant burst above.
> (89–96)

God is not the agent, but one of the topics, along with questions about where snow, wind, and earthquakes originate; apparently God is one of the possible explanations for certain phenomena, like thunder. Heaven seems to work by mysterious laws that precede God, Who (or who) comes into the picture when we search for some explanation for the origin of the world, or the cause of nature. This is in sharp contrast to Theseus' view (examined earlier in another context), which begins with a purposeful God and a clear order, not with some mysterious laws and an abundance of rattling, shaking, and dancing movements from which a godly power might be inferred:

> The Cause and Spring of Motion, from above
> Hung down on earth the Golden Chain of Love:
> Great was th' Effect, and high was his Intent,
> When Peace among the jarring Seeds he sent.
> Fire, Flood, and Earth, and Air by this were bound,
> And Love, the common Link, the new Creation crown'd.
> (3:1024–29)

Having started his Creation speech with God, Theseus keeps returning to "that All-seeing, and All-making Mind" (3:1035), whom he refers to as "some unalter'd Cause" (3:1041), "God the Whole" (3:1042), and "th' Omniscient Pow'r" (3:1054). When we look at Theseus' universe, there is no question Who is behind it all, and no question that all is ordered. For Pythagoras, as his speculations on Creation indicate, these same questions remain questions, and if Theseus focuses steadily on the possible causes and springs behind the new Creation, Pythagoras turns his attention not to causes but to effects. His speech is not so much a First Mover speech as it is an All-Things-Keep-Moving-No-Matter-What speech.

These speeches accomplish something else as well when seen in the context of the history of ideas. Although Dryden is translating Chaucer and Ovid, and enjoying the metaphoric and imaginative play involved in describing or reinventing Creation, he is also describing the kind of processes that were becoming the subject of scientific inquiry. It is not surprising that the poetry of the age often reveals the influence and popularity of natural philosophy. One frequently discovers "scientific imagery," especially in passages on Creation, in descriptions of the Last Judgment, in poetic analyses of such processes as fire, weather, or the geological formation of mountains.[18] If we consider Dryden's Creation speeches in this light, as evidence of his own fascination with the new science that he had celebrated as early as 1663 in his poem to Dr. Charleton, we discover Dryden playing with issues at the center of a continuing controversy, one that divided the French from the English. On one side, there were the Cartesians, who saw the universe as a great clock that, once started by the great clockmaker, needed no further divine intervention. On the other, there was the English counterreaction from such authors as Thomas Sprat, Joseph Glanvill, Walter Charleton, John Ray, and Robert Boyle, who attempted to put God back in where they thought the French had left Him out.[19] Dryden, as a Catholic, an Englishman, and an admirer of Boyle and Charleton (Dryden praises Boyle in his poem to Dr. Charleton), might be expected to argue the English side of the argument, but these two passages on Creation together constitute a broader view. In essence, they summarize the European controversy. Theseus takes the English line, seeing within the wondrous, orderly universe an omnipresent Creator; Pythagoras takes a Cartesian stance, acknowledging a god who may be the motive force, but who then steps aside and disappears from Pythagoras' ensuing discussion. For Pythagoras, the system, however it was started, keeps on moving of its own accord.

Yet despite this difference between the Christian and pagan (or English and French) views, the resulting philosophies are similar in that both speakers see change as the intrinsic pattern of the universe, in one case emanating from an unchanging God, in the other, visible in the universe whatever it may emanate from. Theseus maintains that all forms are "perishable" (3:1033), that only God is "perfect, stable" (3:1046) and all the rest is "Subject to Change" (3:1047), which he proceeds to demonstrate. Theseus' conclusion is for Pythagoras the starting point; it becomes the central theme on which he composes his many variations, which at much greater length recount the many imperfect and unstable things that continually change. And as both speakers expand on this subject, we cannot help noticing that each one delivers an Ages of Man speech (Theseus at 3:1058–80, Pythagoras at 320–53). It almost seems as if Dryden is indulging himself, running through this topic twice out of sheer pleasure in playing with a fruitful theme.[20] In both cases, the discussion of man is included within a larger discussion of nature, and it is not so much the separate stages of man's life that interest Dryden's philosophers as the process of continual change at work, in trees, towns, seasons, and man. Both philosophical discourses, then, contain sections on Creation and on the Ages of Man, and both deal centrally with change, with Christian-Stoic Theseus searching for the stable Cause, and pagan Pythagoras concerning himself with the animated Effects. We can regard these as complementary views, two speakers from different vantage points meeting on a common ground, in which case Pythagoras confirms the informing philosophy Dryden presents at the opening of *Fables*.[21]

This does happen, but this is not all that happens, for the final discourse, while echoing what we have heard before, also alters it; the common ground shifts. The two speakers may both see a universe of change, but Pythagoras sees change as a significantly different process from the one Theseus describes. This becomes more apparent when we consider the slightly different applications of the same image, that of the river, in each speech. Theseus refers to a river briefly, in one of a series of similes illustrating the presence of change in the world:

> So wears the paving Pebble in the Street,
> And Towns and Tow'rs their fatal Periods meet.
> So Rivers, rapid once, now naked lie,
> Forsaken of their Springs; and leave their Channels dry.
> So Man, at first a Drop, dilates with Heat
> Then form'd, the little Heart begins to beat
> (3:1062–67),

and off we go into the similar pattern of change Theseus sees in man. The images Theseus uses make it clear that he sees change moving primarily downhill. Pebbles wear down, towns and towers come to an end, and rivers turn to dry channels. All of this follows the description of the Monarch oak that grows for three centuries, stays supreme for another three, "and in three more decays" (3:1061). Even as we enter the Ages of Man section, then, we are aware of the pattern and are already anticipating the outcome: as rivers dry, men die.

Pythagoras, who uses the same image for the first stage of human life ("some few fruitful Drops, the promise of a Man," 325), includes all this in his speech, but with a different emphasis: nature, time, man, and the river imagery that meanders in and out of the discussion, do not just move toward decay, fatal periods, dry channels. Rather, Pythagoras' river just keeps rolling along,

> or Ebbs, or Flows:
> Ever in motion; she destroys her old,
> And casts new Figures in another Mold.
> Ev'n Times are in perpetual Flux; and run
> Like Rivers from their Fountains rowling on.
> For Time no more than Streams, is at a stay:
> The flying Hour is ever on her way;
> And as the Fountain still supplies her store,
> The Wave behind impels the Wave before.
> (263–71)

Pythagoras sees ends as only temporary states; when nature destroys, she casts anew in the very next line.

Elsewhere in his speech, where Pythagoras discusses geological changes, he too mentions waters that dry up, but in so doing, he describes this not so much as an end of water as a beginning of land:

> The Face of Places, and their Forms decay;
> And that is solid Earth, that once was Sea:
> Seas in their turn retreating from the Shore,
> Make solid Land, what Ocean was before.
> (402–5)

Warming to his subject, Pythagoras goes on for about a dozen lines in the same fashion; I think it significant that he develops the water imagery more fully, for this itself suggests that his main interest is in the continual fluid process. It also may suggest, once again, Dryden's interest in issues raised by the new science. While the notion of a constantly changing universe is as old as Heraclitus and, obviously, Pythagoras, it is also in the seventeenth century a contemporary idea, and one hears in Dryden's translation something reminiscent of Francis Bacon: "Certain it is, that the matter is in a perpetual flux, and never at a stay." [22] Moreover, the idea of seeing within immovable mountains and solid earth a principle of mutability parallels the new philosophical and mathematical speculations about substance (quantities were now seen as functions of what is variable), which were altering the way in which men looked at what appeared to be solid and fixed. Dryden's account of a world "Ever in motion," his ready supply of imagery of flux, his descriptions of a "Nature" that "knows / No stedfast Station" (262–64) constitute a celebration of the Leibnizian and Newtonian approach. The special mathematics of change, infinitesimal calculus and its "fluxions," to use Newton's term, has here its poetic equivalent in Dryden's perpetual flux, in his view of both time and nature as wave upon wave.

Whereas Pythagoras sees perpetual flux everywhere, Theseus has his eye on the end result: the dead oak, the worn pebbles, the dry bed. And where Theseus stops with the end, no end is an end for Pythagoras, who goes on, and on, and on. Not only does ocean become solid land, but the reverse is equally true:

> And what were Fields before, now wash'd and worn
> By falling Floods from high, to Valleys turn,
> And crumbling still descend to level Lands;
> And Lakes, and trembling Bogs are barren Sands:
> And the parch'd Desart floats in Streams unknown;
> Wondring to drink of Waters not her own.
> (408–13)

Rivers appear where there were once fields, but they retreat to leave valleys, as lakes and bogs turn to desert, which then becomes inundated with water, and so it goes, right into the next verse paragraph where Pythagoras continues swimming back and forth:

> Here Nature living Fountains ope's; and there
> Seals up the Wombs where living Fountains were;
> Or Earthquakes stop their ancient Course, and bring
> Diverted Streams to feed a distant Spring.
> So *Lycus*, swallow'd up, is seen no more,
> But far from thence knocks out another Door.
> (414–19)

Apparently, you just cannot keep a good river down—this one verse paragraph includes four changeable rivers—for if it disappears, it will reappear, only to disappear.

There are other speakers in *Fables* whose comments touch upon this issue of change in the universe, most notably Sigismonda and the crone in the "The Wife of Bath Her Tale," which immediately precedes "Of the Pythagorean Philosophy."²³ Whereas Theseus offers the consolations of philosophy to his people in an attempt to reconcile them to the death of Arcite, and Pythagoras addresses an attentive audience (including Numa) seeking the instructions of philosophy, these women both offer private speeches to an audience of one, Sigismonda to her cruel father, and the crone to her reluctant knight-husband, who has just complained that his new bride, unfortunately, is old, ugly, and from "so mean a Race" (368) as to be below the station of a noble knight-rapist like himself. The speeches by these oppressed women are obviously parallel to one another; both deal with nobility, particularly whether or not it is inherited, a crucial issue for Sigismonda, who needs to defend her husband Guiscardo's high worth despite his low birth, and for the crone, who needs to defend her lowly self on the same grounds.²⁴ At the same time, what these women have to say has a bearing on the two philosophical set speeches about change. Consider, for instance, the crone's comments on what happens to virtue over successive generations; after describing the constancy of fire, which will not decay as long as the fuel lasts (412), she contrasts this against man:

> Such is not Man, who mixing better Seed
> With worse, begets a base, degenerate Breed:
> The Bad corrupts the Good, and leaves behind
> No trace of all the great Begetter's Mind.
> (414–17)

What she sees is a pattern of degeneration, so whatever honor a man may possess perpetually corrupts; inevitably, "The Bad corrupts the Good" (416). In families, "The Father sinks within his Son" (418), and as we go further down the line,

> Or Man, or Woman, which soever fails:
> And, oft, the Vigour of the Worse prevails.
> *Æther* with Sulpher blended, alters hue,
> And casts a dusky gleam of *Sodom* blue.
> Thus in a Brute, their ancient Honour ends,
> And the fair Mermaid in a Fish descends.
> (431–36, a passage added by Dryden)

So much for progress. Later on, Cymon the brute will, to the embarrassment of his father, confirm the crone's theory of the worse prevailing in subsequent generations, confirm it with a vengeance, for it takes but one generation for the Cyprian family to reach the brute stage.

It is easy to see that the crone's comment could serve as a contrast to Sigismonda's optimistic view, in a passage where Dryden expands somewhat on his original:

> Thus born alike, from Vertue first began
> The Diff'rence that distinguish'd Man from Man:
> He [Guiscardo] claim'd no Title from Descent of Blood,
> But that which made him Noble, made him Good:
> Warm'd with more Particles of Heav'nly Flame,
> He wing'd his upward Flight, and soar'd to Fame;
> The rest remain'd below, a Tribe without a Name.
> (510–16)

For noble Sigismonda, who starts by looking back to "when the World began" (501), the "common Mass" that "compos'd the Mould of Man" (502) can separate, with the noble rising upward, presumably into a worthy Guiscardo, instead of inexorably downward. What for the crone is the exception to the general operation of honor across the generations is to Sigismonda the rule. But the crone's view, while it contrasts to Sigismonda's, could serve as a gloss on Theseus' remarks, for he too has a dim view of man's "progress":

> He perfect, stable; but imperfect, We,
> Subject to Change, and diff'rent in Degree.
> Plants, Beasts, and Man; and as our Organs are,
> We more or less of his Perfection share.
> But by a long Descent, th' Etherial Fire
> Corrupts; and Forms, the mortal Part, expire.
> (3:1046–51)

We could reasonably arrange the different views of change in a kind of hierarchy. The crone, who looks no further than the family of man, sees change as corruption or degeneration, whereas Theseus accepts that and yet believes that a perfect and stable God allows something to endure, so that "though the Forms decay, / Eternal Matter never wears away" (3:1030–31), which sounds Platonic. That is some consolation, although it may not make decaying forms decay any less. Sigismonda also looks at the operation of the universe, viewing things in a broader context than the crone and in a sunnier light than Theseus. Sigismonda goes back to "the Principles of Things" (500), and she sees those operating so as to separate into a profitable order that allows the good to ascend. Building, rather than decaying, is nature's pattern. But Pythagoras' view is broader still. He sees beyond growth and beyond degeneration and death as well, beyond the present (which is where Sigismonda stops) into subsequent regeneration and rebirth.

All speakers also use fire imagery in ways consistent with this hierarchy.[25] The crone, as we have seen, contrasts the constancy of fire against the corruptibility of man: man sinks, corrupts, declines,

> But Fire, th' enliv'ner of the general Frame
> Is one, its Operation still the same.
> Its Principle is in it self. . . .
> (427–29, a Dryden insertion)

At one point, she likens a heritage of virtue to "a long trail of Light" (441) that rather than endure in her husband, only ends "in thy Smoke" (442). Theseus, looking ever heavenward, sees a pure "Etherial Fire," not a substance independent of man, but an eternal force that descends through man and keeps corrupting. That represents an improvement; the light that is in man may grow steadily dimmer, but man is at least more than smoke and dusky gleams of sulfur. For Sigismonda, the "Particles of Heav'nly Flame" (514) within man, rather than growing dim, remain strong enough to warm him, wing him upward, enable him to soar (515). Pythagoras goes a step further, or several steps further, for he too discusses an "ætherial Flame" (596; the phrase is Dryden's, not Ovid's), not as something contrasted against man's smoldering, nor as an essence from God, nor as a helpful heating agent, but as something more encompassing, something larger than man and something that includes man. For Pythagoras, the "ætherial Flame" is the Phoenix (578–611), a central emblem that succinctly expresses his concept of death and rebirth. In short, the change the crone sees in man, and Theseus sees in all nature, works in one direction, downward toward degeneration, decay, or death, whereas Sigismonda sees change working for the better; Pythagoras, however, sees change going both up and down, not just inevitably destroying, but creating too, in a continual cycle epitomized by the Phoenix.

Pythagoras' contribution to the discussion, then, both confirms the ubiquitousness of change and yet amplifies the issue. "Amplifies" is, I think, the appropriate word, for not only is Pythagoras' speech longer, but his whole vision is more expansive, as we will perhaps notice when we compare his presentation with that of Theseus. Although both speakers see change in nature as well as man, when Theseus offers examples from the natural and the human realms, he selects more or less at random, moving from the Monarch oak, to pebbles, towns, towers, then to rivers, then to man. His purpose is to provide a host of analogues, each of which takes a mere two or three lines, all listed in quick succession to demonstrate that wherever Theseus looks, change is what he sees. Pythagoras, on the other hand, puts things in a causal order. For Theseus, oaks die, pebbles wear away, rivers dry, man sinks, all concurrently; for Pythagoras, man changes because nature changes, and nature changes because elements themselves are in flux.

Pythagoras begins with changes in nature—the rising and setting of the sun, the waxing and waning of the moon. He then discusses changes that cover longer periods of time, namely, the changing of the seasons, which he likens to the changes in man; i.e., Spring is "like Infancy" (299), "Summer grows adult, and ripens into Man" (309), and so on. The sustained comparison serves as a smooth transition to the following Ages of Man passage (320–53); having covered the day, the month, and the year, Pythagoras is now discussing years. And having just spent nearly a hundred lines moving gradually from nature to man, he actually repeats this sequence, but with a difference. The first time around, like a good Baconian, he dealt only with what could be empirically observed. Having made his case at that level, he is free to run through the argument again on a more theoretical plane, looking at things more broadly, getting behind the observable physical facts to the probable acting principles. Thus, in his second grand survey, he talks about the ever-changing elements—earth, air, fire, and water—rather than sun, moon, and seasons, going on to explain that since matter is made of all these elements, and since matter itself persists but changes, "Forms are chang'd" and "nothing can / Continue in the Figure it began" (398–99).

Pythagoras next talks about geological change, which follows from what he has just said about forms: "The Face of Places, and their Forms decay; / And that is solid Earth, that once was Sea" (402–3). Mountains become plains, islands become seas, seas become hills, all of this a consequence of the theory that form, comprised of elements, changes. After a digression to some examples of death that brings forth life (which of course runs counter to Theseus' view of life leading inexorably to death), and a pause to consider the Phoenix, that mythological version of life from death, Pythagoras again makes a transition from nature to man, but this time he discusses man in his civilized capacity, cities and empires, rather than man as an individual moving through stages. Like the terrain, cities sink and rise, and as was the case with his discussion of rivers, Pythagoras tends to balance the contrary movements; if he maintains that "Nature and Empires flourish," he is swift to add "and decay" (626) in the same line. Or, he can perform his balancing act in matched couplets:

> *Mycene, Sparta, Thebes* of mighty Fame
> Are vanish'd out of Substance into Name.
> And *Dardan Rome* that just begins to rise,
> On *Tiber*'s Banks, in time shall mate the Skies.
> (635–38)

The canvas is larger, both because Pythagoras is speaking of man in his collective state and because his time-scale has expanded; instead of the span of a day, or the seasons, we have a geological time-scale stretching back to the prehistoric, and instead of the years of men's lives, we have the ages of civilizations.

Pythagoras' most extended example of crumbling empires is Troy, which has gone the same way as extinct volcanoes and dried-up rivers and has become "the Sepulcher of what she was" (634). Like everything else that apparently dies, from the elements themselves to the Phoenix, Troy's downfall is just the preparation for the next change: though Aeneas may now be "drooping" because "*Ilium* now was in a sinking State" (646–47), the prophet Helenus advises him that he need not droop long, for

> *Troy* in Foreign Lands shall be restor'd.
> In happier Fields a rising Town I see,
> Greater than what e'er was, or is, or e'er shall be:
> And Heav'n yet owes the World a Race deriv'd from Thee.
> (652–55)

This is a suitable way to climax the discussion, since this talk is addressed to Numa, who is now being told what will become of the little town that he is about to shape. Pythagoras, who sees more broadly a power of change that works to build as well as to destroy, ends with this optimistic vision of the civilization to arise from the ashes of Troy:

> Sages, and Chiefs of other Lineage born
> The City shall extend, extended shall adorn:

But from *Julus* he must draw his Birth,
By whom thy *Rome* shall rule the conquer'd Earth.
(656–59)

While such a prediction is both a logical consequence of the foregoing argument and a lesson appropriate to the audience and the occasion, this acclamation may be somewhat unexpected in the context of *Fables* as a whole. This final extended speech, the last word, philosophically speaking, unabashedly celebrates the old heroic code, which, according to many critics, Dryden at this point in his career should be debunking. The peace-loving Pythagoras caps off his argument with the story of Aeneas, and his vision specifically includes a "conquer'd Earth" that we might expect Pythagoras to abhor, particularly since he follows this prediction by reiterating his injunctions against killing; his final verse paragraph begins: "Take not away the Life you cannot give" (705). But like the proper hunt, waged for self defense, certain kinds of conquest are acceptable, even to a man of peace. Caesars are necessary if Rome is to be possible.[26]

In balance, however, Pythagoras laments the destruction of empires even as he praises the rise of new ones. If his lengthy prophecy of Helenus confirms the heroic ideal, his depiction of a Troy "for ten long Years . . . / . . . daily bleeding" (630–31), whose streets are "fill'd with Tombs of her own perish'd Race" (633), and his spirited abhorrence of bloodshed confirm the rampant anti-heroism of *Fables* as well. Just as his view of change is more encompassing than that of Theseus, or the crone, or Sigismonda, so is his view broad enough to include the irreconcilable extremes we encounter in *Fables*, from the bad hunt to the beneficial hunt, from the anti-heroism to the partial heroic ideals. The lamentable destruction of war and the glory of civilization, or more generally the loss and the gain, Pythagoras not only recognizes, but celebrates. He rejoices

to view
My Country Walls rebuilt, and *Troy* reviv'd anew,
Rais'd by the fall: Decreed by Loss to Gain;
Enslav'd but to be free, and conquer'd but to reign.
(664–67)

The man of peace who accepts conquest, who explains that rising and falling, loss and gain, enslavement and freedom, defeat and victory are not only continually oscillating but also connected, the one leading to the other, presents on a philosophical plane the same clash of apparently irreconcilable positions that I have argued pervades *Fables*. As we go from one tale to another, from one group of tales to another possible grouping, from a noble character to his opposite (who is sometimes the same character), from a possible ideal—Christian or pagan, elevated or humble, dutiful wife or confirmed bachelor—to an unravelling of that ideal, we experience the perpetual flux that the Leibnizian Pythagoras praises as the universal process.

"The Cock and the Fox" and "Of the Pythagorean Philosophy," so different in genre, tone, and subject, could nonetheless be said to complement one another by offering commentary of two different sorts, the one comic, the other poised and philosophical. Both are inclusive in different ways: one parodies all, the other comprehends all, with Pythagoras providing us with a view that contains anti-heroic and heroic possibilities, that decries killing as it justifies necessary killing, that sees degeneration as an inescapable stage of regeneration. And both tales shift us outside the anthology to new vantage points: in one case to a position above the barnyard, where we watch with detachment and glee a comic enactment of perpetual flux; in the other, to a position beyond the human kingdom, up there in a philosophical realm from which it appears that perpetual flux is the active principle of all things, of beast, man, civilizations, nature, and time itself. In locating potential informing ideals, and then tracing their subversion, I have suggested that perhaps the ultimate informing ideal of *Fables* is the process of doing and undoing itself. If that is true, then I have done little more than anticipate Pythagoras, whose comment, applied to the universe as a whole, aptly describes what happens in the shifting landscape of *Fables*: "And every moment alters what is done, / And innovates some Act till then unknown" (276–77). "Innovation is" no longer "the Blow of Fate" ("Absalom and Achitophel," 800) that Dryden once dreaded; it is now an inescapable trait of a rapidly changing universe, which Pythagoras not only tolerates but also celebrates. What Pythagoras accepts with equanimity, what the creatures of the beast fable comically enact, is the same conflict of irreconcilable opposites that occurs throughout *Fables*. Dryden's Pythagoras does not so much "harmonize the apparently contradictory elements" (81), as Brooks Otis claims for Ovid's philosopher, as he demonstrates the absence of harmony and the unavoidable presence of contradiction. Both tales could be said to "cap" the entire collection; they repeat the pattern of doing and undoing, thereby confirming the basic strategy of *Fables*. But beyond that, they actually liberate us from irresolution, from unreconciled oppositions, in one case by freeing us into laughter at the whole process, and in the other by providing us with an enlarged understanding, grounded on ancient philosophy as well as on the new science, that perpetual flux, values knitting and unravelling, reforming and dissolving, are all part of a universe whose basic active principle is subversion.

NOTES

1. Brooks Otis, *Ovid as an Epic Poet*, 2nd ed. (Cambridge: Cambridge University Press, 1970), 81.
2. Unstable across Chaucer, and within the tale itself: "The shifting style and the succession of topics never rest long enough to serve a single view or a single doctrine or an unalterable judgment. Other tales adopt norms, then uncover differences according to their lights. This tale celebrates the normality of differences." From Charles Muscatine, *Chaucer and the French Tradition* (1957; rpt. Berkeley: University of California Press, 1966), 242.
3. The alternation of the bestial with the civilized, though implicit in Ovid, is made more overt in Dryden's version. Ovid's Myrrha describes these incestuous activities in a straightforward manner: animals unite ("coëuntque"); it is not considered shameful for the heifer to bear her father from behind ("Ferre patrem tergo"); the he-goat goes in ("init") among the flocks he himself has created ("creavit"). Dryden spices this up by using verbs like "bestride" and "rut," and by adding adjectives such as "lusty" and "salacious." On the other side of the contrast, although Ovid specifically mentions piety ("pietas"), Dryden amplifies this by adding the line about laws (41), and he further heightens the contrast by taking piety from the opening of Myrrha's speech and instead inserting it later on, right next to the "lusty Ram" (45). The Ovid text used is that of *Publii Ovidii Nasonis Operum*, ed. Nicolaus Heinsius, 3 vols. (Amsterdam: Elzevir, 1676), pp. 184–85 [Loeb, lines 324–26].
4. Tom Mason, in "Dryden's Version of the *Wife of Bath's Tale*," *Cambridge Quarterly* 6 (1975): 240–56, seems to have something similar in mind when he describes Dryden's general use of balances and contrasts in *Fables*: "The reader is never for a moment allowed to rest secure in any one set of attitudes but is caught up and led irresistibly and rapidly through a series of varied and delightful surprises so that he comes out more alive both to what is absurd and to what is wonderful in the way men and women behave towards each other" (242–43).
5. Peter Elbow, in *Oppositions in Chaucer* (1973; rpt. Middletown, CT: Wesleyan University Press, 1975), speaking of Chaucer, describes the mistranslation as "at once exactly wrong and exactly right" (107).

6. E. Talbot Donaldson, in *Chaucer's Poetry* (New York: Ronald Press Company, 1958), makes a similar observation about both the Nun's Priest and Chaucer, the fiction-maker behind the fiction-maker: each "survey[s] the world as if he were no part of it, as if he were situated comfortably on the moon looking at a human race whom he knew and loved wholeheartedly but whose ills he was immune from" (944).

7. For a discussion of how Dryden's attitude toward the poet's power and public role developed as early as the 1660s, under the influence of Davenant and in reaction against the "hazy mythic propaganda or brain-teasing intellectual conceit" that characterized poetry just before Dryden, see James Anderson Winn's biography (Winn, especially Chapter 3).

8. Elbow explores a similar ironic undercutting in Chaucer, who relies heavily upon "fancy rhetoric" to depict a Chaunticleer who demonstrates "the ridiculousness of high rhetoric." Preferring to emerge from the contradiction on the positive side, Elbow claims that "the final effect of the whole performance is a *celebration* of the very virtuoso rhetoric that is debunked" (110–12). My discussion merely puts it the other way around, taking the whole performance as a debunking of the virtuoso-rhetoric that is celebrated.

9. Ralph Cudworth, *The True Intellectual System of the Universe* (London, 1678), 370, quoted by S. K. Heninger, Jr., in *Touches of Sweet Harmony: Pythagorean Cosmology and Renaissance Poetics* (Los Angeles: Huntington Library, 1974), 34; Heninger provides a thorough account of the role played by Pythagoras in Renaissance thought, emphasizing that the Pythagorean sect at Croton was the "acknowledged prototype" for both the Academy of Plato and the Lyceum of Aristotle (19). In examining the many sources that combined to form the Pythagoras known to the Renaissance, Heninger suggests that "the classical author who transmitted Pythagorean ideas to the largest number of readers . . . is probably Ovid" (50).

10. As was the case with his translating only part of book thirteen of *Metamorphoses*, Dryden again edits his material rather than translating all of book fifteen. I think this is partially because Ovid gradually moves from Pythagoras to an extended, climactic panegyric for Augustus Caesar; I doubt that Dryden, whose hostility toward his own monarch is everywhere evident in *Fables*, would be interested in praising an Augustus at this point.

11. In seeking Pythagoras, Numa journeys to Crotona and asks for information from "a Senior of the Place" (14), who then tells the complicated history of Crotona, including how the Samian Pythagoras came there. When Pythagoras begins his speech, we are still within the summary offered by the elderly citizen, and it is his version of Pythagoras, rather than Pythagoras' own words, that we actually hear.

12. In *Dryden: The Poetics of Translation* (Toronto: University of Toronto Press, 1985), Judith Sloman, elaborating on her earlier argument that *Fables* moves toward Christian ideals, offers another explanation for Pythagoras' attitude toward meat-eating: "Through his attacks on cannibalism and ultimately on violence itself Dryden defines the true nature of the Eucharist as a banquet of sense and retaliates against the Anglican efforts to represent the Catholic as a weird mixture of cannibal and naïf for his insistence on taking Christ's phrase, 'This is my body', literally" (181). I have doubts about this interpretation, because again it seems to me a strained effort to turn an obviously pagan philoso-

pher into a proto-Christian, or in this case, a proto-Catholic. Sloman does the same thing in discussing Dryden's attitude toward Polybius (as expressed in the Dedication to the *Aeneid*), commenting that "though Polybius was not religious at all, as a pagan exemplar of integrity and in the search for truth he is a proto-Catholic" (32).

13. This is a slight Dryden alteration; Ovid's Pythagoras decries man's desire for forbidden food—"Unde fames homini vetitorum tanta ciborum" (Heinsius, p. 274 [Loeb, line 138]), which Sandys translates as "Whence springs so dire an appetite in man / To interdicted food?" (*Ovids Metamorphoses*, trans. George Sandys, 3rd ed. [London: Andrew Hebb, 1638], lines 138–39). Dryden renders the passage as "From whence, O mortal Men, this gust of Blood / Have you deriv'd, and interdicted Food" (202–3). Although he retains Sandys's translation of "vetitorum . . . ciborum" as "interdicted Food," Dryden adds "gust of Blood," which shifts this criticism of man's uncontrollable hunger into a more pointed denunciation of man's desire to kill.

14. For a thorough discussion of the hunting episodes in *Fables*, see Rachel A. Miller, "Regal Hunting: Dryden's Influence on *Windsor Forest*," *Eighteenth-Century Studies* 13 (1979/80): 169–88. Miller also connects the hunt with warfare and with passion, arguing that "traditionally, the hunt was viewed as a substitute for war, as a release for potentially dangerous passions. But it could inspire the very excessive passions that erupt in warfare" (179). Miller argues that the good hunts are those in which passion is under control (e.g., the joust in "The Flower and the Leaf"), while the evil hunts exhibit uncontrolled passion (e.g., "Meleager and Atalanta"). Jay Arnold Levine, in "John Dryden's Epistle to John Driden," *Journal of English and Germanic Philology* 63 (1964): 450–74, also discusses the connection of war and hunting, specifically examining the political implications of Kinsman Driden's hunt as an "Emblem of Humane Life" that applies to William III, whose sylvan chase is also the chase of James II from the throne (460). See also Eric Rothstein, "*Discordia non Concors*: The Motif of Hunting in Eighteenth-Century Verse," *Journal of English and Germanic Philology* 83 (1984): 330–54, on the ambivalence of the hunt.

15. Brooks Otis comments on similar linking devices in Ovid, at points where Ovid feels responsible for making connections, but where "the linkage in itself is often extremely superficial, often simply an ingenious *tour de force*" (80).

16. Besides adding the couplet about the heaven-sent monarch (714–15), Dryden expands a little on what Numa teaches, or rather, on what Numa's teaching serves to control. In the original, Ovid puts it positively: his sage teaches "sacrificos . . . ritus" (Heinsius, p. 283 [Loeb, line 483]), the source for Dryden's "soft Arts of Peace." Dryden, glancing again at familiar issues, adds that Numa will restrain rapine and lust, neither of which Ovid specifically mentions at this point.

17. Judith Sloman, in *Dryden: The Poetics* (181–83), argues that Theseus, Pythagoras, and Numa, together with other teaching figures like Nestor and the good parson, constitute an apostolic succession, whereby Dryden provides by indirection a Catholic substructure to *Fables*. Since Pythagoras is passing along his teachings orally, since they constitute a "sure Tradition" (76), one that, thanks to Numa, will be "thence transferr'd to *Rome*" (713—Ovid has "populi Latialis," Heinsius, p. 283 [Loeb, line 481]), this looks like a distinct possibility. However, as Sloman also admits, Numa had by tradition been associated with Catholic

superstition and popish ceremonies, and people like Sir Robert Filmer were changing him into the prototype of a worthy Anglican. Although it is possible that Dryden makes Numa a true Catholic apostle, thereby rescuing him from "both the positive Anglican image and the negative anti-Catholic image" (183), it is also possible that Dryden's Numa is, as he appears to be, the pupil of a pagan Pythagoras. I see no need to make pagan exemplars (including such as Baucis and Philemon) represent particular Christian traditions in order to appreciate the values they embody.

18. Although he does not deal specifically with Dryden's poetry, William Powell Jones, in *The Rhetoric of Science: A Study of Scientific Ideas and Imagery in Eighteenth-Century English Poetry* (Berkeley: University of California Press, 1966), assembles an impressive range of examples of the ways in which "scientific imagery" (36) pervades poetry dealing with these and other themes. Most pertinent to the age of Dryden is Jones's second chapter, "The Continuity of Old Ideas After 1700" (33–78), which actually begins with English poetry before 1700.

19. See William Powell Jones's *The Rhetoric of Science*, especially Chapter 1, "The Background of Science and Ideas" (1–32), for a discussion of this controversy and an account of the contributions made by these and other authors. Jones points out that the mechanical philosophy of Descartes was not as godless as the English attackers assumed, but that "to them the atheistic implications in Cartesian materialism revealed by Hobbes made it necessary to distinguish between their philosophy and Descartes's" (8).

20. Fruitful, and traditional. Although the topic is perhaps best known to modern readers from Jaques's Seven Ages of Man speech in *As You Like It*, the history of this attractive topos is long and complicated. See Samuel C. Chew, "'This Strange Eventful History,'" from *Joseph Quincy Adams: Memorial Studies*, ed. James G. McManaway, Giles E. Dawson, and Edwin E. Willoughby (Washington, DC: Folger Shakespeare Library, 1948), 157–82. Chew handily summarizes some of the treatments: "Aristotle had made three divisions; Pythagoras, Horace, and Ovid, four; Marcus Varro, five; Solon, St. Augustine, Avicenna, Isidore of Seville, and the Venerable Bede, six; Hippocrates, the famous seven" (159). Although Dryden is translating Ovid (who is presenting Pythagoras' view), the emphasis is on the process of change, not on the discrete steps, however many there may be.

21. Judith Sloman, in "The Structure of Dryden's *Fables*," Ph.D. diss., University of Minnesota, 1968, also compares the views of Pythagoras and Theseus, seeing the former as concerned with "the universality of change" (107) and the latter with "the stability beneath change" (108). The two speeches set "an idealistic against a realistic view of nature, leading a reader to consider both before arriving at a complete view" (108). Although this is a possible arrangement, I question whether a Christian who accepts death and dwells on the subject is necessarily more idealistic than a pagan who sees new empires arising from the ashes of the old. Nor do I believe that a "complete view" lies outside of both tales (Sloman is, I think, referring to the brief Christian portraits that follow), but rather that Pythagoras offers the broader view of the two, and that the quest for a complete view may be merely our natural desire to fix what, as Pythagoras argues, is ever in flux.

22. From Francis Bacon's "Essay: Of Vicissitude of Things" (1625), in *The*

Works of Francis Bacon, ed. James Spedding, Robert Leslie Ellis, and Douglas Denon Heath, 14 vols. (London: Longman & Company, 1858–74), 4:512. I am not arguing for direct influence here, even though "perpetual Flux" and "never at a stay" make Bacon and Dryden sound rather close. My point is that, with the widespread popularity of natural philosophy, it would be normal to find Dryden and Bacon relying upon a similar store of ideas, and at times a similar vocabulary. Bacon's essay is quite unlike the speech of Pythagoras in tone and purpose; yet, as some index to what kinds of ideas were in the air, one might note that Bacon too discusses deluges, earthquakes, mountains, wars, and the decay of empires. Bacon even ends his essay with an Ages of Man trope.

23. In *Dryden's Poetry* (Bloomington: Indiana University Press, 1967), Earl Miner, accounting for the links between "Of the Pythagorean Philosophy" and the preceding "The Wife of Bath Her Tale," stresses the importance of the resonances between Pythagoras' speech and that of the crone: "The real connection is between the philosophical nature of this selection and the long philosophical passage added or changed by Dryden towards the end of the preceding (386–484), which also introduces Roman history for examples of virtue (448 ff.)" (299–300). Judith Sloman, in *Dryden: The Poetics*, explores another interesting linkage, reading the crone's speech alongside the kinsman poem and "Cymon and Iphigenia" (197).

24. In his Preface, Dryden specifically acknowledges this parallel, although he makes it sound accidental; having already translated the Wife of Bath's tale, "when I took up *Boccace*, unawares I fell on the same Argument of preferring Virtue to Nobility of Blood, and Titles, in the Story of *Sigismonda*; which I had certainly avoided for the Resemblance of the two Discourses, if my Memory had not fail'd me" (Kinsley, 4:1460). Though the connection may have been accidental, it may also have been subconscious. At any event, having discovered the duplication, Dryden, despite his disclaimer, includes both tales in his collection, offering this advice: "Let the Reader weigh them both" (Kinsley, 4:1460).

25. James D. Garrison, in "The Universe of Dryden's *Fables*," *Studies in English Literature* 21 (1981): 409–23, examines many examples of fire imagery, including its appearance in these passages from "Palamon and Arcite," "Sigismonda and Guiscardo," "The Wife of Bath Her Tale," and "Of the Pythagorean Philosophy." Garrison sees two kinds of fire, one "a private fire potentially destructive of civilization," the other "a public fire that enhances and preserves it" (415). In tracing the many implications of the fire imagery, he establishes "sharply contrasting attitudes" (416) and "alternative paradigms of narrative within the universe of the *Fables*" (417), which he finds to be "in ultimate equilibrium" as "two phases of a single, repeated cycle" (423). Although I agree with much of Garrison's argument, especially in its attempt to illustrate "alternative paradigms," I disagree on the issue of Dryden's achieving "ultimate equilibrium"; this may be an imposition of order on conflicting views that Garrison himself admits are "problematic" (420) and difficult to understand in moral terms.

26. At the risk of inventing yet another grouping of tales, I might remind the reader that in his Preface, Dryden reports that he began *Fables* by translating the following works, in this order: the first book of the *Iliad*, the twelfth book of Ovid (The Battle of the Centaurs), "The Speeches of Ajax and Ulysses," and

then "Of the Pythagorean Philosophy." One could reasonably consider the last tale as part of the whole set dealing with the heroic code, and it is perhaps significant to note that Dryden placed it not next to the others, but toward the end of the entire collection, where it serves to summarize a great many other tales not in this initial grouping.

Chapter Seven

THE OLD POET AND THE
NEW POETIC MODE

$\mathcal{C}$RITICS have long wrestled with the idea of two-sided, irreconcilable Dryden. When the contraries entailed eulogizing Cromwell and then celebrating the Restoration of Charles, or defending Anglicanism against the gainful trading Catholics and then becoming a Catholic himself, Dryden's two-sidedness was hypocrisy and opportunism; he was shifting with the wind and merely saving himself as cheaply as he could. That kind of accusation died away when the issues, and Dryden's enemies, died away, at which point Dryden's crime matured into inconsistency, that hobgoblin of skeptical minds. Even his defender, Sir Walter Scott, saw Dryden as a "powerful mind" that could "entangle itself in sophistical toils of its own weaving," and went on to comment that Dryden's "opinions, doubtless, are often inconsistent, and sometimes absolutely contradictory."[1] Thomas H. Fujimura, Elias J. Chiasson, Phillip Harth, and Sanford Budick gradually turned this view around by establishing Dryden's skeptical procedure as a positive philosophical operation rather than an anti-rationalistic propensity for disconcerting vacillation.[2] At the same time, scholars like Bernard N. Schilling, Alan Roper, and Earl Miner approached the poetry looking for a unified, comprehensive Dryden.[3] Inconsistency gradually lost its force as a damaging accusation, and it was possible, and even normal, to speak of a unified Dryden; certainly, there was irony and paradox, but it served a coherent purpose, with differences being reconciled rather than ever clashing.[4]

Like the Pythagorean universe, all this may be changing again, for with the recent advent of post-structuralism, we are beginning to hear yet another reappraisal of Dryden in some quarters, a reappraisal that rejects the quest for organic unity. Instead of attempting to pull contradictions into coherence, some critics have done just the opposite, emphasizing Dryden's reiteration of contradiction, his disparities, dualities, disjunctions, his irreconcilable oppositions.[5] The very inconsistencies that had once bothered Scott and George Saintsbury, and that constituted a problem that another generation of critics needed to solve, are gradually becoming not merely acceptable but praiseworthy. We seem to be coming around in a full circle, in ways Dryden would no doubt have appreciated; we have become inconsistent about inconsistency. Now that playful contraries are in fashion, Dryden's worst failing is well on its way to becoming his chief virtue.

In speaking about a process of doing and undoing, about a text that subverts itself and presents irreconcilable alternatives, I perhaps sound close to this deconstructionist position. To some, I may seem to be moving dangerously close to the brink, although I suspect (and hope) I am not moving at all far enough for the satisfaction of those who regard deconstruction as the truth (to be consistent, they would also have to claim it is not the truth). I should stress, then, that I am talking about something different, and that I disagree with the deconstructionist position. I do not think that the subversive process I am describing is an inescapable property of all texts, but rather a particular quality, serving a particular strategic purpose, in *Fables*. In some cases, we can see Dryden choosing his material so as to create this effect, perhaps most noticeably when he follows his translation of *Metamorphoses*, book twelve, that vigorous grotesque of heroic exploits, with just enough of book thirteen to end with the tribute to Ajax and a sigh at the loss of heroic greatness. After thoroughly debasing the heroic code, Dryden ends with a tribute to it, and it is his choice of what to include and where to stop that creates the reversal.

In other cases, by comparing some of Dryden's translations to their originals, we can discover how Dryden has *made* his material subversive, by emphasizing contradictions, heightening tensions, disallowing resolutions. In the tale of Cymon, discussed previously, Dryden both amplifies the regeneration of this brute (supporting the "progress" with a "Poeta Loquitur," adding a Virgilian passage on this new Creation, etc.) and deepens the degeneration as well, pushing the Cymons further apart.

He treats Sigismonda similarly; he makes his heroine better (by making Tancred worse), depicting her as a wronged daughter, as a patriot steadfastly resisting a tyrannical monarch, and as a wife whose father has no right to complain about her choice of a second husband. At the same time that Dryden fortifies his Sigismonda, he also undermines her, by making her motives for "loving" Guiscardo more suspect and by adding the peculiar marriage scene that I examined earlier. What makes that scene especially interesting is that it works to contrary ends and in a way epitomizes the subversive process I have been exploring; the scene establishes a sacred marriage and removes Sigismonda's crime, but in the process nearly destroys the sanctimony of the act, as we watch the harried priest rush offstage to prevent being corrupted by the wild passion he has just made holy. Whatever the conflict may be between Ghismonda's behavior and her self-justification, or between improved Cymon and debased Cymon in the Boccaccio originals, Dryden's additions widen the extremes, keep the conflicts constantly before us, and turn possible resolutions into the irreconcilable; it is not the stories that break apart, but Dryden who does the disassembling.

Even an original work such as "Alexander's Feast" offers evidence of added tensions, although here we are looking not at an original Dryden has altered, but at a tradition involving the story of Timotheus. Dryden follows the basic tale used by Spenser, John Case, Tom Durfey, and Jeremy Collier, whereby Timotheus enrages and calms Alexander. However, Dryden reverses the standard sequence, and where the original Timotheuses calm Alexander before he can wreak any havoc, Dryden's Timotheus does just the opposite, with Dryden emphasizing the destructive power of Timotheus' craft.[6] Yet Dryden's emphasis does more than just the opposite; the destruction does not cancel out the miraculous power of Timotheus, which I think Dryden is genuinely celebrating. Dryden's twisting of the traditional story manages to complicate the glorious power of the artist with the suggestion of its possibly dangerous consequences. Like the figure of the poet in "The Cock and the Fox," the poet-rhetorician Timotheus is both a testament to Dryden's divine craft and a manipulator who could lead to destruction. In any case, Dryden has made the Timotheus figure as troublesome as Cymon and Sigismonda, in similar ways, for they all command respect for their apparent virtues, which is challenged or undone by their frailties.

What we have in these examples, and I think throughout *Fables*, is a purposeful disjunctive strategy. Furthermore, it is a strategy that represents a new poetic mode, not something discontinuous with Dryden the laureate, but something developing naturally out of his earlier habits of mind. The skeptical Dryden, able to argue both sides of an argument, much to the consternation of critics, has long been with us. But the earlier skeptic who examined different sides of an issue used that technique for polemical purposes. In arguing for the superiority of the Ancients, and then for the advantages of the Moderns, for French drama, then English drama, in taking the Shaftesbury side, and then the Charles side, Dryden may have played with opposites, but there is little doubt as to what side of the case wins. However tenuous they may sometimes sound to modern ears, resolutions emerge, and if we hear Catholic arguments that seem to endanger the Anglican purpose of "Religio Laici," we nonetheless find that this poem ends with an Anglican conclusion. The inconsistent Dryden who changed his mind—about blank verse vs. rhyme in tragedy, about Anglicanism and Catholicism—may have argued opposites sides of each case, but at any given point, he shaped his argument toward a resolution and took a position, which he usually made appear to be a mean between extremes.

After 1688, however, Dryden becomes more ambiguous, in part because this had become necessary given the political circumstances. Something happened, something had to happen, as the prophet-laureate lost his privileged position, as this former spokesman in "The Public Mode" watched his ideals going one way while the nation went another.[7] Furthermore, Dryden's verse becomes more disjunctive because his views have altered, his previous visionary accords and many of his ideals having crumbled, making synthesis and resolution no longer possible. What happened to Dryden has an important bearing on *Fables*; far from being an autonomous object that self-destructs, *Fables*, I would argue, is a deeply personal work, expressing Dryden's own struggles as a poet in a hostile clime.[8]

A SUBJECT AND HIS KINGS

That Dryden's voice has become more disjunctive will perhaps become clearer if we take a familiar Dryden theme, like the dangerous power of kings, and listen to how his treatment of that issue shifts, while his words seem to be offering the same conservative, wary advice as ever. That kingship was always a topic dear to Dryden needs no proving; he either celebrated or criticized (or both) every leader from Cromwell through William III. Throughout *Fables*, Dryden seems almost obsessed with the issue, using any available opening, and making openings when we least expect them (e.g., by adding the tyrant's den for Tancred in "Sigismonda and Guiscardo"), to comment on usurping William and his military policies.

The first pointed comment occurs in the opening poem, "To the Dutchess of Ormond," where after likening the duchess and the duke to Emily and Palamon, Dryden suggests that the duke deserves to be sent by "Conqu'ring *Theseus* . . . / . . . to guide the *Theban* Government" (36–37).[9] In the tale to follow, Theseus burns and sacks Thebes, so this amounts to a polite suggestion that James Butler, the duke of Ormond, would make a proper, constructive appointee to rule a conquered country. This is more than hypothetical praise, for Butler had just visited Ireland, a country recently ravaged by William when, by mounting a major military offensive, he managed to defeat the Jacobites decisively at the Battle of Boyne (1690). Butler's mission was to reconcile the hostile Irish to William's rule, and thus Dryden's comment expresses his approval of the duke's qualifications in that specific role. What makes Ormond especially appropriate, besides the noble qualities of his character, is that he is Irish. His is "a venerable Name; / His Father and his Grandsire [were] known to Fame" (55–56). When the duchess goes forth to Ireland first, as "*Ormond*'s Harbinger" (62), the Irish will fall prostrate and adore this "Pledge of her expected Lord" (54):

> Aw'd by that House, accustom'd to command,
> The sturdy *Kerns* in due Subjection stand;
> Nor hear the Reins in any Foreign Hand.
> (57–59)

What is praise of the Ormond peace mission, as we cannot help but notice, is also criticism of William, for Dryden contrasts the "Gen'rous" (37) duke against "Conqu'ring *Theseus*," just as he contrasts the restorative powers of the duchess against the "Waste of Civil Wars" (64); she is the "mighty Recompence" for the "Blood, Rapines, Massacres" (68–69) William inflicted on Ireland.

As we hear Dryden distinguishing this "due Subjection" of the Irish to the Ormonds from the undue subjection of obeying "any Foreign Hand," it is difficult not to think of Dryden's penchant for complaining about Dutch William. Dryden had done something similar when he compared foreign kings to England's native St. George in the final tableau of *King Arthur* (1691). Here, in the Ormond poem, Dryden takes advantage of a delicious irony that history made possible: backward Ireland, of all places, the home of Flecknoe and the easternmost boundary of Shadwell's empty kingdom, is the blessed land about to receive a "second Coming" (80), while the source of barbarism that has nearly destroyed that "happy Clyme" (87) is William. In other words, Dryden has turned a common ethnic joke around: William is *worse* than Irish—he is Dutch.

With this kind of innuendo running throughout the poem and, indeed, throughout *Fables*, we are likely to be alert to the political significance of a later passage in the Ormond poem, in which Dryden, instead of merely complaining about William, offers some concrete advice to his monarch:

> A Subject in his Prince may claim a Right,
> Nor suffer him with Strength impair'd to fight;
> Till Force returns, his Ardour we restrain,
> And curb his Warlike Wish to cross the Main.
> (107–10)

There is nothing vague about this. It sounds like the standard Opposition line, which consistently attacked William's attempts to strengthen the military.[10] The unpopular Nine Years War, still called by historians "King William's War," had come to an end with the 1697 Treaty of Rijswijk. In order to prevent further aggression by Louis XIV, William was pushing for a Standing Army, and England, weary of the war and saddled with a war debt of £5,500,000, resisted William. What we have here is the first of Dryden's many remarks in *Fables* on the maintenance of the Standing Army, which was also being attacked by a flood of pamphlets beginning in 1697. William's third Parliament (1697–98) fought over this issue, with things finally coming to a head in the fourth Parliament, which, in December 1698, voted to reduce William's land forces drastically. Parliament also voted to exclude from those forces all but natural-born subjects, which meant doing away with the Dutch Guards, whose presence had served as an irritating reminder of William's foreignness. In this context, Dryden's lines defend the right of the English to do what the English and the new Country Party had just done: to curb the apparently warlike wishes of the "Conqu'ring *Theseus*" who had just dragged England through a costly, unpopular war.

Glancing back a few years, we can discover a similar warning levied against the military predilections of another king. It occurs in "Britannia Rediviva" (1688), the last major poem Dryden wrote before losing the laureateship. Now that a son, the so-called "warming-pan" baby, had been born to James II, thus promising the Catholic succession so greatly feared by the English, Dryden performs his laureate's task of acclaiming the event, somewhat frantically, because he is well aware of the shaky state of James's throne. The panegyric seems edgy, with Dryden not so much celebrating the guaranteed succession as praying that "Thy Father's Angel and Thy Father joyn / To keep Possession, and secure the Line" (45–46). Toward the end of the poem, Dryden turns to his king, taking advantage of what was to be his last chance to remind James of the impending disaster that might result from the king's continued high-handedness:[11]

> The Name of Great, your Martial mind will sute,
> But Justice, is your Darling Attribute:
> ·
> Some Kings the name of Conq'rours have assum'd,
> Some to be Great, some to be Gods presum'd;
> But boundless pow'r, and arbitrary Lust
> Made Tyrants still abhor the Name of Just:
> They shun'd the praise this Godlike Virtue gives,
> And fear'd a Title, that reproach'd their Lives.
> (333–34, 339–44)

The political circumstances are different, and this is a different king, but the warning sounds the same; the passage in the Ormond poem on the rights of a subject to curb the warlike instincts of his prince sounds like a defense of the very stance taken by subject Dryden in the lines above.

If, however, we consider the entire context of Dryden's remarks, we discover that the familiar-sounding voice is saying things rather differently in these two poems. In "Britannia," the context of the passage serves to confirm Dryden's advice to his king. The poem is filled with supporting examples of the destruction resulting from the exercise of tyrannical power. England itself has been too "Prompt to Revenge" (283) and should, like James, incline toward charity and moderation rather than aggressiveness and severity:

> By living well, let us secure his days,
> Mod'rate in hopes, and humble in our ways.
> No force the Free-born Spirit can constrain,
> But Charity, and great Examples gain.
> Forgiveness is our thanks, for such a day;
> 'Tis Godlike, God in his own Coyn to pay.
>
> (298–303)

Just as James's martial mind should instead incline toward justice, so should England incline toward moderation, whereby the prince and the people will reaffirm one another. And Dryden's warnings to James are consonant with Dryden's depiction of England's past behavior:

> Enough of Ills our dire Rebellion wrought,
> When, to the Dregs, we drank the bitter draught;
> Then airy Atoms did in Plagues conspire,
> Nor did th' avenging Angel yet retire,
> But purg'd our still encreasing Crimes with Fire.
> Then perjur'd Plots, the still impending Test,
> And worse; but Charity conceals the Rest:
> Here stop the Current of the sanguine flood,
> Require not, Gracious God, thy Martyrs Blood;
> But let their dying pangs, their living toyl,
> Spread a Rich Harvest through their Native Soil:
> A Harvest ripening for another Reign,
> Of which the Royal Babe may reap the Grain.
>
> (152–64)

Bloodshed only begets more bloodshed, as England's rebellion only brought an avenging angel, in the form of the Plague and the Great Fire. The advice for moderation, for stopping the "sanguine flood," is equally applicable to England and to James, to the past and to the future. Dryden is bringing past political history and natural phenomena into one accord, and the patterns he arranges out of such events confirm the advice he gives to James. "When will the Minister of Wrath give o're?" (175), a line applied to the years of rebellion, becomes equally applicable to James, who leans too much to "Resistless Force" (349). A line like "Tempests have force unbounded to destroy" (351), applied to James, is equally applicable to Dryden's version of England's "dire Rebellion" and its consequences. The warning addressed to the king about the dangers of "arbitrary Lust" (341) is also applicable to the country and to the poet himself, as implied by Dryden's earlier confessional statement, "In Lusts we wallow" (281), where the "we" includes England and Dryden, both guilty of the vice that threatens to undo James II.

This is not the case with the interesting passage from the Ormond poem on a subject's right to restrain his prince, for here we find instances and circumstances that undercut rather than confirm the words addressed to the king. The justification for restraining a warlike king, which I think is an unavoidable implication of the subject-prince passage, pulls against the immediate context of the passage. Dryden has just described the duchess as an emissary of peace, a redemptive force whose visit to Ireland will restore that war-torn country:

> So, when You came, with loud repeated Cries,
> The Nation took an Omen from your Eyes,
> And God advanc'd his Rainbow in the Skies,
> To sign inviolable Peace restor'd;
> The Saints with solemn Shouts proclaim'd the new accord.
> (75–79)

But then, after amplifying on the restorative powers that this Venus-like, Christlike, St. Patrick-like figure promises to offer Ireland, Dryden comes to the turning point considered earlier, and begins speculating on the duchess's illness, advising her not to travel to Ireland again until she has fully recovered: he dare not "trust so soft a Messenger, / New from her Sickness, to that Northern Air" (101–2). Now comes the subject-prince passage, and its basic sense is that the duchess should not engage in this venture until her health, her "Force," returns; Dryden as a subject is claiming his right to restrain her from this generous act lest she endanger herself further:

> A Subject in his Prince may claim a Right,
> Nor suffer him with Strength impair'd to fight;
> Till Force returns, his Ardour we restrain,
> And curb his Warlike Wish to cross the Main.
> (107–10)

In short, the prince is both the warlike William and the peace-bringing duchess who, like the "Dove returning, bore the Mark / Of Earth restor'd" (70–71). The desire "to cross the Main" is both a potentially warlike act, presumably against France, and the duchess's restorative mission to a devastated Ireland, devastated by none other than the warlike prince.

As was the case when I earlier built an argument for Dryden's anti-heroism and then argued for the existence of partial heroic ideals, or when I defended the cause of noble Sigismonda and then made a case for an ignobled Sigismonda, I have dealt with two opposing interpretations of the subject-prince passage separately and rather deliberately, for convenience. But this is not a matter of reading the passage either one way *or* the other. We are in the realm of "both/and," trying to adjust somehow to two opposing pulls that exert their force simultaneously.[12] This is quite a different experience from what "Britannia Rediviva" offers; in the 1688 poem, the historical background and the events in the poem conspire to validate the political innuendo. For the Ormond poem, our knowledge of the historical circumstances, our awareness of Dryden's other poems ripe with political criticism, and our consciousness of Dryden's personal situation—what else can one expect from an outcast who disliked the administration that had cast him out?—make the criticism of William inescapable. But the local context of the events in the poem subverts rather than confirms this reading, creating a clash between that "Warlike Wish" suitable to William and "inviolable Peace restor'd" in the person of the duchess.

It would be oversimplifying things to imply that the earlier passage on James II is straightforward. Obviously, irony abounds in Dryden, where, even in the non-satires, praise accompanies its contrary, blame (in the satires, of course, praise can *be* blame). The lines on James also cut two ways, in part because Dryden is sweetening his criticism by coating it with praise, hoping that James will lean toward justice and rule with a "steady Hand" (360) rather than give in to "boundless pow'r, and arbitrary Lust" (341). But the oppositions here are cooperative rather than subversive. Instead of a clash of the irreconcilable, here the qualities attributed to the king are those that Dryden desires; they comprise a standard against which Dryden's more frightening image of the martial king can be measured. James should be the one, steady, restrained, and constructive, but he is all too probably the other, boundless in his power and dangerously arbitrary; the "Prince" in the passage from the Ormond poem, on the other hand, is simultaneously constructive and warmongering.

Antitheses in Dryden, both in his poetry and his career, have been the primary reason the poet has been blamed, or more recently praised, for inconsistency. As in the case of two-sided James, Dryden often uses divisions as contrasts acting together for a clear rhetorical end.[13] Speaking of divided kings, we can find further evidence of this kind of cooperative contrast by briefly examining how Dryden treats Charles II in "Absalom and Achitophel" (1681). Under the cover of praise, Dryden's famous opening lines establish clearly Charles's most memorable hobby, his "Promiscuous use of Concubine and Bride" (6), supposedly not a sin in those pious times when polygamy was standard. In detailing the immediate effects (and lack of same) of Charles's behavior, Dryden introduces a key epithet that will reappear later in the poem:

> *Michal*, of Royal blood, the Crown did wear,
> A Soyl ungratefull to the Tiller's care:
> Not so the rest; for several Mothers bore
> To Godlike *David*, several Sons before.
> (11–14)

A king who fornicates with the same finesse as a ploughman plying his trade is scarcely Godlike, although he may be David-like.[14] Part of the humor comes from the unsuitability of "Godlike *David*," from our recognizing the disparity between Charles's graphically described behavior and his responsibilities as God's agent. Dryden drives the joke home a few lines later when he singles out Absalom-Monmouth as an especially worthy heir because he may have been "inspir'd by some diviner Lust" (19); "divine" is just as inappropriate to lust as "Godlike" is to this seed-scattering David.

Throughout the poem, Dryden continues his criticism of this "indulgent *David*" (31) who is too easy, both in managing the body politic and in managing his own body. In praising his father, Absalom-Monmouth stresses these softer traits, describing Charles as "Mild, Easy, Humble, . . . / Enclin'd to Mercy, and averse from Blood" (325–26); Achitophel-Shaftesbury, in his second temptation speech, maintains that such mildness attests to a serious deficiency: "Not that your Father's Mildness I condemn, / But Manly Force becomes the diadem" (381–82). True, these are Dryden's deluded and deluding characters rather than the omniscient persona, but they emphasize the same thing about Charles that Dryden usually emphasized, the king's "mildness," his disposition toward mercy rather than toughness, which could be either a good thing or a bad thing. For instance, in "Threnodia Augustalis" (1685), Charles is "That all forgiving King" (257), and the first of the various "Vertues of a Royal Mind" (335) that Dryden lists is forgiveness (336); here, a mild and forgiving nature is taken as a virtue, made clearer by contrasting Charles with his successor James, "A Warlike Prince" who "ascends the Regal State" (429). As "Britannia Rediviva" demonstrates, Dryden would soon complain about too much manly force in James and too little mercy, but in the days of Charles, things were the other way around.

In "Absalom and Achitophel," when Charles finally speaks, he demonstrates the accuracy of Monmouth's characterization of him, mentioning that he has long been swayed "by native mercy" (939), admitting that he has been "So willing to forgive th' Offending Age" (941), lamenting that his "Clemency" (943), his "Forgiving Right" (944), and his "tenderness of Blood" (947) have been misconstrued as weaknesses. Gradually, and reluctantly—"Must I at length the Sword of Justice draw?" (1002)—Charles asserts his lawful power to punish, moving finally away from forgiveness and toward the manly, and kingly, force that befits the diadem.[15] His last words amount to a threat; once "Factious crowds" (1018) expend their "Brutal Rage" (1019), he will then

> urge the fight,
> And rise upon 'em with redoubled might:
> For Lawfull Pow'r is still Superiour found,
> When long driven back, at length it stands the ground.
> (1022–25)

Despite Charles' inclination toward mercy and tolerance, when push comes to shove, kings will ultimately be kings, by God.

> He [David-Charles] said. Th' Almighty, nodding, gave Consent;
> And Peals of Thunder shook the Firmament.
> Henceforth a Series of new time began,
> The mighty Years in long Procession ran:
> Once more the Godlike *David* was Restor'd,
> And willing Nations knew their Lawfull Lord.
> (1026–1031)

Charles assumes kingliness literally "by God," Who approves the royal pronouncement with a nod followed by impressive theatrical effects. We no longer read "Godlike *David*" as ironic, for the Charles figure, having fallen comically short of this standard at the beginning of the poem, has finally risen to fulfill the ideal by the end of the poem. This marks his second Restoration in at least two ways: first, his assertion of power establishes once more the proper Stuart succession, triumphant over wicked Shaftesbury, illegitimate Monmouth, and the fractious rabble; second, the Charles figure has been restored to the sacred ideal of kingship. The over-indulgent, dissipated monarch has become a consolidation of lawful power forcefully applied, and then confirmed by heavenly thunderbolts. Like his earlier model of poetic power, Anne Killigrew, Dryden has just endowed his monarch with a "Warlike Mind" and "Soul devoid of Fear" (131), in hopes of urging his too-easy monarch to adopt these traits.

As was the case with James in "Britannia Rediviva," we again have two opposing images of the king, although Charles seems to progress from one to the other, whereas James's progression is what Dryden urgently pleads for.[16] The contrasting images, one mild and merciful, the other manly and forceful, do not remain in conflict, but rather imply resolutions; Charles is either the one (usually) or the other (eventually); in "Britannia," James should be the one, but is too much the other. In either case, the opposites combine in defining kingship, suggesting what a king should be by showing how he falls short of certain desirable virtues, and this, I think, is how doubleness so often works in Dryden. We are accustomed to discovering a set of analogues, of illuminating patterns, implicit ideals, and underlying values, as Earl Miner does when he sees in "MacFlecknoe" a testament of Dryden's "assurance of abiding ideals and values to which lesser realities might be referred with ease" (*Dryden's Poetry*, 84). These distinctly lesser realities are kings of another stamp, but a similar cooperative contrast is at work. The king of bad poetry is likened to Augustus and Romulus; bad playwrights are compared to Fletcher, Jonson, and Etherege, as well as to the legendary Arion; the "last great Prophet of Tautology" (30) and his spiritual father are likened to such prophets as John the Baptist, Elijah, and Elisha. Aside from providing humor, this sustained disparity also serves to establish informing ideals, both artistic and moral, against which Flecknoe and Shadwell can be measured and found wanting.

Yet, as I have tried to demonstrate, when we search for informing ideals in *Fables*, we find instead unresolved oppositions, as the local example of the two-sided prince and duchess illustrates. This is true of the ideal Christian figures, who cannot replace or be replaced by those vestiges of noble heroism, who run counter to the anti-heroes; true of the heroic Sigismonda, who is also self-deluding fleshpot; of the visionary Timotheus, who is also a manipulating flatterer; of the improved Cymon, who is still Cymon the brute. The clash within a passage, within a tale, across tales, between groups of tales does not lead toward resolution, but rather establishes hosts of contradictions that remain irreconcilable.

DRYDEN'S FINAL POETIC MODE

Like the deconstructive critics, I see "doubleness," "disjunction and incommensurability," and "failure to reconcile," but even so, I think what I am describing is significantly different.[17] Speaking of Dryden's "failure to reconcile" suggests a deficiency in the poetry, whereas I would maintain that Dryden's process of establishing contrary positions, like his skepticism, amounts to a purposeful strategy, with Dryden firmly in control. The history of favorable critical responses to *Fables* suggests that we are dealing not with a poet who fails, but rather with one who has succeeded remarkably well. I am also uncomfortable with the deconstructionists' tendency to slight the issues in favor of appreciating clever duplicities, an approach I find unsatisfactory for a poet like Dryden, so deeply embroiled in the political turmoil and religious controversies of a turbulent age.[18] Dryden's lifelong concern with the moral responsibilities of a poet, on which he reflects sometimes with pride, and sometimes with guilt and self-consciousness, should encourage us to participate sympathetically in his struggles, which is not what happens when we stand back from the poems and list the contradictions.[19] Appreciating contrariness, treating Dryden's poetry as purposeless exercises in paradox and contrariety, not only abstracts us from the very issues Dryden thought crucial, but also often privileges the reader, quirks and all, to the exclusion of the author, his purposes, and his times. Deconstructive criticism too often skims over this necessary context, and the result, to my mind, is line-by-line readings that are frequently idiosyncratic, solipsistic, and defiantly ahistorical. Ultimately, such an approach reveals more about the psychology of the individual reader, or about the process of reading itself, than about the work under consideration and about the author's intentions.

By insisting on the significance of the historical context, and by daring to mention that sinful word immoralized by Wimsatt and Beardsley, "intention," I am taking advantage of one of the healthy developments emerging from the trembling wake of deconstruction. In defending themselves against the new wave, many who have been grounded in New Critical principles have been forced to reexamine their own beliefs, and there seems to be a growing tendency to respect those very contexts New Criticism officially regarded as extraneous to the poem itself, namely, history and the author's intention.[20] It now may be possible to move unapologetically in a direction that not long ago would have been closed off, as James A. Winn does when, after criticizing deconstructionists who seem absorbed in studying their own minds, he insists upon weighing the author's intention: though this remains unknowable in its entirety, it is still pertinent, because even if "we can never gain perfect access to the mind of any writer, . . . most readers will be more interested in a partial account of a poet's mind than in a partial account of a critic's."[21]

A partial account of Dryden's mind must take into consideration his changed position after he lost the laureateship. At one level, having lost his privilege to comment and criticize as the king's poet, from within the system, Dryden had to resort to indirect, partially veiled criticism. This is not to argue that as laureate he relied upon bludgeoning in making his political criticisms; "there is still a vast difference betwixt the slovenly Butchering of a Man, and the fineness of a stroak that separates the Head from the Body, and leaves it standing in its place" ("Discourse concerning the Original and Progress of Satire," *Works*, 4:71). Indirection was always part of the game, but now the game went underground. Dryden could not, as at the end of "Absalom and Achitophel," pronounce ringingly his ideas of kingship, or, for that matter, denounce the Williamite settlement as blatantly as in "The Medall" he had indicted the "Frogs and Toads, and all the Tadpole Train" (304) who followed that "formidable Cripple" (272) Shaftesbury; if that is Dryden's idea of a fine stroke, it is only as fine as a sledgehammer would allow. Dryden, always capable of the deftly aimed sidelong slash, could also be bold and forthright in his commentary; after 1688, however, he had to choose his weapons more carefully.

Dryden had to be wary about political reprisals, about active persecution, about the possibility of being charged with treason, which I doubt troubled him when he used the word "promiscuous" in describing Charles.[22] By November of 1688, when William's invasion was underway and James's hasty departure (23 December) imminent, miscellaneous, disorganized persecution of Catholics began, with general rioting and looting that included attacks upon Catholic chapels. Dryden, like any Catholic, probably hoped to maintain a low profile, but that would have been difficult, what with opportunistic hack authors attacking the old laureate in print; Tom Brown, for instance, published a pamphlet, *The Reasons for Mr. Bays Changing his Religion*, in the Fall and had another attack ready even before James left the country (although Brown did not publish the sequel until 1690). Once James had departed and William had started to settle in, mob violence dwindled, order was restored, and the persecution became better organized, as selected Catholics, particularly prominent ones, were arrested and imprisoned, including the Catholic scholar Obidiah Walker (January 1689), who may have been tutor to Dryden's son John, Jr.

Along with direct arrests came a more insidious form of persecution, beginning as early as 22 December 1688 (the day before James's flight), when "a great meeting of the lords spiritual and temporal at Westminster" decided "to banish papists 10 miles from London" (Luttrell, 1:490). Dryden was technically safe, since the quasi-legal order excluded those who had been in residence for the past three years, but who could tell how far the new government would go in carrying out its threats? It would have been impossible for Dryden to feel secure, especially when, in February of 1689, constables were charged with taking a census of Papists living in London, and they accordingly counted Dryden, "a poet in Gerrard Street," mistakenly registering him as one William Dayton (so much for the idea that municipal officials might have been familiar with poetry). One suspects this would have been unnerving, all the more so when on 13 March 1689 a proclamation banning Catholics from living in London made the earlier ad hoc order official (Luttrell, 1:533).

Although we have little evidence concerning Dryden's activities during this period, he probably laid low in his house in Gerrard street, or possibly slipped off to visit his Northamptonshire relatives until things cooled down. In his first play after the Bloodless Revolution, *Don Sebastian* (first acted 4 December 1689, in print by 6 January 1690), we get a glimpse of Dryden's altered circumstances. He closes the Dedication (to the earl of Leicester) with a quotation pieced together from two letters written by Cicero and sent as he left for banishment in 58 B.C., which includes the remark: "ego nimirum, idem sum. Inimici mei mea mihi non meipsum ademerunt" ("I am still the same. My enemies have robbed me of all I had; but they have not robbed me of myself").[23] What I find intriguing about this self-consciously noble stance—Dryden as a second Cicero staunchly remaining true to himself and resisting a dictatorship—is how indirectly Dryden assumes it, through analogy, in another tongue, through another author, without naming enemies or dictators who may have dispossessed him. Dryden is taking a firm stand, but seems to be taking it as quietly as possible, saying enough to satisfy his own scruples, and yet not enough to make him too conspicuous a target.

With less posturing, Dryden alludes to his troubles again towards the beginning of the Preface. Speaking of himself in the third person, he freely acknowledges that "misfortunes have once more brought him against his will, upon the Stage," and then makes fun of "these bad circumstances" (*Works*, 15:65), which he has just regarded as dire consequences visited upon a stoic Cicero. Dryden laughs off the inconveniences he has had to endure: in the Prologue that follows, he mentions specifically the prohibition against Catholics owning a horse worth more than five pounds, and the double tax rates imposed upon Catholics, hoping that his audience will "Fine him to daily Drudging and Inditing; / And let him pay his Taxes out, in Writing" (Prologue, 45–46). Dryden, a man without a pension since July 1688, who was now in all likelihood supporting his previously self-employed sons, Charles and John, Jr., would probably have regarded doubled taxes as more than a minor aggravation, and yet he makes his financial difficulties sound like a petty annoyance he is above.[24] What we get is a glimpse of high seriousness, a dramatic, noble pose, asserted quietly, and then further softened by good-humored acceptance of his plight; Dryden manages to take his stand and seem acquiescent at the same time. He also takes a political stand in the play itself, although whenever we find passages bristling with innuendo, we are likely to discover that they are generally applicable, not just pointed. When characters denounce tyranny or mob violence, we can assume Dryden has some local examples in mind, yet what sane, responsible subject-playwright would *not* abhor tyranny and mob rule?

Even when Dryden glances toward the new regime, he tends to avert his gaze before he can be caught.[25]

In retrospect, we can see that Dryden had little to fear, that he was considered harmless, that he managed to write and publish with his usual energy—four plays, an opera, contributions to two collections of verse (*Satires of Juvenal & Persius, Examen Poeticum*), a steady flow of occasional poems, prologues, epilogues, not to mention his translation of Virgil, and, of course, *Fables*. The initial hysteria, before William had consolidated his power, gradually died down, and Dryden was never arrested, as easy a target as he must have been (perhaps they were all looking for William Dayton). Though there may have been factions foaming at the mouth, they were not quite threatening to devour the old Papist. That Dryden could make light of his troubles in the Prologue to *Don Sebastian*, that he could continue to acknowledge his Catholicism publicly, that he could persist in criticizing William and his policies almost every time he set pen to paper, attests to the comparative tolerance of the Protestant regime. At times, that tolerance actually helped Dryden get away with criticism without him having to set pen to paper, as was the case when Queen Mary on 28 May 1689 ordered the revival of Dryden's *The Spanish Fryar*, which she attended only to be embarrassed when the Protestant play she had requested happened to include a typically Drydenian advocacy of legitimate succession. Dryden must have enjoyed scoring a palpable hit without even having to draw his sword.

Hindsight, however, may tempt us to overestimate Dryden's sense of confidence and freedom from fear—*Don Sebastian* does not sound like the work of a harassed man—but we should pause to consider that, from where Dryden stood, things looked far more dangerous.[26] He could not know how tolerant the regime would continue to be; he could not know that he would emerge unscathed and would be able to continue publishing, and in the volatile political atmosphere of the 1690s, no Catholic could regard himself as secure, at least not for very long. If Dryden had been confident enough about his own safety when he wrote *Don Sebastian*, he probably would have felt uneasy when, in June of 1690, a conspiracy was revealed, and more people were arrested and held in the Tower awaiting trial, "being committed for high treason in being reconciled to the church of Rome" (Luttrell, 2:10–11). If mere suspicion of a man's being Catholic could result in his arrest, if houses were being searched "for disaffected persons" (Luttrell, 2:67), then one would imagine that the author of "The Hind and the Panther," the Mr. Bays who had changed his religion and was making no secret about it, might have good reason to be distressed. On 22 June 1690 his friend Samuel Pepys (at whose suggestion Dryden was to write "The Character of a Good Parson") was arrested and charged with high treason. That too passed. Pepys was released after three months. No harm befell Dryden. He may have relaxed when that crisis cooled, yet everything could heat up at any moment. Much later, on 25 February 1696, a failed plot to assassinate the king as he went hunting in Richmond park was revealed, which led to more arrests, including Dryden's friends Henry Sheeres, Sir Roger L'Estrange, and Colonel James Graham. The former vice-master of Magdalen College (Oxford), Robert Charnock, known to Dryden's son John, Jr., was executed for his part in the conspiracy on 18 March. One suspects that Dryden, no stranger to what "inborn Broyles . . . / Or Wars of Exil'd Heirs" could do to a "Temp'rate Isle" ("The Medall," 318–19, 248), would know that even periods of apparent tolerance were at best temporary and should be viewed with caution.

We can sense Dryden's attitude, an interesting combination of confidence and uncertainty, from some of his correspondence during this period. In a late letter, written while he was working on *Fables*, "still drudgeing at a Book of Miscellanyes," as he tells his correspondent, Elizabeth Steward, he seems to feel that he is no longer in any real danger:

> We poor Catholiques daily expect a most Severe Proclamation to come out against us; & at the same time are satisfyed, that the King is very Unwilling to persecute us; considering us to be but an handfull, & those disarmd: But the Archbishop of Canterbury is our heavy Enemy; & heavy He is indeed, in all respects.
>
> (#59, dated 4 March 1699, *Letters*, p. 112)

Dryden sounds relieved, but he also sounds nervous; first, he fears hostile governmental action, then he persuades himself that nothing much is likely to come of it. Having put his mind at ease on that score, he worries about another enemy, only to disarm that threat immediately with a joke at the archbishop's expense. I suppose this sounds like Dryden's usual give and take, but in this case I see it not as a strategy but as personal ambivalence, combining a wise reading of the stable political situation he thinks likely with a wariness about what might happen should this probable tolerance evaporate. Having survived occasional conspiracies, having escaped arrests when friends, acquaintances, and even distant relatives around him were being seized, he had reasons to feel safe; yet, as he feared, severe proclamations against Catholics, including new prohibitions against their owning or inheriting land, were forthcoming.

Political reprisals and arrests aside, Dryden was beset by other sustained troubles throughout these final years; he was perpetually badgered, attacked in pamphlets, plagued by a succession of exasperations. He wrote knowing that his works would likely be scrutinized for any hint of treasonable ideas. Having turned to the stage to secure an income, Dryden had to worry not only about the financial success of his plays, but also about whether or not he would be allowed to present them. The story of his attempts to get *Cleomenes* produced demonstrates the uncertainty of his position and the certainty of irritating annoyances. The play was complete in October 1691, but delayed thanks to a temporary suspension of acting in December and an already crowded theatrical season. Then Shadwell, eager to strike back at the author of "Mac-Flecknoe," managed to delay *Cleomenes* further by complaining in a letter to Dorset (16 January 1692) that Durfey and Dryden's plays were given too much priority. Shadwell urged that Nicholas Brady's play be acted next, which further postponed Dryden's production. *Cleomenes* was finally ready to be acted in April 1692, only to be banned by the lord chamberlain at the instruction of Queen Mary. Dryden had to scramble to get supporters, including the earl of Rochester, whom he persuaded of the innocence of *Cleomenes* by reading the play in the presence of Rochester's family. Dryden also called upon Anthony Carey, viscount Falkland, for assistance, and the ban was lifted once Falkland testified that he and Dryden had discussed possible subjects for a tragedy, including this one, back in 1684 and 1685, which "proved" that any resemblance between an exiled king in *Cleomenes* and kings deposed since 1684–85 was entirely coincidental. This is scarcely what one would consider an airtight alibi for a renowned satirist, but it apparently worked, for after these frustrating interruptions, *Cleomenes* was finally produced in the Fall of 1692. Little wonder that Dryden might sound confident and fearful simultaneously, since he was alternately being regarded as harmless and threatening.

That Dryden had to resort to such stratagems, that he found himself continually appealing to relatives (Sir Robert Howard), friends (the earl of Dorset), acquaintances he scarcely knew (the earl of Abingdon), people of opposing political and religious views (the earl of Leicester, William Levenson-Gower), and even one-time enemies (Charles Montague), all of whom might afford Dryden timely protection, reinforces this image of a troubled, harassed poet, by his own account struggling on with "fitts of Sickness & so much other unpleasant business" (#60, dated 11 July [1699], *Letters*, p. 114). It was not just that Dryden had to keep from being thought of as an enemy of the country, but rather that he had somehow to do this while remaining loyal to his political and religious principles. He was, in a way, trapped between irreconcilable demands, caught between his prudence and his scruples. Since he could be attacked as a Jacobite at any moment, it was wise to "sheath his cutting Satyr" (Prologue, 33) as he jokingly promised in the Prologue to *Don Sebastian* (1690). Yet his own conscience necessitated that he remain not merely acquiescent, but still a spokesman, defender of his personal beliefs; if prudence encouraged restraint, still, "Satire will have room, where e're I write" (94)," as he accurately put it a few years later in his poem to Godfrey Kneller (1694).

Again, turning to Dryden's correspondence gives us a sense of his predicament during this period. In a letter to his sons (3 September 1697), for instance, Dryden admits to the struggle he endures in trying to remain silent:

> I remember the Counsell you give me in your letter: but dissembling, though lawfull in some Cases, is not my talent: yet for your sake I will struggle, with the plain openness of my nature, & keep in my just resentments against that degenerate Order.
>
> (#47, *Letters*, p. 93)

In an often-quoted later letter written to Mrs. Elizabeth Steward (7 November [1699]), Dryden demonstrates that this struggle is continual, and plain openness is winning; as he had promised his sons, the poet again grudgingly agrees to endure the political system he cannot abide:

> If they [the Court] will consider me as a Man, who have done my best to improve the Language, & Especially the Poetry, & will be content with my acquiescence under the present Government, & forbearing satire on it, that I can promise, because I can perform it: but I can neither take the Oaths, nor forsake my Religion.
>
> (#67, *Letters*, p. 123)

Dryden's willingness to acquiesce is accompanied by the inevitable "but," his promise to cease satirical attack being followed later in the same letter by a complaint about William's desire to maintain a Standing Army, "& make the stirr in Scotland his pretence for it" (*Letters*, p. 124). Dryden may technically be forbearing satire, but he cannot forbear from criticizing William, from making his opposition known in the very act of dismissing his opposition.

Satire *would* have room wherever he wrote, although when it came to published poetry, rather than private correspondence, more caution was necessary. The trick for Dryden was to wield the weapon of satire effectively but invisibly, and this is what I mean by the increased indirectness in his poetry during those difficult final years. He managed to take his conservative stand, launch his satirical bolts, hit his targets, but without completely revealing his position. In "To my Dear Friend Mr. Congreve" (1694), for example, consider the way Dryden slips into a potentially dangerous remark, lets it do its damage, and then backs off. He is talking ostensibly about his own loss of the laureate, complaining that instead of the rightful poet, Congreve, inheriting the laurel, a nonlineal succession has taken place. Naturally, the idea of succession suggests a political parallel:

> Oh that your Brows my Lawrel had sustain'd,
> Well had I been Depos'd, if You had reign'd!
> The Father had descended for the Son;
> For only You are lineal to the Throne.
> Thus when the State one *Edward* did depose;
> A Greater *Edward* in his room arose.
> But now, not I, but Poetry is curs'd;
> For *Tom* the Second reigns like *Tom* the first.
> (41–48)

In terms of the poetic succession, Dryden would gladly have surrendered the laureate to Congreve, but unfortunately, the wrong men have assumed Dryden's posts, Thomas Shadwell by acquiring the laureate in 1688, Thomas Rymer by taking over the position of historiographer royal after Shadwell's death in 1692. But of course poetry is like politics, and just as the laureate has gone the wrong way, so has kingship; where we might have hoped for a greater Edward III to ascend the throne after the deposition of the rightful monarch, all we have is . . . , and he is as bad for the country as Shadwell and Rymer are to the kingdom of literature. I use ellipses because Dryden stops short of naming names—he makes the political parallel obvious, but instead of pursuing it, returns quickly to the tenor of the metaphor, poetry.

The same is true, I think, in "To Sir Godfrey Kneller" (1694), where Dryden, while apparently discussing the sad fate of the arts following the classical era, sees an opening for satirical political commentary and marches in:

> *Rome* rais'd not Art, but barely kept alive;
> And with Old *Greece*, unequally did strive:
> Till *Goths* and *Vandals*, a rude Northern Race,
> Did all the matchless Monuments deface.
> Then all the Muses in one ruine lye;
> And Rhyme began t' enervate Poetry.
> Thus in a stupid Military State,
> The Pen and Pencil find an equal Fate.
>
> (45–52)

In tone and import, this sounds like the many thrusts aimed, throughout *Fables*, at conquering Theseuses, brutal Tancreds, and Standing Armies. Dutch William, who is also an invader from a northern race, is now like the barbarian hordes that desecrated the ancient splendors, and we have no difficulty in hearing Dryden's general statement about the fate of the artist in "the Dark Ages" as a comment specifically relevant to his own personal situation. But Dryden no sooner touches upon his own plight in the hostile present, than he shifts back to the ostensible topic, the history of art; the next verse paragraph traces the reawakening of classical values in "*Raphael*'s Age" (59), and Dryden moves from Raphael (who is like Homer) and Titian (who is like Virgil) to the painter who supposedly combines the qualities of all these artists, Godfrey Kneller. William's stupid military state is implicated, but William is not overtly named, with Dryden tossing off a rapier thrust while pretending to talk about the distant past, or to be speaking generally about military states. In both poems, Dryden makes his personal plight and his criticism clear enough, lashing out briefly at the government, giving us a glimpse of his own fate as an outcast, and then returning swiftly to the safe side of the line.

One would expect fewer certainties, less resolution, more ambiguity in a poet protecting himself by adopting modes of disguise, and that is part of the reason for the increased indirectness and disjunctiveness in Dryden's late verse. But I think the irreconciliation in *Fables* has its basis at another, deeper level, as Dryden's long-held conservative vision, which had served him so well in his poems from the 1680s, gradually began to crumble. In those earlier years, Dryden could steadfastly believe that England would return to its true sovereign, the "Godlike *David*" whose pronouncement of order, resoundingly confirmed by God, ends "Absalom and Achitophel" (1681). In Dryden's view, which the subsequent events of the 1680s verified, the proper, established order sooner or later would resume once rebellion and disruptions had run their course and dissipated their energies. To Dryden, that was simply the way of the world. He could end a poem like "The Medall" (1682) with a comfortable prediction of the return of order:

> Thus inborn Broyles the Factions wou'd ingage,
> Or Wars of Exil'd Heirs, or Foreign Rage,
> Till halting Vengeance overtook our Age:
> And our wild Labours, wearied into Rest,
> Reclin'd us on a rightfull Monarch's Breast.
> (318–22)

The final couplet alludes to the earlier image in the poem of Samson (England) slumbering on the breast of Delilah, waiting to be shorn (73–74); should England's "native Strength" (72) be cut and, in the metaphor of the medal, clipped by the Philistine-Whigs, ultimately Samson's power will be reaffirmed, and the poem not only depicts the inevitable return of "true Succession" (289), but also closes in peace, rest, composing all England in the bosom of her king.

By the time of *Fables*, however, Dryden can no longer tie things together so neatly, and that in itself helps explain why *Fables* abounds in divisions and irreconciliation. He cannot confidently assert the return of England to a rightful monarch's breast when clearly the rightful monarch is on the run. Moreover, as Dryden's nervous address to James in "Britannia Rediviva" (1688) implies, Dryden by 1688 had begun to see that the rightful monarch might not be the *right* monarch. However popular James was when he served as lord high admiral, or when he crushed Monmouth's Rebellion in June and July of 1685, James's exercise of royal prerogative and his swift expansion of power, starting as early as 1686, rapidly demonstrated his leaden-handed authoritarianism. Dryden, not one to be naive about misuses of kingly power, could scarcely help noticing this; in a letter to Etherege (16 February 1687), Dryden frets that James "will not much advance his affaires by Stirring," and wishes instead that the new monarch would emulate the "noble idleness" of Charles, the same trait that, ironically, Dryden himself had repeatedly criticized (#13, *Letters*, p. 27).[27]

We sense Dryden's uneasiness in "Britannia Rediviva," a poem that, in a familiar fashion, pulls past and present together into an accord to validate the Stuart succession. Yet despite the effort at synthesis, and the familiar realms of order corroborating one another, Dryden's poem moves toward a curious ending, a resolution that to me seems apprehensive; in the final verse paragraph, Dryden establishes an apparent image of stability, James holding a balance in his steady hand, but Dryden also produces a series of images and warnings that seem to endanger that balance:

> Resistless Force and Immortality
> Make but a Lame, Imperfect Deity:
> Tempests have force unbounded to destroy,
> And Deathless Being ev'n the Damn'd enjoy,
> And yet Heav'ns Attributes, both last and first,
> One without life, and one with life accurst;
> But Justice is Heav'ns self, so strictly He,
> That cou'd it fail, the God-head cou'd not be.
> This Virtue is your own; but Life and State
> Are One to Fortune subject, One to Fate:
> Equal to all, you justly frown or smile,
> Nor Hopes, nor Fears your steady Hand beguile;
> Your self our Ballance hold, the Worlds, our Isle.
>   (349–61)

In "Annus Mirabilis" (1667), Dryden had treated Charles similarly, not as holding the balance, exactly, but rather as being one-half of it, the peaceful king set against "martial people," each acting as "poize and counter-ballance" (47–48) to the other. Yet now the balance is placed in the hands that belong not to a moderator, but to a great and martial (333) king who must be advised about the dangers of "Kings" who "the name of Conq'rours have assum'd" (339). The emphasis on "Resistless Force" (349), "boundless pow'r" (341), and the prophetic image of the destruction that will occur from "force unbounded" (351) suggest that the final image of order is urgently desired rather than actually achieved. The portrait of James, bristling with admonitions, hints that the steady hand may be too heavy to hold the desirable balance properly.[28]

Dryden was right to be apprehensive, for within a few weeks resistless force tipped the scales, and "Britannia Rediviva" reveals that Dryden could see this coming. More important for our purposes, Dryden was also wrong: the political vision that had sustained him during the turbulent 1680s, that informs his poems from that period, is endangered. He invokes that vision in this borderline poem, his final performance as laureate, but he cannot quite get it to work, as boundless power and tempests threaten the future of the true and proper Stuart succession. As time passed, it became increasingly clear that peace and "true Succession," which Dryden customarily had regarded as coextensive, were becoming mutually exclusive; peace and stability would not occur through the true succession, but on the contrary, would ultimately be achieved thanks to a foreign, usurping, warlike king. This time it was the revolutionaries who were ultimately to bring order. Dryden must somehow deal not just with a particular political reversal and its associated inconveniences, but also with the loss of the political vision that had sustained him through most of his poetic career.

In assembling his systems of belief back in the 1680s, Dryden had recourse to entire sets of analogues, most of them already established in prose tracts and minor poetry, which he combined into his own particular poetic vision. His habit of mind involved making connections, revelling in the parallels, so as to sanction his own view, adding the weight of authority and precedent to his own judgments.[29] The rebellion of Satan, the rebellion of Adam, the rebellion of Absalom, and the rebellion of the Puritans were all parallels in Dryden's poetic universe, with Dryden pulling episodes from diverse sources together into a grand accord, typologically justifying the proper succession and, in his eyes, the consequent political stability. We see the same process of synthesizing different realms of human experience early in Dryden's career, as in the poem to Dr. Charleton (1663), in which we discover that the restoration of scientific knowledge from the "longest Tyranny" (1) of Aristotle, and the restoration of Charles II from the tyranny of Puritan rule, are parallel and mutually supportive. The Charleton poem is not about the new science or about the recovered monarchy so much as it is about restoration, which Dryden sees as coextensive in science and politics, each realm explicating and validating the other.[30] This sort of doubleness (or sometimes tripleness), with intertwined restorations, or rebellions that echo rebellions that echo rebellions, is continually at work in Dryden, not at cross-purposes as some might argue, but cooperatively. As in science, so in politics; as in Adam's fall, so in Monmouth's; as in Satan's rebellion, so in Shaftesbury's. Wherever Dryden looked—in science, recent history, biblical history—he found analogues that confirmed and substantiated his view of Charles's Restoration, or of his New Restoration after the Exclusion Crisis.

By the time Dryden was writing *Fables*, however, such a synthesis would no longer work. History would not cooperate. William had consolidated his authority; James II had been soundly defeated at the Battle of Boyne (1690), with the Irish Jacobites surrendering at Limerick in 1691, ending any hopes that the true succession might yet occur. Though Dryden still on occasion longs for James's return, he expresses his hopes in such a fashion as to suggest that, realistically, this is a "lost Cause," which is exactly how he refers to his position in the Fall of 1690, in the immediate wake of the Jacobite defeat (Dedication to *Amphitryon*, *Works*, 15:224). As time passed, the significance of that defeat could only have become more obvious. In a letter to Chesterfield (17 February 1697), Dryden explains that

> My Translation of Virgil is already in the Press and I can not possibly deferr the publication of it any Longer than Midsummer Term at farthes. I have hinder'd it thus long in hopes of his return, for whom, and for my Conscience I have sufferd, that I might have layd my Authour at his feet: But now finding that Gods time for ending our miseries is not yet, I have been advis'd to make three severall Dedications, of the Eclogues, the Georgics, and the Eneis.
>
> (#41, *Letters*, pp. 85–86)

As a matter of principle, Dryden makes his continued allegiance clear, but he is more the patient (and breast-beating) sufferer than the hopeful Jacobite. Although he leaves open the possibility of a time "for ending our miseries" arriving, one notices that he is not going to wait for it any longer, but rather proceed with publication immediately.

Not only was the Williamite government more securely entrenched, but it had also concluded the unpopular Nine Years War with the Treaty of Rijswijk (1697), bringing peace to England, at least temporarily. Faced with a king who represented everything hostile, dangerous, and illegal, and faced as well with a stable throne and a nation no longer at war, Dryden found himself caught between two long-standing but now contradictory principles, one being his Jacobite allegiance to the rightful monarch, the other his pragmatic belief in the necessity of a secure throne and a peaceful state. As he had argued in "Absalom and Achitophel," whatever the rights of the people to make and unmake kings, "What Prudent men a setled Throne woud shake?" (796). In 1681–82, Dryden could argue that way and at the same time support the rightful monarch, but now he must weigh his desire for political stability against his distaste for the illegal warring king who had achieved that stability. Dryden's uncertainty about James as a monarch, which we sense in "Britannia Rediviva," and Dryden's moral bind, impelled to speak yet be still, caught between conflicting principles, by the late 1690s could only be "resolved" into a more fixed uncertainty.[31] There are no new restorations on the horizon and no more convenient syntheses of values, no more grand prophetic visions of order.

I have attempted to demonstrate how it is the tales in *Fables* offer potential informing ideals, how different patterns emerge, with Dryden suggesting connections, which is what occurs throughout Dryden's poetry. He does, indeed, assemble his realities so as to construct "abiding ideals and values" (to use Earl Miner's phrase again), but now Dryden's abiding values have failed him. Things no longer connect in the way they once did, because the world has changed, and worldly change, significantly, is the basic principle on which Pythagoras expounds: "All Things are alter'd" (388). Whatever Dryden might have once endorsed, he has learned to see "that nothing can / Continue in the Figure it began" (398–99), including his own values. Dryden, who had long dreamed of writing an epic, who took pride in his successful translation of Virgil, who had celebrated the heroic virtue of occasional Almanzors, now demeans all that, and yet cherishes the possibility of heroism as well. Dryden, who had celebrated his share of Cleopatras and Almeydas, now undoes the nobility of a Sigismonda, exposes the human failure to achieve the desired ideals, and yet in an Alcyone, reaffirms the familiar ideal. Dryden, who had wrestled his way toward Catholicism, now presents exemplars of the redemptive power of Christianity, the duchess and the kinsman, the ideal parson and the fair maiden lady, who are by turns inspiring and incomplete, powerful yet limited in efficacy. Dryden, who kept returning to discussions of the poet's important moral responsibility in his occasional essays, his prefaces, his ode to Anne Killigrew, now punctures that self-centered posturing with the eloquent but wicked fox and the silver-tongued but foolish cock, and elsewhere offers a "Poeta Loquitur" that is Dryden's final claim to moral responsibility, a claim that the tale to follow first fulfills, and then denies. The attempt to find systems of value persists, but now we find that opposing possibilities cannot be reconciled. Destruction and restoration are now coextensive, inextricably intertwined; warlike princes *are* peace-bringing duchesses, and razing Troy means raising Rome.

What *Fables* expresses is Dryden's own plight, caught between conflicting principles, unable to resolve issues in the synthetic, visionary manner he had so often employed. The irreconciliation that characterizes *Fables* is an expression of the very process Dryden is experiencing in dealing with a changed world, a world in which the wrong monarch persists in being wrong but is the right monarch for a stable England, a world where all the abiding ideals Dryden can muster are both necessary and insufficient simultaneously. All things have changed. What is perhaps unexpected, and what has probably contributed to the warmth with which *Fables* has so often been regarded, is Dryden's attitude toward this state of affairs. Having learned that "Our Lives unteach the Doctrine we believe" ("Britannia Rediviva," 284), Dryden does not resort to a bitter, anti-visionary *Dunciad*, a poem that ends with the hand of the great Anarch dropping the final curtain and universal darkness burying all. On the contrary, Dryden seems to revel in the collapse of his poetic kingdoms, celebrating the changing world instead of denouncing the change in *his* world. Pythagoras' description of nature's operation—

> Nature knows
> No stedfast Station, but, or Ebbs, or Flows:
> Ever in motion; she destroys her old,
> And casts new Figures in another Mold.
> (262–65)

—applies as well to the experience of Dryden's own life in those final years.[32] It applies, in a broader sense, to his whole career of changeable and changing positions, a lifetime of casting new figures in another mold. In the troublesome 1690s, rather than lamenting the loss of his previously held values, Dryden celebrates the process, seeing, like Pythagoras, that what collapses also rises. Even though Dryden's poetic universe reveals the fragility of various systems of value, and the futility of discovering any abiding ideals in a universe of perpetual flux, it also reveals a poet who actively engages in a human quest rather than surrendering to nihilism or retreating into despair. It is this quest, this attempt to accommodate oneself to a changing, subversive world, that is, I think, the central issue in Dryden's life in the 1690s. And, I think it is the "informing ideal"—not a static issue abstracted from the poems, but a process—in this last major work of Dryden's career.

NOTES

1. Walter Scott, *The Life of John Dryden*, ed. Bernard Kreissman (Lincoln: University of Nebraska Press, 1963), 427–28. Scott has just mentioned "Religio Laici," and he is speaking in general about Dryden's philosophy.

2. Thomas H. Fujimura, "Dryden's *Religio Laici*: An Anglican Poem," *PMLA* 76 (1961): 205–17; Elias J. Chiasson, "Dryden's Apparent Scepticism," *Harvard Theological Review* 54 (1961): 207–21; Phillip Harth, *Contexts of Dryden's Thought* (Chicago: University of Chicago Press, 1968); Sanford Budick, *Dryden and the Abyss of Light: A Study of 'Religio Laici' and 'The Hind and the Panther'* (New Haven: Yale University Press, 1970). As is well known, these authors were challenging the view of Dryden as Pyrrhonist offered by Louis I. Bredvold in *The Intellectual Milieu of John Dryden: Studies in Some Aspects of Seventeenth-Century Thought*, University of Michigan Publications: Language and Literature, 12 (Ann Arbor: University of Michigan Press, 1934).

3. Bernard N. Schilling, *Dryden and the Conservative Myth: A Reading of 'Absalom and Achitophel'* (New Haven: Yale University Press, 1961); Alan Roper, *Dryden's Poetic Kingdoms* (London: Routledge & Kegan Paul, 1965); Earl Miner, *Dryden's Poetry* (Bloomington: Indiana University Press, 1967).

4. For some good critical analyses of paradox and irony that nonetheless regard Dryden's poetry as purposively coherent and unified, see Earl R. Wasserman's analysis of the double-subject (science and politics) in "Dryden's *Epistle to Charleton*," *Journal of English and Germanic Philology* 55 (1956): 201–12, rpt. in *The Subtler Language: Critical Readings of Neoclassic and Romantic Poems* (1959; rpt. Baltimore, MD: Johns Hopkins Press, 1968); David M. Vieth's "Irony in Dryden's Ode to Anne Killigrew," *Studies in Philology* 62 (1965): 91–100; and Dustin Griffin's "Dryden's 'Oldham' and the Perils of Writing," *Modern Language Quarterly* 37 (1976): 133–50.

5. See particularly Laura Brown's "The Ideology of Restoration Poetic Form: John Dryden," *PMLA* 97 (1982): 395–407; and Ruth Salvaggio's *Dryden's Dualities*, English Literary Monograph Series, 29 (Victoria, British Columbia: University of Victoria Press, 1983). Brown reverses the quest for unity, for Dryden's "successful reconciliation of opposites" and "artful joining of disparate images, perspectives, or experiences," arguing instead that "Dryden's form is not organic. It does not produce unity from disparity. . . . It is defined precisely by its failure to reconcile, by its persistent reiteration of contradiction" (405). Sal-

vaggio takes this a step further by revelling in the dualities; she considers Dryden as not "an 'integrated person' at all, but ultimately torn between the dual structures which he himself continually creates" (19). See my review of Salvaggio's book in *The Eighteenth-Century: Theory and Interpretation* 27 (1986): 188–93, for a full explanation of my reasons for disagreeing with her position.

6. As Douglas Murray puts it, in "Dryden's Inversion to Disorder in *Alexander's Feast*," *Scriblerian* 16 (1984): 182, "the traditional form of the story extols the miraculous power of music, but Dryden's poem emphasizes the destruction and disorder of Timotheus' playing" (182). I do not see this as an either/or distinction, but rather as Dryden both extolling the power of music and emphasizing its potential destructiveness. Robert P. Maccubbin, in "The Ironies of Dryden's 'Alexander's Feast; or The Power of Musique': Text and Contexts," *Mosaic* 18, no. 4 (1985):33–47, fortifies Murray's point with a host of examples, from other poems, from history, from painting, all of which demonstrate just how surprisingly different Dryden's treatment of Alexander was from traditional treatments.

7. To borrow the term used by Alan Roper in *Dryden's Poetic Kingdoms* (15–34), and by Earl Miner in *The Restoration Mode from Milton to Dryden* (Princeton: Princeton University Press, 1974), 14–15.

8. Thomas H. Fujimura, in "The Personal Element in Dryden's Poetry," *PMLA* 89 (1974): 1007–23, argues that after 1685, "the exigencies of his own life increasingly drove Dryden in the direction of more personal themes" (1007). Also pertinent to my argument is Steven N. Zwicker's observation, in *Politics and Language in Dryden's Poetry: The Arts of Disguise* (Princeton: Princeton University Press, 1984), that what we find in *Fables* "are not new themes, but their handling and coloration . . . seems more personal than before" (159).

9. In the following discussion, I am borrowing liberally from my own article, "Dryden's Final Poetic Mode: 'To the Dutchess of Ormond' and *Fables*," *The Eighteenth Century: Theory and Interpretation* 26 (1985): 3–21.

10. The historical information in this paragraph is based upon J. R. Jones, *Country and Court: England, 1658–1714* (Cambridge, MA: Harvard University Press, 1978), 279–85; David Ogg, *England in the Reigns of James II and William III* (Oxford: Clarendon Press, 1955), 407–50; and Henry Horwitz, *Parliament, Policy and Politics in the Reign of William III* (Newark: University of Delaware Press, 1977), 222–50.

11. The baby was born 10 June 1688; Dryden's poem was licensed only nine days later (*Works*, 3:472); by June 30th, Whig and Tory leaders had signed an invitation for William of Orange to take over the government. Charles E. Ward discusses all this and comments that Dryden "seems to have been convinced that disaster was inevitable" (*Life*, 238), which accounts for what Ward hears as "a despairing voice" (237) in "Britannia Rediviva." James Anderson Winn does not so much hear despair as he does self-criticism, with Dryden including his own failings with those of the nation so as to gain "a moral perspective" from which he can "bravely glance at the vindictive nature of the King" (Winn, Chapter 12).

12. As evidence that this represents a continuation of Dryden's habit of thought, one might note that this is the way in which Edward Pechter, in *Dryden's Classical Theory of Literature* (London: Cambridge University Press,

1975), specifically describes Dryden's basic critical approach: Pechter maintains that Dryden perceived "literary qualities in terms of complementaries—both/ and; a statement of preferences in an exclusive sense, either/or, tends to be the last kind of statement that Dryden wishes to make" (12). This may sound similar to the position taken by G. Douglas Atkins, an applied deconstructionist, in *Reading Deconstruction: Deconstructive Reading* (Lexington: University Press of Kentucky, 1983): "Literary texts, born of language, partake of a both/and nature, both preserving and undoing meaning at once, though we try desperately to stop the ceaseless oscillation and reduce the complication, and interimplica- tion, to the either/or thinking that evidently characterizes Western thinking" (4). However, both Pechter and I are talking about a purposeful Drydenian approach, about a "kind of statement that Dryden wishes to make," and we do not regard this both/and strategy as a property inherent in all literary texts or in language itself.

13. It is possible to view the subject-prince passage in this way, taking the duchess as an ideal, seeing in her the values Dryden advocates and uses to con- demn William and his policies. This is essentially how Alan Roper, in *Dryden's Poetic Kingdoms*, understands the passage: "William III, then, the foreigner, the conqueror, and the warlike prince, promoter of discord and strife is present in the poem—by indirection and allusion—as the antithesis of the peace-bringing Ormondes. . . . Just as satire in its largely negative attack upon vice and folly will often take time to touch briefly upon the opposed positive or virtue, so its rhe- torical converse of panegyric may properly set its celebration of virtue into high relief by touching upon the opposed vice" (122–23). Although I agree with the second half of Roper's statement, that this is how oppositions often work in Dry- den, I think this is not applicable to the Ormond poem, or *Fables* as a whole, where oppositions tend to remain unresolved.

14. David's promiscuities could be regarded as "gallantries," which is how Gibbon referred to them (according to Schilling, 147); in Dryden's version, Dav- id's promiscuous tilling does not quite retain the connotation of gallantry.

15. James Anderson Winn demonstrates that during the Exclusion Crisis Charles became, for once in his career, severe and vindictive (Winn, Chapter 10), which suggests that he acted in the forceful, decisive way Dryden's "Godlike David" was supposed to act (Steven N. Zwicker also sees Dryden advocating uncompromising measures, in *Politics and Language*, 99–100). Winn, however, argues that Dryden's emphasis on mercy was meant to temper the king's vindic- tiveness. I agree that this is one of the effects of combining softness with hard- ness, but I think that, given Charles's notorious mildness, Dryden was advocating decisiveness here.

16. William Frost, in his edition of *Selected Works of John Dryden*, 2nd ed. (1953; San Francisco: Rinehart Press, 1971), also argues for the development of Charles-David from a "symbol of weakness . . . to a symbol of stability and dis- interested justice" (12). Steven N. Zwicker, in *Dryden's Political Poetry: The Typology of King and Nation* (Providence, RI: Brown University Press, 1972), argues against Frost and against the idea of a transformation of Charles. Instead, Zwicker sees a sustained separation of "the person of the king from the office of kingship" (88), so that Charles is both earthly and heavenly throughout the poem. Although I agree with Frost on this issue, Zwicker's interpretation still

supports my point: he sees a two-sided Charles figure, with both sides working in concert, subsumed in the larger "figural design of the poem as a whole" (90–91), a design based on biblical typology.

17. It is Ruth Salvaggio, in *Dryden's Dualities*, who repeatedly stresses Dryden's doubleness; Laura Brown, in "Ideology," emphasizes "disjunction and incommensurability" (401) and speaks about Dryden's "failure to reconcile" (405).

18. This characterizes Salvaggio's approach; on "Religio Laici," for instance, she comments: "I am not sure that the function of the images is simply to highlight some religious message in the poem. And that is why I prefer to treat them as reflective of Dryden's double poetic strategy" (84). The religious issues, which, I think it fair to say, genuinely engaged Dryden throughout his life, are for Salvaggio secondary to his duplicity, and we are advised to watch as "he worked dualisms into a specifically religious discourse" (88), as if he could as readily have used any topic for the game of doubling.

19. As Laura Brown does, for example, when she finds in "Dryden's poetic language . . . a common structural core: the equation of drowning and the successful crossing of the seas, of ravishment and security, of strength and disarmament, of ill success and happiness, of whoring and pious polygamy, of prophecy and tautology, of painting and cosmetics, of triumph and regret—an equation that . . . strives to join disparate and usually contradictory sentiments, qualities, or effects" (397–98). The fact of "formal contradiction" (397) or the implied solidity of "structural core" interests me less than the dynamic effect and the purpose of the conflicts. For a healthy rejoinder to Brown, see Harold Love's "Dryden's Rationale of Paradox," *ELH* 51 (1984): 297–313, where Love argues that pluralism is a better term than inconsistency, and that Dryden, rather than manifesting "fundamental confusion," employs "a conscious intellectual strategy" (302). Similarly, Judith Sloman, in *Dryden: The Poetics of Translation* (Toronto: University of Toronto Press, 1985), appreciates Dryden's pluralism: "I do not think that any poem in *Fables* should be read one-sidedly," Sloman advises; "Dryden created a moral labyrinth, not a series of virtues and vices" (91). Sloman's labyrinth has something in it.

20. It should be noted that the best of the New Critics contravene the Intentional Fallacy all the time, and although they concentrate on the text itself and not the background, they tacitly rely on history and biography. Despite the knowledge of matters outside the poem that help some New Critics become perceptive readers, the Wimsatt-Beardsley law nonetheless remains in force. For instance, J. Douglas Canfield, reviewing G. Douglas Atkins's pre-deconstructionist *The Faith of John Dryden: Change and Continuity* (Lexington: University Press of Kentucky, 1980), in *Yearbook of English Studies* 14 (1984): 316–17, finds that "the real problem with Professor Atkins's analysis throughout is theoretical: he infers Dryden's own personal beliefs from his works" (316). Although this may merely be a criticism of too casual inference, it also reveals a distrust in intentionality.

21. Winn criticizes deconstructionists who "no longer subject their critical ideas to the explicit historical testing most earlier critics thought necessary," and whose "readings therefore tell us more about their minds than about the minds of the authors whose texts they are considering." I cannot help thinking that this

sounds a bit like "The Tides of Ignorance, and Pride" ("Religio Laici," 428) combined, and by "pride," we might recall that Dryden had in mind the presumptuous, zealous interpreters "itching to *expound*" (410), too reliant on "private Reason" (447), deaf to "what unsuspected Ancients say" (436; i.e., deaf to previous scholarship). Winn's comments appear in a recent *Scriblerian* forum of brief (and readable) essays on the relevance of deconstruction to eighteenth-century studies, which begins with G. Douglas Atkins, "Going Against the Grain: Deconstruction and the Scriblerians," *Scriblerian* 17 (1985): 113–17, followed by James A. Winn, "Some Doubts about Deconstruction," 117–21 (the passages quoted appear on page 118). Then, Wallace Jackson responds in "Exorcising Prometheus and Narcissus," *Scriblerian* 18 (1985): 5–7, followed by Brian McCrea's response to the response, "The Inevitability of Derrida," 7–9. Winn and McCrea are by no means alone in their esimate. John Sitter, in *Scriblerian* 16 (1983): 55–57, reviewing Maynard Mack's *Collected in Himself: Essays Critical, Biographical, and Bibliographical on Pope and Some of His Contemporaries* (Newark: University of Delaware Press, 1982), makes the commonsensical point that "whatever austerities literary study, history, philosophy, or psychology may impose upon themselves in the academy, readers will persist in being interested in the relation of human intentions to human productions" (57). The justice of Sitter's remark is, I think, confirmed by recent eighteenth-century scholarship, which features such works as James A. Winn, *A Window in the Bosom: The Letters of Alexander Pope* (Hamden, CT: Archon Books, 1977); *The Author in His Work: Essays on a Problem in Criticism*, ed. Louis L. Martz and Aubrey Williams (New Haven: Yale University Press, 1978); Dustin H. Griffin, *Alexander Pope: The Poet in the Poems* (Princeton: Princeton University Press, 1978); not to mention the major biographies of Swift and Pope: Irvin Ehrenpreis, *Swift: His Life, His Works, His Times*, 3 vols. (London: Methuen, 1962–83); Maynard Mack, *Alexander Pope: A Life* (New York and New Haven: W. W. Norton and Yale University Press, 1986). In Dryden scholarship, we have the forthcoming major biography of Dryden by Winn, as well as a series of articles by Thomas H. Fujimura exploring biographical elements in Dryden's poetry: "The Personal Element in Dryden's Poetry"; "Dryden's Virgil: Translation as Autobiography," *Studies in Philology* 80 (1983): 67–83; and "'Autobiography' in Dryden's Later Work," *Restoration* 8 (1984): 17–29.

22. The biographical and historical material in the following pages is based on Winn's forthcoming biography (Winn, Chapters 12 and 13), which supplements the detailed commentary in *Works* (3, 10, and 15) and supplants Ward's account in *Life* (especially 239ff.). One of Winn's important historical sources, which I will allude to parenthetically, is Narcissus Luttrell's *A Brief Historical Relation of State Affairs from September 1678 to April 1714*, 6 vols. (Oxford: Oxford University Press, 1857).

23. *Works*, 15:64 (the English version of the Cicero quotation is that of the Loeb translation). Earl Miner discusses the significance of Dryden's pastiche from Cicero in his notes to this passage (15:411–12), as does Fujimura in "Autobiography" (18–19). Miner also provides a handy description of the "anti-Catholic hysteria" in his commentary on *Don Sebastian* (*Works*, 15:405–6).

24. As Winn argues (Winn, Chapter 12), Dryden may even have moved from

Longacre to Gerrard Street in the first place, possibly in the winter of 1688–89, in order to reduce expenses (i.e., because of lower tax rates, a smaller house, fewer servants, etc.).

25. Winn examines the critical innuendo in *Don Sebastian*, noting at one point that some "passages are so clearly aimed at the new regime that I wonder how Dryden got away with them"; however, Winn explains how by demonstrating the general, as opposed to Jacobite, significance of key passages. He also adds that overtly dangerous commentary might have been suppressed during performances, all of which, I think, implies that Dryden consciously avoided the direct assault, yet managed to reach his target by an alternate route (Winn, Chapter 12).

26. Winn speculates that Dryden might have been "trying to hide in the early months of 1689," but that "his fears were quieted by the end of the year" or he would not have made open references to his plight in *Don Sebastian* (Winn, Chapter 12). I agree, but I would stress that such a relaxation of fears was at best short-lived; Dryden would spend those last years alternately confident and fearful, depending on the circumstances.

27. Louis I. Bredvold, whom Ward cites, discusses this letter and adds that the fable of the swallows in "The Hind and the Panther" (1687), 3:461ff., is "the discreet expression of Catholic disapproval of James and his policies, . . . the tragic end of the swallows . . . symbolizing what the Catholics were expecting with deep apprehension" (*Intellectual Milieu*, 183). Winn also finds in this poem "considerable criticism of James's advisors and policies" (Winn, Chapter 11), and in the fable of the swallows, sees Dryden "not shrink[ing] from attempting to give the King advice" (Winn, Chapter 12).

28. As Earl Miner points out in his commentary for the California Dryden, there may be innuendo even in the praise Dryden affords James, which would further undermine the apparent stability of the final lines. Dryden has made James powerful rather than wise, has made his "Darling Attribute" (334) justice rather than mercy, and that twists things: "Since earthly kings, and indeed all men, should mirror the divine King, whose essence is reason and whose prime attribute is mercy, it is clear that, however obliquely and theologically, Dryden criticizes James" (*Works*, 3:482–83).

29. The classic study of Dryden as a synthesizer is still Alan Roper's *Dryden's Poetic Kingdoms*, which explores what Roper, speaking specifically of "The Medall," describes as Dryden's "creative and witty use of analogy" that "often consists in effective correspondence between analogies drawn from different sources and applied to the same object or tenor" (27). Steven N. Zwicker focuses more specifically on the biblical analogies in *Dryden's Political Poetry*; he observes that "Dryden's career as political poet can be read as a series of attempts to forge a sacred history for the English nation. . . . Dryden sets the particular events—the return and restoration of the king—against restorative moments in the redemptive history—the Old and the New Testament" (x). Zwicker ends his examination of typology in the political poems with a discussion of "Britannia Rediviva," in which he implies that Dryden is no longer pulling all things together as he had before; Zwicker notices Dryden losing "the ability so supplely and powerfully demonstrated in *Absalom and Achitophel* to see nation and king

unified in terms of sacred metaphor" (109). My interest here is in the voice that emerges when this powerful, imaginative unification no longer works.

30. As Earl R. Wasserman argues, in *The Subtler Language*, 13–31. While discussing what he calls the "double reference" (19) throughout the Charleton poem, Wasserman also mentions similar parallels between restorations in "To Sir Robert Howard" (1660), where "Howard has restored order to letters" just as "Charles will restore sobriety to the state, neither assertion being subordinate to the other" (16). In the poem to Howard, it is poetry and politics, in the Charleton poem, science and politics, that Dryden pulls together.

31. Judith Sloman discusses Dryden's "struggle between detachment and political involvement," which she argues accounts for his stance of detachment, his striving for a "mellow, Christian Epicureanism in his old age," his turning the "English country setting into an image of the life of retirement," and so forth (*Dryden: The Poetics*, 147). It seems to me that, if we consider both sides of the struggle, Dryden's divided allegiances would also account for his inability to endorse ideals of retirement completely, and would thus support my argument that such figures as Kinsman Driden, the good parson, and the like, may present attractive ideals, but ideals that are finally insufficient.

32. Steven N. Zwicker, in *Politics and Language*, makes a similar observation: "Through the encounter with Ovid's 'Pythagorean philosophy' Dryden came to some accommodation with the changes that had come over his own life and with those that had come over the nation in the 1690s. The attempt to understand the Pythagorean mysteries is less a celebration of pagan religious philosophy than an attempt to derive consolation from the mysterious laws of flux" (171).

BIBLIOGRAPHY

TEXTS AND TRANSLATIONS

Boccaccio

The Decameron. Trans. G. H. McWilliam. 1972; rpt. Harmondsworth, England: Penguin Books, 1980.

The Decameron, Preserved to Posterity by Giovanni Boccaccio and Translated into English Anno 1620. [Trans. John Florio], intro. Edward Hutton. 4 vols. 1909; rpt. New York: AMS Press, 1967.

Giovanni Boccaccio: Decameron, Filocolo, Ameto, Fiammetta. Ed. Enricho Bianchi, Carlo Salinari, and Natalino Sapegno. Milan: Riccardo Ricciardi Editore, [1952].

Chaucer

Chaucer's Poetry: An Anthology for the Modern Reader. Ed. E. Talbot Donaldson. New York: Ronald Press Company, 1958.

The Complete Poetry and Prose of Geoffrey Chaucer. Ed. John H. Fisher. New York: Holt, Rinehart & Winston, 1977.

Dryden, John. *Fables Ancient and Modern Translated into Verse from Homer, Ovid, Boccace, & Chaucer: With Original Poems*. London: Jacob Tonson, 1700 [the Chaucer texts included at the end are from Thomas Speght's 1687 edition of Chaucer].

Dryden

The Letters of John Dryden: With Letters Addressed to Him. Ed. Charles E. Ward. Durham, NC: Duke University Press, 1942.

The Poems of John Dryden. Ed. James Kinsley. 4 vols. Oxford: Clarendon Press, 1958.

The Works of John Dryden. Ed. Edward Niles Hooker, H. T. Swedenberg, et. al. 20 vols. Berkeley: University of California Press, 1955–.

The Works of John Dryden. Ed. Walter Scott. 18 vols. London: William Miller, 1808.

Bibliography

Homer

Chapman's Homer: The Iliad, the Odyssey, and the Lesser Homerica. Trans. George Chapman, ed. Allardyce Nicoll. Bollingen Series, 41. 2 vols. New York: Pantheon Books, 1956 [*Iliad* appears in vol. 1].

Homer His Iliads translated, Adorn'd with Sculpture, and Illustrated with Annotations. Trans. John Ogilby. London: James Flesher, 1669.

The Iliad of Homer. Trans. Richard Lattimore. 1951; rpt. Chicago: University of Chicago Press, 1963.

Ovid

Ovid: Metamorphoses [Loeb Classical Library]. Trans. Frank Justus Miller. 3rd ed., rev. G. P. Goold. 2 vols. 1st ed., 1916; 3rd ed., 1977; rpt. Cambridge, MA: Harvard University Press, 1984.

Ovids Metamorphosis Englished. Trans. George Sandys. 3rd ed. London: Andrew Hebb, 1638.

Publii Ovidii Nasonis Operum. Ed. Nicolaus Heinsius. 3 vols. Amsterdam: Elzevir, 1676 [*Metamorphoses* appears in vol. 2].

OTHER TEXTS

Bacon, Francis. *The Works of Francis Bacon.* Ed. James Spedding, Robert Leslie Ellis, and Douglas Denon Heath. 14 vols. London: Longman & Company, 1858–74.

Byron, George Gordon. *Byron's Letters and Journals.* Ed. Leslie A. Marchand. 10 vols. Cambridge, MA: Harvard University Press, 1973–80.

Chamberlayne, William. "Pharonnida[: A Heroick Poem (1659)]." In *Minor Poets of the Caroline Period.* Ed. George Saintsbury. Vol. 1. 1905; rpt. Oxford: Clarendon Press, 1968.

Cicero: Letters to Atticus [Loeb Classical Library]. Trans. E. O. Winstedt. 3 vols. New York: Macmillan, 1912–18.

Congreve, William. *The Works of William Congreve.* Ed. Montague Summers. 4 vols. 1924; rpt. New York: Russell & Russell, 1964.

Johnson, Samuel. *Lives of the English Poets.* Ed. George Birkbeck Hill. 3 vols. Oxford: Clarendon Press, 1905.

Pope, Alexander. *The Correspondence of Alexander Pope.* Ed. George Sherburn. 5 vols. Oxford: Clarendon Press, 1956.

Warton, Joseph. *Essay on the Genius and Writings of Pope.* 4th ed. 2 vols. London: J. Dodsley, 1782.

DRYDEN BIOGRAPHICAL MATERIAL

Luttrell, Narcissus. *A Brief Historical relation of State Affairs from September 1678 to April 1714.* 6 vols. Oxford: Oxford University Press, 1857.

Scott, Walter. *The Life of John Dryden.* Ed. Bernard Kreissman. Lincoln: University of Nebraska Press, 1963 [originally published in 1808 as vol. 1 in Scott's edition of Dryden's *Works*; Kreissman's edition is a photo-reproduction of the 1834 text, edited by John Lockhart].

Ward, Charles E. *The Life of John Dryden.* Chapel Hill: University of North Carolina Press, 1961.

Winn, James Anderson. *John Dryden and His World.* New Haven: Yale University Press, 1987.

MODERN SCHOLARLY WORKS

REFERRED TO IN TEXT

Amarasinghe, Upali. *Dryden and Pope in the Early Nineteenth Century: A Study of Changing Literary Taste, 1800–1830.* Cambridge: Cambridge University Press, 1962.

Atkins, G. Douglas. "Going Against the Grain: Deconstruction and the Scriblerians." *Scriblerian* 17 (1985): 113–17.

———. *Reading Deconstruction: Deconstructive Reading.* Lexington: University Press of Kentucky, 1983.

———. *The Faith of John Dryden: Change and Continuity.* Lexington: University Press of Kentucky, 1980.

Bell, Robert H. "Dryden's 'Aeneid' as English Augustan Epic." *Criticism* 19 (1977): 34–50.

Bossy, John. *The English Catholic Community, 1570–1850.* New York: Oxford University Press, 1976.

Bottkol, J. McG. "Dryden's Latin Scholarship." *Modern Philology* 40 (1943): 241–54.

Bredvold, Louis I. *The Intellectual Milieu of John Dryden: Studies in Some Aspects of Seventeenth-Century Thought.* University of Michigan Publications: Language and Literature, 12. Ann Arbor: University of Michigan Press, 1934.

Brewer, Wilmon. *Ovid's Metamorphoses in European Culture.* Included in *Ovid's Metamorphoses.* Trans. Brooks More. Rev. ed. 2 vols. Francestown, NH: Marshall Jones, 1978.

Brown, Laura. "The Ideology of Restoration Poetic Form: John Dryden." *PMLA* 97 (1982): 395–407.

Buck, John Dawson Carl. "The Ascetic's Banquet: The Morality of *Alexander's Feast.*" *Texas Studies in Literature and Language* 17 (1975): 573–89.

Budick, Sanford. *Dryden and the Abyss of Light: A Study of 'Religio Laici' and 'The Hind and the Panther.'* New Haven: Yale University Press, 1970.

Canfield, J. Douglas. "The Image of the Circle in Dryden's 'To My Honour'd Kinsman.'" *Papers on Language and Literature* 11 (1975): 168–76.

———. *Yearbook of English Studies* 14 (1984): 316–17 [review of G. Douglas Atkins's *The Faith of John Dryden*].

Chew, Samuel C. "'This Strange Eventful History.'" Pp. 157–82 of *Joseph*

Bibliography

Quincy Adams: Memorial Studies. Ed. James G. McManaway, Giles E. Dawson, and Edwin E. Willoughby. Washington, DC: Folger Shakespeare Library, 1948.

Chiasson, Elias J. "Dryden's Apparent Scepticism." *Harvard Theological Review* 54 (1961): 207–21.

Daly, Robert. "Dryden's Ode to Anne Killigrew and the Communal Work of Poets." *Texas Studies in Literature and Language* 18 (1976): 184–97.

Duthie, Elizabeth. "'A Memorial of My Own Principles': Dryden's 'To My Honour'd Kinsman.'" *ELH* 47 (1980): 682–704.

Ehrenpreis, Irvin. *Swift: His Life, His Works, His Times*. 3 vols. London: Methuen, 1962–83.

Elbow, Peter. *Oppositions in Chaucer*. 1973; rpt. Middletown, CT: Wesleyan University Press, 1975.

Frost, William. "Dryden's Versions of Ovid." *Comparative Literature* 3 (1974): 193–202.

———. *Dryden and the Art of Translation*. 1955; rpt. Hamden, CT: Archon Books, 1969.

———. Introduction to *The Twickenham Edition of the Poems of Alexander Pope*. Vol. 7 (*Pope's Iliad*). Ed. Maynard Mack. New Haven: Yale University Press, 1967.

———(ed.). *Selected Works of John Dryden*. 2nd ed. 1953; rpt. San Francisco: Rinehart Press, 1971.

Fujimura, Thomas H. "'Autobiography' in Dryden's Later Work." *Restoration* 8 (1984): 17–29.

———. "Dryden's *Religio Laici*: An Anglican Poem." *PMLA* 76 (1961): 205–17.

———. "Dryden's Virgil: Translation as Autobiography." *Studies in Philology* 80 (1983): 67–83.

———. "John Dryden and the Myth of the Golden Age." *Papers on Language and Literature* 11 (1975): 149–67.

———. "The Personal Element in Dryden's Poetry." *PMLA* 89 (1974): 1007–23.

Garrison, James D. "The Universe of Dryden's *Fables*." *Studies in English Literature* 21 (1981): 409–23.

Griffin, Dustin H. *Alexander Pope: The Poet in the Poems*. Princeton: Princeton University Press, 1978.

———. "Dryden's 'Oldham' and the Perils of Writing." *Modern Language Quarterly* 37 (1976): 133–50.

Hagstrum, Jean H. *Sex and Sensibility: Ideal and Erotic Love from Milton to Mozart*. Chicago: University of Chicago Press, 1980.

Harth, Phillip. *Contexts of Dryden's Thought*. Chicago: University of Chicago Press, 1968.

Heninger, S. K., Jr. *Touches of Sweet Harmony: Pythagorean Cosmology and Renaissance Poetics*. Los Angeles: Huntington Library, 1974.

Hollander, John. *The Untuning of the Sky: Ideas of Music in English Poetry, 1550–1700*. 1961; rpt. New York: W. W. Norton, 1970.

Hopkins, D. W. "Dryden's 'Baucis and Philemon.'" *Comparative Literature* 28 (1976): 135–43.

Horwitz, Henry. *Parliament, Policy and Politics in the Reign of William III*. Newark: University of Delaware Press, 1977.

Hughes, Derek. *Dryden's Heroic Plays*. Lincoln: University of Nebraska Press, 1981.

Hume, Robert D. *Dryden's Criticism*. Ithaca: Cornell University Press, 1970.

Husk, William Henry. *An Account of the Musical Celebrations of St. Cecilia's Day*. London: Bell & Daldy, 1857.

Jackson, Wallace. "Exorcising Prometheus and Narcissus." *Scriblerian* 18 (1985): 5–7.

Jones, Emrys. "Dryden's Sigismonda." Pp. 279–90 of *English Renaissance Studies: Essays Presented to Dame Helen Gardner in Honour of Her Seventieth Birthday*. Ed. John Carey. Oxford: Clarendon Press, 1980.

Jones, J. R. *Country and Court: England, 1658–1714*. Cambridge, MA: Harvard University Press, 1978.

Jones, William Powell. *The Rhetoric of Science: A Study of Scientific Ideas and Imagery in Eighteenth-Century English Poetry*. Berkeley: University of California Press, 1966.

Kinsley, James. "Dryden and the *Encomium Musicae*." *Review of English Studies* 4 (1953): 263–67.

———, and Helen Kinsley (eds.). *Dryden: The Critical Heritage*. London: Routledge & Kegan Paul, 1971.

Levine, Jay Arnold. "John Dryden's Epistle to John Driden." *Journal of English and Germanic Philology* 63 (1964): 450–74.

Love, Harold. "Dryden's Rationale of Paradox." *ELH* 51 (1984): 297–313.

McCrea, Brian. "The Inevitability of Derrida." *Scriblerian* 18 (1985): 7–9.

Maccubbin, Robert P. "The Ironies of Dryden's 'Alexander's Feast; or The Power of Musique': Text and Contexts." *Mosaic* 18, no. 4 (1985): 33–47.

Mace, Dean T. "A Reply to Mr. H. Neville Davies's 'Dryden and Vossius: A Reconsideration.'" *Journal of the Warburg and Courtauld Institutes* 29 (1966): 296–310.

———. "Musical Humanism, the Doctrine of Rhythmus, and the Saint Cecilia Odes of Dryden." *Journal of the Warburg and Courtauld Institutes* 27 (1964): 251–92.

Mack, Maynard. *Alexander Pope: A Life*. New York and New Haven: W. W. Norton and Yale University Press, 1986.

Martz, Louis L., and Aubrey Williams (eds.). *The Author in His Work: Essays on a Problem in Criticism*. New Haven: Yale University Press, 1978.

Mason, H. A. *To Homer through Pope: An Introduction to Homer's 'Iliad' and Pope's Translation*. New York: Barnes & Noble, 1972.

Mason, Tom. "Dryden's Version of the *Wife of Bath's Tale*." *Cambridge Quarterly* 6 (1975): 240–56.

Middleton, Anne. "The Modern Art of Fortifying: *Palamon and Arcite* as Epicurean Epic." *Chaucer Review* 3 (1968): 124–43.

Miller, Rachel A. "Regal Hunting: Dryden's Influence on *Windsor Forest*." *Eighteenth-Century Studies* 13 (1979/80): 169–88.

Miner, Earl. "Chaucer in Dryden's *Fables*." Pp. 58–72 of *Studies in Criticism and Aesthetics, 1660–1800: Essays in Honor of Samuel Holt Monk*. Ed. Howard Anderson and John S. Shea. Minneapolis: University of Minnesota Press, 1967.

Bibliography

——. "Dryden's Admired Acquaintance, Mr. Milton." *Milton Studies* 11 (1978): 3–27.

——. *Dryden's Poetry*. Bloomington: Indiana University Press, 1967.

——. "Forms and Motives of Narrative Poetry." Pp. 234–66 of *Writers and Their Background: John Dryden*. Ed. Miner. Athens: Ohio University Press, 1972.

——. *The Restoration Mode from Milton to Dryden*. Princeton: Princeton University Press, 1974.

——. "Time, Sequence, and Plot in Restoration Literature." Pp. 67–85 of *Studies in Eighteenth-Century Culture*. Vol. 5. Ed. Ronald C. Rosbottom. Madison: University of Wisconsin Press, 1976.

Murray, Douglas. "Dryden's Inversion to Disorder in *Alexander's Feast*." *Scriblerian* 16 (1984): 182.

Muscatine, Charles. *Chaucer and the French Tradition*. 1957; rpt. Berkeley: University of California Press, 1966.

Myers, Robert Manson. *Handel, Dryden, and Milton*. London: Bowes & Bowes, 1956.

Myers, William. *Dryden*. London: Hutchinson, 1973.

Ogg, David. *England in the Reigns of James II and William III*. Oxford: Clarendon Press, 1955.

Otis, Brooks. *Ovid as an Epic Poet*. 2nd ed. Cambridge: Cambridge University Press, 1970.

Pechter, Edward. *Dryden's Classical Theory of Literature*. London: Cambridge University Press, 1975.

Proffitt, Bessie. "Political Satire in Dryden's *Alexander's Feast*." *Texas Studies in Language and Literature* 11 (1970): 1307–16.

Rabkin, Norman. *Shakespeare and the Problem of Meaning*. Chicago: University of Chicago Press, 1981.

Reverand, Cedric D., II. "Double, Double Dryden." *The Eighteenth-Century: Theory and Interpretation* 27 (1986): 188–93 [review of Ruth Salvaggio's *Dryden's Dualities*].

——. "Dryden's 'Essay of Dramatick Poesie': The Poet and the World of Affairs." *Studies in English Literature* 22 (1982): 375–93.

——. "Dryden's Final Poetic Mode: 'To the Dutchess of Ormond' and *Fables*." *The Eighteenth Century: Theory and Interpretation* 26 (1985): 3–21.

Roper, Alan. *Dryden's Poetic Kingdoms*. London: Routledge & Kegan Paul, 1965.

Rothstein, Eric. "*Discordia non Concors*: The Motif of Hunting in Eighteenth-Century Verse." *Journal of English and Germanic Philology* 83 (1984): 330–54.

Ruggiers, Paul G. *The Art of the Canterbury Tales*. 1965; rpt. Madison: University of Wisconsin Press, 1967.

Salvaggio, Ruth. *Dryden's Dualities*. English Literary Monograph Series, 29. Victoria, British Columbia: University of Victoria Press, 1983.

Schilling, Bernard N. *Dryden and the Conservative Myth: A Reading of 'Absalom and Achitophel.'* New Haven: Yale University Press, 1961.

Sitter, John. *Scriblerian* 16 (1983): 55–57 [review of Maynard Mack's *Collected in Himself: Essays Critical, Biographical, and Bibliographical on Pope and Some of His Contemporaries*. Newark: University of Delaware Press, 1982].

Sloman, Judith. "An Interpretation of Dryden's *Fables*." *Eighteenth-Century Studies* 4 (1970/71): 199–211.

———. "Dryden's Originality in *Sigismonda and Guiscardo*." *Studies in English Literature* 12 (1972): 445–57.

———. *Dryden: The Poetics of Translation*. Toronto: University of Toronto Press, 1985.

———. "The Structure of Dryden's *Fables*." Ph.D. diss., University of Minnesota, 1968.

Trickett, Rachel. *The Honest Muse: A Study in Augustan Verse*. Oxford: Clarendon Press, 1967.

Van Doren, Mark. *The Poetry of John Dryden*. New York: Harcourt, Brace & Howe, 1920. Rev. and retitled *John Dryden: A Study of His Poetry*. 1946; rpt. Bloomington: Indiana University Press, 1963.

Verdurmen, J. Peter. "Dryden's Cymon and Iphigenia at Century's End: Ploughshares into Swords." *Revue des langues vivantes* 44 (1978): 285–300.

Vieth, David M. "Introduction." *Papers on Language and Literature* 18 (1982): 227–33.

———. "Irony in Dryden's Ode to Anne Killigrew." *Studies in Philology* 62 (1965): 91–100.

Wasserman, Earl R. "Dryden's *Epistle to Charleton*." *Journal of English and Germanic Philology* 55 (1956): 201–12. Rpt., pp. 15–33 of *The Subtler Language: Critical Readings of Neoclassic and Romantic Poems*. 1959; rpt. Baltimore, MD: Johns Hopkins Press, 1968.

Weinbrot, Howard D. "Recent Studies in the Restoration and Eighteenth Century." *Studies in English Literature* 25 (1985): 671–710 [includes review of Steven N. Zwicker's *Politics and Language*].

West, Michael. "Dryden and the Disintegration of Renaissance Heroic Ideals." *Costerus* 7 (1973): 193–222.

———. "Dryden's Ambivalence as a Translator of Heroic Themes." *Huntington Library Quarterly* 36 (1973): 347–66.

Winn, James Anderson. *A Window in the Bosom: The Letters of Alexander Pope*. Hamden, CT: Archon Books, 1977.

———. "Some Doubts about Deconstruction." *Scriblerian* 17 (1985): 117–21.

Zwicker, Steven N. *Dryden's Political Poetry: The Typology of King and Nation*. Providence, RI: Brown University Press, 1972.

———. *Politics and Language in Dryden's Poetry: The Arts of Disguise*. Princeton: Princeton University Press, 1984.

INDEX

239